INDY® RACING

Legends

Tony Sakkis

Motorbooks International
Publishers & Wholesalers ®

First published in 1996 by Motorbooks International Publishers & Wholesalers, 729 Prospect Avenue, PO Box 1, Osceola, WI 54020 USA

Indy® is a registered trademark of the Indianapolis Motor Speedway, used under license from IMS Properties

Library of Congress Cataloging-in-Publication Data

Sakkis, Tony.
    Indy racing legends/Tony Sakkis.
        p. cm.
    Includes index.
    ISBN 0-7603-0123-9 (pbk.: alk. paper)
    1. Automobile racing drivers—Biography. 2. Indianapolis Speedway Race—History. I. Title.
    GV1032.A1S27   1996
    796.7'2'0922—dc20   96-6083

On the front cover: A.J. Foyt in 1967 driving a Coyote-Ford in the Indianapolis 500. Foyt went on to win the race, his third "500" victory.

On the back cover: (top) Mario Andretti, one of racing's most charismatic racers, speeds along the main straightaway during the Indy 500 in 1969. (bottom) In 1970, Al Unser Sr. captured both the pole for the Indy 500 as well as the race itself.

Printed in the United States of America

Contents

Acknowledgments

It would be simplistic to assume that the spirit of each of these men or women has been captured here in just a few pages. Trying to fit the career of a Mario Andretti, an Al Unser, or an A.J. Foyt into just seven pages each is simply impossible. These are people who deserve volumes, and I have only managed two thousand words.

What I have done is try to capture an essence; a sort of underlying theme in each individual's life. Although I have listed cursory achievements of each person, there will be some fact, some trait, or some success that I omitted due to space constraints.

As I said in my last book, *Heroes of Drag Racing*, there is no way I can really know these people. I am a member of the press; they are private people living public lives, competing against one another and grappling with the specter of death while doing business. The best I can hope to accomplish is to describe what it is they have held up for us to see.

I must also say that Indy Car racing, no matter what one would like to believe, belongs to the world, not just the United States. The racing, which took place on the board tracks, dirt ovals, paved ovals, dirt mountain roads, and paved road courses of America is not, contrary to Gordon Johncock's belief, separate from European Grand Prix racing, but an integral part of it.

The people contained within these pages, therefore, have been chosen for their contribution to the sport of racing as it affected American open-wheel racing—Championship cars, Indy Cars, IndyCars, CART cars or whatever else they will be known as in the future. But this is not simply about Indy Car racing, but rather a record of sports car drivers, Grand Prix drivers and stock car drivers, all of whom became famous, ultimately, for their contribution to Indy Cars.

What follows is a description of a group of drivers who contended the speedways of the United States with success. They have changed the way the world looks at open-wheel racing and have given us small pieces of themselves in the process. They are, in every sense of the word, heroes.

Thanks to: Mario Andretti, Tom Blattler, Susan Bradshaw, Emerson Fittipaldi, Andy Granatelli, Dan Gurney, Janet Guthrie, Jim Hall, Parnelli Jones, Gordon Johncock, Jim McGee, Chris Mears, Rick Mears, Pat Patrick, Bobby Rahal, Patty Reid, Johnny Rutherford, Tom Sneva, Judy Stropus, Danny Sullivan, Al Unser Jr., for their help and patience.
Special thanks to the great people at IndyCar, Adam Saal, Kevin Wilkerson and especially John Precida. And to Russ Lake, Bob Tronolone and Brian Craig, whose photos have captured the real essence of the heroes in this book. A very special thanks to Ned Wicker, Editor-in-Chief of *Indy Car Racing Magazine,* and Kevin Davey of IMS Properties.

Introduction

A few years later and they might have been called "DetroitCars," these open wheeled marvels of speed and agility, America's greatest contribution to motorsport.

But the fledgling auto industry was immersed in the industrial center of Indianapolis, Indiana at the infancy of the automobile's creation. Who could have known that Detroit would supplant it as the center of automotive creation. It was a young machine, and it was a young sport.

More than anything else, Indianapolis was where the best cars of the epoch went to prove themselves. To the Speedway. And the place where one man, Anton Hulman, star of Yale football and track, took a dying tradition and made it into what is now called the greatest spectacle in sports. The Indianapolis 500.

The story of The Speedway began almost forty years before Hulman came on the scene. Carl Fisher, a local entrepreneur, had witnessed first hand the incredible Bennett Cup races in Europe and immediately saw the wisdom of using the captivating speed of racing to increase sales of the automobile. A competitive racer in his own right, Fisher decided to build an enclosed circuit somewhere in the center of Indianapolis for both racing and testing for the local manufacturers—manufacturers whose production eventually ranked Indianapolis as the second largest car producer in the country. Since Indianapolis, it seemed, was about to become home to American car building, Fisher reasoned that it would be he who would bring it that distinction.

In Autumn of 1908 the idea flourished. The one mile oval was to be built on farmland that had been used as grazing land for sheep.

A *one mile* oval.

In fact, if it hadn't been for the expansive piece of land that dwarfed the oval, it may have been just another circle track. Instead, Fisher, on a whim, took the straights and extended them until they more or less occupied the land adequately. What he came up with was four corners that measure four-hundred-forty yards each with two long straights of five-eigths-of-a-mile in length and two shorter straights at one-eighth-of-a-mile each. Two and a half miles total. It

could have as easily have been three miles, but he felt it was just as simple to make the 2.5 miler. He had planned on eventually adding a road racing track through the infield, which never happened.

The Indianapolis Motor Speedway's first race was, strangely, a hot air balloon race. The balloon race was a success, but the first motor races—a series of auto and motorcycle races—were disastrous.

Freshly laid crushed gravel and a tar surface wore the inefficient tires horribly. Accident after accident occurred, killing several participants as well as a handful of fans. The final day of the outing was canceled and the circuit was closed. Undaunted, a month later Fisher regrouped and the tar surface was covered with about three-and-a-half million bricks. Laid on their side and cemented in place, the job was completed in just over two months. The Brickyard was born.

A new set of races was announced and planned for Memorial Day then again on July Fourth. Although 40,000 had shown up for the balloon race, only about ten percent of that number showed for the Memorial Day race. Management decided two races was not a lucrative arrangement. More to the point, they could ill-afford to hold the race twice a year. They decided on one big push and one big race. A day of racing, calculating speeds of the time, would give the fans eight hours of racing in five hundred miles. May 30, 1911. The Indianapolis 500 had its start.

The track opened its gates for practice on the first of May and 44 entries appeared to contest the event. Qualification was held Thursday through Saturday just prior to the race, and those who managed to average seventy-five miles through the speed traps were allowed to compete, running numbers painted on the sides of the car which matched the order in which they entered—not the order in which they qualified which was normal for the times.

Throughout the first years of the Indy 500, foreign cars were the class of the Indy field. Dawson's American-made National, built by an Indianapolis carmaker, took the second race when Ralph DePalma lost a connecting rod—which forced him out of the car and onto the track to give the huge 4.5 liter Mercedes a push. Dawson and his American car won,

DePalma failed, but the Indy 500 was seen as a serious spectator race.

By the 1924 season, Fisher had relinquished control of his track to one of his junior partners, James Allison (founder of Allison Diesel). By 1927 the facility would be sold to WWI flying ace, Eddie Rickenbacker, who had created an automobile after his own name following his return from the war in the skies over Europe.

The inter-war period in Europe was producing a new wave of creative talent in the arts and in politics. In the racing world, where innovation, individuality and creativity were standard operating procedure, designers stepped up development of race cars. But as the high-tech race builders began to appear, the high-society players suddenly dropped out of sight as the stock market crash of October 24th, 1929 dropped the country into recession and subsequently depression. The era which followed at the Brickyard was called the Junk Era, and the majority of the field were cars literally compiled of parts found in salvage yards.

The world went to war once more. The Brickyard—which was now bricks only on the front straight while the rest of the circuit was paved with asphalt—shut down for three seasons. Rickenbacker became president of Eastern Airlines and had become increasingly involved in politics. Auto racing had taken a backseat to his personal life and the Speedway floundered.

When it reopened, it was under the command of three-time Indy winner Wilbur Shaw, who was appalled at the condition of this the most famous of American race tracks. Shaw was testing tires for Firestone at The Speedway during the war and saw first hand how the track had deteriorated. There were huge cracks in the asphalt and grass was growing between the bricks on the straightaway. The wooden grandstands looked as if they were about to fall apart.

Shaw was said to have had nightmares about the fate of the facility and approached Rickenbacker about a sale. He agreed, and Shaw went about finding a suitable syndicate of buyers. He avoided the offers of most of the corporations due to what he felt was their intention to make the Speedway a huge billboard for their products. Then he found Anton Hulman.

"Unlike most of the individuals on my original list of prospects, "Shaw wrote in his autobiography, "Mr. Hulman had no important business interests in anything connected with the automotive industry. He would be free to do whatever was necessary for the good of the Speedway and racing in general, without any selfish interests to influence his decisions."

Hulman was a wholesale grocer who founded Clabber Girl baking powder, gas companies, a brewery and a Coca Cola bottling plant. He had been enthralled by the Dawson and DePalma spectacle of 1912 and had seen his first 500 in 1914 when Jules Goux won in the Peugeot. He had been a big fan of the race ever since.

After a few cursory meetings, the negotiations got down to brass tacks, so to speak. Hulman wanted to buy the Speedway, not for its commercial value as much as it's value to the state of Indiana.

"I don't care whether or not I make any money out of it," he said to Shaw, "The Speedway always has been a part of Indiana, as the Derby has been part of Kentucky. The five-hundred mile race should be continued. But I don't want to get into something that will require additional capital each year to keep it going. I'd like to be sure of sufficient income so we could make a few improvements each year and build the Speedway into something everyone could really be proud of."

Shaw convinced Hulman that it would do as he requested, that its appeal was still in tact, and Hulman purchased it from Rickenbacker on November 14, 1945 for something rumored to be about $700,000.

The race had not been run since 1941 and with only a few months before May, the family hurriedly sent out entry sheets and advertised for this first race. To Hulman's surprise the event was jammed to the gills with both fans and participants. The Indy 500 had returned and Hulman, a benevolent dictator, was driving it.

Wilbur Shaw was president, and Hulman became chairman of the board. In the first four seasons, they renovated the grandstand area, changing them from dilapidated wood to steel and concrete structures, built the golf course and charted a course where each year some upgrade was done.

Although the speedway never gives attendance results, the race draws an annual crowd now of about a half-million race fans. It has become not just the largest auto race, or even the largest sporting event, but the largest regular social gathering in the world. All thanks to Tony Hulman.

The race survived and evolved into what it is today largely because of Hulman's purchase of it in 1945. Had the track had been purchased by a huge corporation with no interest in preserving anything but shareholder capital, The Speedway might have gone the way that many other tracks did: to the developer's bulldoze—just a memory. Hulman saw to it that race fans from generations to come would be able to enjoy something that is so much an integral part of American culture and history.

Chapter 1

Mario Andretti

When you're fifty-six years old and your name is used in pop music, you know you've transcended the level of your sport. Mario Andretti has.

If Coca-Cola is the most recognized trade name in the world, Andretti is the most recognizable sportsman's name in the world. Ask someone's mother, niece, sister, uncle, priest, second cousin who Michael Schumacher is, and you're likely to get a blank stare. Ask them about Andretti, and they'll say, "Race car driver, right?"

Ask a race fan, and you'll see a change in attitude. Maybe it will be a twinkle in the eye, a memory of some Andretti stunt. A smile for sure. Andretti. Yes. Race car driver. The best in the world.

Of all the people in this book, of all the personalities in this sport, Mario Andretti is without a doubt the greatest. Just listing his accomplishments without editorial takes the space of most other drivers.

Europeans remember his Formula One Word Championship; Americans, his Indy Car and dirt track victories. And Italians, well, that he is one of theirs, and a Ferrari driver. Andretti is racing's history personified and racing's present exemplified. He is as fashionable now as he was thirty years ago. He is more than just a name, he is an attitude. The name, the attitude means speed and courage.

For most people, a sportsman is a time capsule, a type of memory that, like a particular sight and smell, can evoke images of the past. Think about Vince Lom-

When one thinks of Indy Cars, the name Mario Andretti quickly comes to mind. Perhaps one of racing's most colorful personalities, Mario is pictured here at the Indianapolis 500 in 1968. Bob Tronolone

bardi, and you remember the Green Bay dynasty of the 1960s, and players with short hair doing battle on windswept, snowy gridirons. Think of Jerry West and remember the seventies, with wild hair and wild last minute shots. The eighties bring memories of Reggie Jackson and the money, the show business of baseball, out there on the natural grass of the diamond. And into the nineties, well, those memories are still forming.

But through it all, if you thought about auto racing, Andretti was there and was a part of each and every aspect of his sport. He was a part of the roadster age of the sixties when hair was short and tempers long; and drove sprint cars when that was the path to paved oval racing. He drove stock cars when guys like Fireball Roberts and Junior Johnson still drove stock cars around bull rings in the south; and drove at Le Mans during the famous Ford/Ferrari fights. He drove at The Speedway when cars moved from front to rear engines and then to turbine power. He drove in F1 during the era of technology, of ground effects; and in Indy Cars when they became CART cars; he drove in sports cars when the Porsche 956 was the premier challenger; and drove Indy Cars when they became IndyCars and Nigel Mansell made them a worldwide commodity.

If it went fast, Mario Andretti drove it. More incredibly, he drove it well. And when he didn't drive well, he drove as if life depended on it, taking chances, never giving quarter, qualifying up front and staying in the fight. For more than thirty seasons.

Mario won the title in his first year, the 1965 season, with a lone victory. Here he leads a Dan Gurney Eagle while carrying number one. He absolutely obliterated the competition in 1966, winning eight of sixteen events of the season, qualifying on the pole of the Indy 500 and winning the championship hands-down. Russ Lake, Milwaukee Mile

"I admire Mario Andretti every day of the week," ex-F1 and Indy Car driver Derek Daly said. "For a man to dedicate his life and remain motivated and driven to make the commitment to being successful in rac-ing for as long as he did, having lost the desire to be a racing driver myself when I was thirty-nine and to know that Mario held that until he was well into his fifties, I admire him so much for that. Not just that he was a racing car driver, but that he was a *competitive* racing car driver.

"Fast. And would still chop your nose off at fifty years of age just like he did when he was twenty-five. He was always good. He was always hard. He was always difficult to pass. He always had an opinion. And that never changed whether he was World Champion or if he was on the back of the grid at an Indy car race. And he knew what both ends of the grid were like. He is a man to be admired from an athlete standpoint as well as a personal standpoint. He's an ambassador. A class act that you can only hope to emulate."

Andretti certainly was—is—an ambassador. There are few like him. He practically drips charisma but has, simultaneously, both a boyish humility and a supreme confidence that commands immediate respect. For journalists, he is a joy, not just because he answers questions with sincerity and thoughtfulness, but because even if he had a bad day, you come away feeling somehow different about racing. A chat with Mario will make you remember the good parts of the sport. To him, racing is not a chore, but a way of life. It is not a vocation but an avocation.

Andretti exiting Turn Two. Not only did Andretti win the Indianapolis 500 in 1969, but he set a speed record for the time of 156.867mph. Bob Tronolone

Often he drove the best machinery. But he did so because with his talent and feel for the car he could. And although he drove stock cars and sports cars, his raison d'etre was directed to single seaters.

"Let me put it this way," Andretti said, "obviously you have to look at where my main effort went during my career. My cup of tea has always been single seaters and open wheel cars and the categories, of course, Indy Car and Formula One. The Formula One World Championship, for me, was the star of the show because Formula One was certainly my first love when I was a teenager. It got me into the sport to begin with because of my background. Yes, I pursued Indy Car because obviously being in America at a young age that was the natural thing to do, but my sights were always in Formula One.

"But I pride myself very much on what I've been able to accomplish in Indy Car mainly because of the versatility of that series. I won some championships where I won races on the dirt which counted on points—the Pike's Peak hillclimb even counted toward the championship—and then road races and super speedways. And so from a skill satisfaction standpoint, there was no equal to that. I've been very, very fortunate to experience all these highs throughout my life and in a nutshell, yes, I'd like to say my feature events were single seater events. The sideshow was always whatever else I could fill in which was stock cars and sports cars and the like."

Mario was born February 28, 1940 in Montona, Italy. Born during the Second World War, Mario's family was displaced when Montona became part of Yugoslavia, and thus communist. The family moved to a camp in Lucca. If the abundant concern for the Italian family was not enough, times were difficult for the Andretti clan in general, sometimes having little food. In 1955, with a sense of relief, Andretti, his twin brother Aldo, his mother and father moved to America.

His first exposure to automobiles was parking other people's cars as a valet in Italy, and his first participation in racing was in Formula Junior in Ancona, a port city of Italy on the Adriatic Sea. As an Italian kid, Andretti followed the sport of auto racing, and admired men like Alberto Ascari. He understood the inner workings of cars, a skill that would be of paramount importance later in life.

His first race wasn't on a well-groomed road course with the likes of a Fangio, Hill, or a Surtees, but on a rough, dangerous dirt oval called Langhorne with a guy named A.J. Foyt. And Foyt beat him. But within time, Andretti had turned his focus from the dreams of European road courses to winning at home in Pennsylvania, which he did prolifically, sometimes racing as often as five days a week.

By 1964, Andretti had entered his first Indy Car race at Trenton, New Jersey, finishing 11th. Ironically, A.J. Foyt won that one as well. But by 1965 he was determined to win in Indy Cars, and he ran the entire

Andretti and the Hawk at speed. After winning the Indianapolis 500 this season, Andretti would go on to win the Pike's Peak Hillclimb and seven other races, winning the championship, his third championship in just five seasons of racing. Courtesy Ford Racing

series, winning his first event at an Indianapolis road course in a Hawk-Ford. He qualified fourth and finished third at Indy, clinching Rookie of the year honors and winning the Indy Car championship in his first season.

In 1966, with his confidence rising, he contended the series again, this time absolutely obliterating the competition, winning eight of sixteen events of the season, qualifying on the pole of the Indy 500 and winning the championship hands-down. In 1967 he won the Daytona 500 race, the Sebring 12 Hours, sat on the pole at Indy and finished second in the championship to A.J. Foyt. In 1968 he finished runner up again to Bobby Unser, winning four races and qualifying on the pole for his first Grand Prix race, the US GP at Watkins Glen. He was driving a Lotus, and retired early with mechanical problems.

In 1969 he succeeded at a track where he would later have notoriously bad luck: the Indianapolis Motor Speedway. Driving for Andy Granatelli, Andretti won in his back-up car. He went on to win seven other races that season, clinching his third Indy Car title. He also contested three more Grands Prix and was named ABC's Wide World Of Sports Athlete Of The Year. In 1970 he won at Sebring, qualified on pole at the 24 hours of Daytona, drove five races in a March-Ford, finishing fifteenth in the F1 World Championship, won once in Indy Cars, and finished fifth in the championship.

The following season, 1971, he began his association with Ferrari, fulfilling a childhood dream. He won his first event for Ferrari, in South Africa, finishing eighth in the championship with only five starts. He finished ninth in the Indy Car championship that season. In 1972, he finished ninth in the F1 World Championship for Ferrari in five starts, and won four endurance events for Ferrari, including the 24 Hours of Daytona, the Sebring 12 Hours, Brands Hatch and Watkins Glen. In 1973, he was back to Indy Cars, running fifteen of sixteen races, winning,

Mario Andretti in 1969 in the Clint Brawner, Jim McGee STP Hawk-Ford. Andretti was supposed to have driven the Lotus this year, but this Indy 500 win, the only one of his long career, was accomplished in what served as a back-up car. Courtesy Texaco Racing, Hank Ives

once at Trenton and finishing fifth in the championship. In 1974 he won the USAC Dirt Track Championship (but finished out of the top ten in the Indy Car series). He also just missed the championship in the prestigious Formula 5000 championship. In 1975 he ran 12 of 14 Grand Prix races in a dismal season which saw him score no poles and no wins. He finished second again in the Formula 5000 series in the US.

In 1976, his career took a dramatic change. The first two races of the season were in the ill-performing Parnelli, which would soon disband and leave him stranded without a ride. But quickly enough, he signed with Colin Chapman and Lotus, and finally, he qualified in the front of the grid, winning once in Japan. That same season he hooked up with Roger Penske, and posted fastest speed for the Indy 500. On both sides of the ocean, Andretti was driving for the best teams.

"Colin Chapman and I had a period where we had the perfect relationship," Andretti said. "It was so special because the timing was perfect in the sense that we joined forces when he was at a new low in his career, but so was I. This was a point in my career when I had decided to do Formula One full time and things were crumbling around me because Firestone and Parnelli Jones decided to just pull back and pull out of it. I was contracted and, God, my whole world just fell in on me. This was in 1976.

"At that point, at the beginning of the season, Colin Chapman didn't qualify for an event at Long Beach. It was the first time he hadn't qualified for an event. At that point, it's a long story, but we got together and I saw a whole new commitment from his side. A total commitment."

1978 was his watershed season as he won Grand Prix races in Long Beach, Argentina, Spain, France,

Germany, and Holland. He captured his first Grand Prix World Championship with Lotus. It was, he says, his pinnacle. He still managed to race Indy Cars, winning in Trenton, New Jersey, but finishing out of the top ten in the championship standings.

In 1979, with the change to CART, Andretti missed his one and only Indy 500 while defending his crown, finishing a poor tenth in the championship, but winning the championship in the International Race Of Champions. In 1980, he raced for Lotus, contending every race, finishing 20th, but was also back in the United States, where he raced four times and won once in the new CART Indy Car series at Michigan with Penske. In 1981 he moved from Lotus to Alfa Romeo in F1 and finished 17th in the championship, and won his second Indy 500 driving for Patrick—sort of. He finished the race behind Bobby Unser, but was shown as the winner that evening because Unser had been disqualified for a rules infraction. It was later reversed and Andretti was declared second.

But by that point, he was back to America full-time, racing each race of the 1982 series, failing to win, but finishing third in the championship. In 1983 he began his twelve-year association with Carl Haas. It was also the first time he co-drove a car with his son, Michael, at Le Mans, where they finished third overall. In 1984 Mario won the Indy Car title for the fourth time. The championship had changed a great deal since his last Indy Car championship. There was a different sanctioning body, a different sort of racing and a different group of people to whom it now appealed. But it was racing, and Mario was to dominate the series with six wins, eight poles and ten track records.

He would concentrate on CART and Indy Cars and finish no worse than seventh in the championship until just before his final season in 1994, where he finished out of the top ten.

Mario's best moments have just been listed. But he had many bad ones as well. Most fans remember the temper, which flared quickly but always subsided. It was part of the man. He was critical of many things, but then took it all in stride. But still, there were some bad times.

"The best experiences, of course, are the championships and the events I've been able to put together, and the worst experiences have been naturally the disappointments—and I've had plenty of those," he smiles. "But if you're in it for the long pull, with so many years and so many events, you're always going to experience that. It's not always going to be a bed of roses. As a matter of fact, I look at a career as peaks and valleys. And we spend more time in the valleys than we do at the peaks, unfortunately. But that's what makes those peaks so much brighter and so much more important. They're so scarce.

"Probably one of the worst experiences of my career was when I was in the race and (my son) Jeff was injured—at Indianapolis. The rest takes care of itself. A failure, not being able to finish an important race when you were leading, that's negative, but it will pass. But the injury side—which I must say we've been very fortunate throughout—it's very traumatic, and when I think about it, it still isn't easy on me. It's a tough one for me. I had many friends that are not here with us any longer. Ronnie (Peterson) was one. Billy Foster, back in the sixties was a driver who's not known today, but he would have been had he been here. He and I were just like brothers and we lost him at Riverside, in a NASCAR race. And of course there were others. Lucien Bianchi is another one that comes to mind. He was a good friend of mine, a terrific sports car driver. He was killed in practice at Le Mans. We were going to team together. Those are the dark sides of the sport and those are the dark sides of my career."

Mario was sometimes critical of the sport. But in hindsight, Andretti has been a catalyst of change. He was one of the few men who stood up to combat needless hazards of racing.

"I would like to think that I'm a shaker and mover in that area certainly," he said, "And there are times when if you've been around long enough people have attention to listen to you.

"The drivers didn't talk about it because you were supposed to accept that about racing. And as time progressed lots of deaths occurred. A lot of us got a little smarter and started addressing not only the race car safety, but the track safety so and so forth."

Andretti changed American racing. Besides Phil Hill, Andretti is America's only World Champion. He brought attention to race tracks both in the United States and overseas. And in the process, his name has become synonymous with speed and competition.

In 1996, Mario is devoting himself full-time to winning the one major event he has never captured, the 24 Hours Of Le Mans.

"Right now is the first time in my career that I can devote full attention to that event," he said in the fall of 1995. "Before it was, 'Gosh, I'm going to try to

The 1987 Chevy-Lola, Chevy's entry into modern Indy Car racing. Mario would win this race at Long Beach, Chevy's first, and win once again at Elkhart Lake, finishing sixth in the championship. This weekend was the first time Andretti raced as a grandfather.
Texaco Racing, Hank Ives

Mario Andretti leads the pack to the first corner at Milwaukee in August of 1966. He would win this race after posting fastest qualifying time. This was the second time in 1966 that he would win at Milwaukee from pole. Russ Lake, Milwaukee Mile

squeak it in.' It was at the height of the season and it was always a real effort to just get there, immediately from one race and then immediately rush to the next race. Right now I can prepare mentally and physically and just enjoy the hell out of it at the same time. And that's exactly what I'm doing.

"That's the spark that keeps me going and makes me feel good about myself. I pushed my envelope as far as I could age-wise, but at the same time, last year I sure as hell didn't feel like I should have retired. I feel as strong as I ever have and I feel like I have something

left in me and this gives me an opportunity to fulfill something else.

"I never ever during my career set a goal for myself and said, 'If I accomplish that, then I'll quit and not do it again.' I love racing and I'll keep doing it as long as I can. I'll sort of assess my position every year but as long as I can win Le Mans, say this year, I would still make the same effort to win again next year. I'm doing it, yes, to win it, but I'm doing it because I love to race."

And for thirty years, we've loved to watch him do it.

Chapter 2

Michael Andretti

On a hot afternoon on the Highveld Plain outside Johannesburg, South Africa Michael Andretti nervously coasted his McLaren Ford to the fifth row of the grid and prepared for the start of the South African Grand Prix.

Andretti, long-awaited America F1 challenger, Indy Car champion, and son of former Grand Prix World Champion Mario Andretti, had never started a race in the traditional European standing start. Predictably, he was apprehensive, and in several practice starts, he had stalled his car.

The problems of the start would be compounded by the fact that he was not on the front row. Up front, he only needed to concern himself with those behind him; in back, he had to not only worry about those behind him but also of those in front.

Andretti's teammate, Ayrton Senna, had missed pole, but managed to put his Marlboro McLaren on the front row alongside then three-time World Champion Alain Prost. Observers had a direct comparison for the American's performance—even though it was to two seasoned veterans who were at the time easily reckoned as the best in the world.

So it was with that mindset—and the pressure of the moment, of this, his first career Grand Prix start—

Michael Andretti, back in Newman-Haas colors in 1995. Although he would win twice in 1995, the season was not as successful as he might have hoped. He was still struggling to get back to the form he enjoyed in 1991 and 1992.
Courtesy IndyCar

that Andretti parked the McLaren on the front straight at Circuito Nelson Piquet and waited. For what was an endless period, Andretti looked from the cockpit at the race cars in front of him as the final rows of the field filed into their starting positions behind him and stopped, also waiting.

A marshall signaled that the field was assembled and in proper order and the light flashed red. The revs of the entire field rose to an ear-splitting cacophony of reciprocating engines. When it changed to green, the symphony of engines turned to a howl of tires and full throttles all straining to get away.

Just before the light changed, Andretti's clutch began to slip and the car began to creep forward. Before he could react, the car stalled. By then, the light had changed. Off sped the field, with Andretti stuck on the grid. The car got restarted and he charged after the pack—down a full lap. On the fourth lap, while trying to pass Derek Warwick's Footwork, Andretti ran into him and damaged his car, ending his race.

It was Andretti's first Grand Prix race.
Some say it was also his last.
Although the young man took the grid twelve more times in the sixteen-race season, he failed to

Michael in the pits in 1995. In the background his father Mario watches (far left, in black shirt). "I know Michael," Mario said at season's end. "With the right team he would be World Championship material. Absolutely. His way of driving really, really falls into the way you drive in Formula One. Aggressiveness right at the beginning. The guy has such focus and I think he's got all the qualities to be a good Formula One driver." Courtesy IndyCar

deliver the performance he had shown in Indy Car racing for so many years. He posted one podium finish—at Monza—and collected seven points at season's end, but mostly he was labeled as an also-ran in Formula One. Maybe in America, they'd said, but not in Europe. Not where the best in the world race.

Barry Green belts Andretti into his March. Green was instrumental in providing Andretti a competitive car which helped him gain experience at the top level. Green, here as Team Manager, formed his own team in 1994. Courtesy Kraco Racing

Only thirty-three years old as this book is being penned, Andretti already sits in fifth position of all-time victors with thirty-one wins. His father, who has raced in the top ranks for twenty more years, has fifty-two and sits second behind AJ Foyt, the all-time leader with sixty-seven. He is also sixth in all-time poles with about half in 1996 of what his father had (67 poles). Here, he drives the Kraco March in 1988. Courtesy Kraco Racing

Somehow, he believed it.

He ultimately abandoned the series, choosing to return to Indy Cars and familiar people, in familiar surroundings. To people who knew how good he was.

The stint in F1 was a turning point in Andretti's life. It was like a slap in the face to the man who had known few failures. Instead of the support and respect he had received in America, he was confronted with resentment and back-biting. Even McLaren, his own team had seemingly abandoned him.

And although Andretti had come back in 1994 to win his first race back on the Indy Car circuit, he was not quite the same man who went to South Africa. Things had changed. He had seen the world. And it had not been altogether friendly toward him.

"I think that since he's been back he has struggled to get back to the level he was at when he went over there," ex-Indy Car and F1 driver Derek Daly said at the conclusion of Andretti's second season back. "He had a supreme level of confidence when he went over there. He drove on instinct and considerable talent. He struggled to get back to that level (since his return).

"I look at where he went to the Ganassi team, a new team, and won a couple of races, then it went lackluster by his standards. Newman Haas this year (1995) wasn't a great season. Things broke. A lot of things happened for no good reason, really. Next year he needs to clear his head and get back to the confidence level he had before he left."

For anyone else, the failure in 1993 would have been insignificant. Mika Hakkinen, who filled in and eventually became the number one driver for McLaren did only slightly better. He wasn't watched as vigorously, analyzed as closely, nor chastised as openly. But then, he wasn't the son of Mario Andretti nor the personified Indy car driver, as Andretti was.

Daly said, "It gave the European fraternity to throw at Indy car saying, 'I told you we were better.' I don't think that's necessarily true. I believe Jacques Villeneuve—we saw him win here—he'll be successful eventually. Mansell was successful here and was a disaster the second year. It depends on the situation. Indy Cars ten years ago could not boast of having some of the world's finest drivers. Now undoubtedly it can. With Michael, Jacques Villeneuve, Gil de Ferran, people like that who compete in Indy Car are world class drivers."

It was too much for any man—even an Andretti—to take. That doesn't mean he wasn't up to it. It also doesn't mean the effort has ended.

"I still think that if Michael were in Formula One today," mused Daly, "he has as much talent as everybody there. Possibly not (World Champion Michael) Schumacher. It might take him a couple of seasons to get as fast as Schumacher. But I believe he's as fast as every other driver out there."

Michael Andretti's father had no doubts, saying, "Let me give you my view on that: you're darn right. That's very disappointing to me. I love Formula One

Here in the McLaren in 1992, Michael looks confident. He would start an unlucky thirteen times in the sixteen-race season, but fail to deliver the performance he had shown in Indy Car racing for so many years. He posted one podium finish—at Monza—and collected seven points at season's end, but mostly his foray into Grand Prix racing was unsuccessful. Courtesy Marlboro Racing

and had the same desires. He tried to do a full stint in Formula One, but unfortunately he left from a real high here. And because of that he earned himself a position on the leading team. But the timing turned out to be terrible for a number of reasons. Number one, the team was going through a terrible transition. They lost their star, the Honda engine. And just a few weeks before the season, literally weeks before the first event, they didn't know which engine they were going to have. So Michael was deprived of any testing. He only did three tests before he signed the contract and all of them were in the wet.

"Then he was not able to get any feel for the car before he went to he first event in South Africa. To add a problem to that is that two weeks before the season started they came out with this new rule that said, number one, you could not test at any of the venues prior to the event. Not like in the past where you could run a few weeks before. You could not test before the event at all! And number two, they limited the amount of laps you could do in timed and untimed practice. So he shows up at South Africa; he had never seen the course before in his life and I couldn't even explain it to him because Kyalami had been changed dramatically. I couldn't even give him any tips. He didn't know the car, but still he qualified, in I think eight-tenths away from Senna.

"As the season progressed, I think he showed some real sparks of brilliance. At Donington I was there and in the wet when he was quickest until the last three minutes, and then he was like third quickest. He was up against the best in Ayrton, who had full

When his father was winning his World Championship, Michael Andretti was winning in go karts, capturing fifty of seventy-five races he entered between 1972 and 1979. Eventually a seat was created on the Newman-Haas team for both Andrettis, the first father/son combination in Indy Car racing. Here, in 1992, both generations confer. Eva Vega

confidence in the car. He went to Interlagos and he was less than a second behind Senna without ever seeing the place.

"But somehow he never got the support of the teams. Senna hadn't signed. He kept (McLaren in) a very doubtful situation. He didn't sign the contract until after Monaco. That forced (McLaren boss) Ron Dennis' hand to hire Mika Hakkinen away from Lotus to protect himself. Then Senna signed and all of the sudden you have Mika who has to have some seat time. So all of the sudden it took Michael away from all of the testing. Michael was *begging* to test. You know, the critical press said, 'Oh, Michael couldn't wait to get home. That was a bunch of bull. The guy was begging to test whenever he could, but obviously they felt obligated to Mika. He was catching it from all sides. Nobody was trying to reflect on the job he was doing. I could have never come close to doing what he was doing.

"McLaren and Ron Dennis chose to not support him. They didn't fire him, they just chose not to pick up his option. They were going to keep him on ice to see what Senna was going to do (for 1994), and Michael was afraid he was going to be left without a

ride and it's too early in his career to take a sabbatical, so he decided to come back here. But it was with a heavy heart, I can tell you.

"But I know Michael. With the right team he would be World Championship material. Absolutely. His way of driving really, really falls into the way you drive in Formula One. Aggressiveness right at the beginning. The guy has such focus and I think he's got all the qualities to be a good Formula One driver. In Formula One it's a different story there. You can't say, 'Okay I'm smart,' like Rick Mears and wait for the race to come back to you. They don't come back to you there. There are no yellows. You just go for it. You've got to be aggressive continuously. And he's got all of that. In an nutshell he went with the best possible team at the worst possible time."

But after the 1993 performance, that will be a hard point to make to the F1 players. As Daly said, it gave the Grand Prix fraternity some ammunition with which to attack the Indy Car fraternity. And, unfortunately, Andretti feels responsibility for that condition.

He came as the American hope and the son of a former World Champion. Few famous baseball players have sons that become famous playing their father's game. Auto racing, on the other hand, is more of a learned skill. It takes natural ability, which Andretti undoubtedly has. But more important, it takes understanding. It takes teaching. Who could be a better teacher than Mario Andretti?

While his father was winning his World Championship, Michael Andretti was winning in go karts, capturing fifty of seventy-five races he entered between 1972 and 1979. While Mario was returning to America and Indy Cars, Michael was moving to SCCA and racing for the first time in Formula Fords. All throughout the maturing process of Michael, Mario was alongside, providing invaluable information and technique.

Andretti began racing go-karts at the age of ten. He proved to be a phenomenal competitor. By 1981 he had won six times in Formula Ford, capturing the Northeast Divisional title. The following season he moved up to SCCA Super Vee, a class similar to Atlantic, but with water-cooled VW engines. The series had already graduated men like Geoff Brabham and Al Unser Jr., among others. Andretti won six races in that class, and won his second championship.

In 1983, after studying at a junior college in business administration, Andretti turned to motor racing as a career, starting the 1983 24 Heures du Le Mans with his father as well as moving into Indy Cars, making his debut in Las Vegas. The next year he finished ninth in the standings with five third place finishes, then finished ninth in 1985. In 1986, after a proper orientation of sorts, he won his first race, then his second, and later that year, his third. He finished second that season to Bobby Rahal.

The next season, he repeated the effort and finished runner up to Rahal again, even though he won four races to Rahal's three. In 1988 he won once and finished in the top five seven times. The 1989 season saw him teamed with his father in a historic contract that was the first ever with father and son. He won twice and finished third in the championship. In 1990, he won five times and finished one-two with his father at Mid-Ohio.

By this time, Andretti had hit stride. He was consistently quicker than his old man and showed an assertiveness that made most people take note. He was clearly a heady young man with ambition.

In 1991 he converted the possibilities into results, as he won an astounding eight races and captured the championship for the first time. The next season was more of the same as he won five races, with seven poles and just missed the title to nemesis Bobby Rahal by a mere four points 192-196. Following the 1992 season he moved to McLaren.

Only thirty-three years old as this book is being penned, Andretti already sits in fifth position of all-time victors with thirty-one wins. His father, who has raced in the top ranks for twenty more years has fifty-two and sits second behind A.J. Foyt, the all-time leader with sixty-seven. He is also sixth in all-time poles with about half in 1996 of what his father had (67 poles).

So success abounds. Yet Andretti's failure in Grand Prix, at this point of his career, is almost more important than his successes in Indy Car racing. Andretti has proven that he has the talent and wherewithal to become the best ever. He could go from here to become World Champion, or he could toil in relative mediocrity (given his talent) as he did in 1994 and 1995.

The years leading up to 1993 were the formative years and he proved himself a formidable competitor—one of the best motor racing has ever seen. But it will be the next half-dozen where he will consolidate that reputation. Indy Car racing will be better for it. So will Michael Andretti.

Although Andretti came back in 1994 to win his first race back on the Indy Car circuit, he was not quite the same man who went to South Africa. Things had changed. Here Andretti moves the Lola-Ford around a street circuit confidently. Courtesy IndyCar

Chapter 3

Jack Brabham

Its fame notwithstanding, Sebring has never been kind to cars or drivers. It is usually oppressively hot and humid, and if not hot and humid, it was always dusty. The old track surface, really just a series of airbase runways joined together by service roads, was never properly juxtaposed and the cars kind of bounced from surface to surface. Even in modern times, the track has been known to kill a top-class racing effort. At Sebring, rarely did the favorite take home the spoils.

And so it was in 1959. The ninth and final round of the Grand Prix World Championship was down to Sebring and its flat, featureless 5.176 miles of road course. It was the first and last time the venue ever hosted a World Championship Grand Prix.

Jack Brabham with Goodyear executive Leo Mehl. Brabham was one of the first professional racers who made it with very little personal financial backing. He might have accomplished even more had he had better machinery early on. Courtesy Goodyear Tire

Australian Jack Brabham and his Cooper-Climax were leading the standings and could clinch the championship over Tony Brooks' Ferrari and Sterling Moss' Cooper-Climax if they performed well at Sebring.

Brabham had won at Monaco and Great Britain; Brooks had won in France and Germany. Brabham had been in the top five four other times where Brooks only scored twice in the top five other than his two wins. All Brabham had to do was finish ahead of either man for the title. In fact, depending on where they finished, if Brabham was directly behind, or within a few points, he would still clinch the title. Moss had captured pole, but Brabham was on the front row next to him.

At the race's outset, Brooks was forced into the pits when he was rammed by his teammate Wolfgang von Tripps. Brooks' machine was repaired and he returned, but by that point Brabham had assumed the lead from Moss, who'd gone out with a transmission problem. Brabham was fighting with Maurice Trintignant's Cooper for the lead, and when he passed he led the majority of the race and looked certain to take the win.

With a lap to go, Trintignant and Bruce McLaren, Brabham's teammate, were within feet of Brabham. Although Brooks had forged steadily through the field, he was still in fact in fourth—out of the World Championship.

But racing being what it is and Sebring being what it is, the championship was far from over. What has been described as a fuel malfunction or often just a lack of fuel, Brabham's Cooper simply sputtered, coughed and slowed just a half-mile from the finish line. McLaren swerved and inherited the lead, winning the race. Trintignant was second and, with Brabham out, Brooks finished third, more than three minutes behind the leaders.

Brabham was out of the championship unless . . .

To clinch the championship, all Brabham had to do was get the car over the line in fourth.

He jumped from the car and began pushing it the final half-mile. Exhausted from a day of racing at Sebring, he kept at it while fans watched the perseverance of the man known as "Black Jack" Brabham. Almost five minutes later, and with Innes Ireland's Lotus closing in, Brabham pushed the Cooper over the stripe for fourth and the World Championship.

If nothing else, Jack Brabham was a stubborn man. Not in the sense that he was mean-spirited, but that he would do more than most men if he thought he was right. His driving prowess brought him three Grand Prix World Championships—1959, then again in 1960 and 1966. His perseverance brought him to Indianapolis.

Jack Brabham had had early experience in oval track racing. His career began, in fact, in a midget car back in Sydney. Brabham's father had been a vegetable merchant and the young Brabham had both driven and worked on his father's cars and trucks. Driving was clearly *not* his ambition—but the engineering was. By the time he was old enough to drive legally, he knew far more than most mechanics did about the internal combustion engine.

In the army, Brabham was working as a mechanic in the Royal Australian Air Force. When he left the Air Force in 1946, Brabham immediately opened up a repair shop which catered to not only street cars, but to race cars. Brabham being a designer as well as a mechanic, the business flourished. Most of the business in construction came, of course, from race car drivers.

Contracted by a local business man to build him a midget car, Brabham built a dominant car which was hugely successful for his customer. Brabham was completely disinterested in midget racing, which he saw as reckless and dangerous, but when his customer gave up racing, he convinced Brabham to take the car and run it in some local races. Brabham re-purchased the car and promptly won the midget car championships of New South Wales, South Australia and Australia.

By 1951, success assured in midgets, Brabham was hill climbing and winning there as well. In 1953 he entered his first race out of Australia—at a non-championship New Zealand Grand Prix (where he was sixth) and decided that international competition was what he was destined for. He went to England in 1955 with his wife and bought a Cooper-Alta. As the car proved to be noncompetitive, he talked John Cooper into allowing him to build one of his cars at the Cooper plant in England. Cooper agreed and Brabham turned a sports car into a Formula One car and was on his own, running the World Championship. Unfortunately, he had little success that year.

He tried a Maserati 250, which also failed him. He had not enough money to buy or build a competitive car, but he was determined to race. Cooper had offered him a job of driving sports cars and F2, so he took that, all the time working out engineering problems in his mind. He captured the British F2 championship in 1957 and when the opportunity came to move back to F1 he took it. Still driving a Cooper for the factory, Brabham finally scored his first championship points in 1958 with a fourth at Monaco. He won the championship in 1959, then won five of nine races in 1960 to become back-to-back World Champion.

Up until 1961 the World Championship had included the Indianapolis 500 as part of the series. Since only about two-thirds of the races generally counted toward the championship, most serious Grand Prix drivers omitted the trip to Indianapolis.

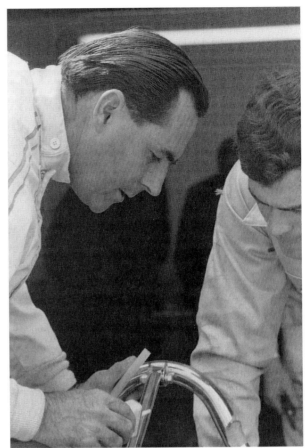

Brabham was a technician before he was a driver and always knew as much about his machinery or more than anyone who worked on his car. Here in 1968, he sorts out some engine problems. John Mahoney

The F1 championship in those days—although of paramount importance—was far more a collection of races than it was a championship. In other words, those with some cash could enter their home Grand

Sir Jack with son, Geoff in 1981. Geoff Brabham finished 5th at the Indianapolis Motor Speedway that season. John Mahoney

At Indy in 1969. Brabham (number 95) heads for the pits as A.J. Foyt passes. Although competitive, he was never as conspicuous as he was at the beginning of the decade. John Mahoney

Prix for the glory, with no intention of contesting the entire season.

Brabham didn't have the money or the inkling to race at Indy. The cars were different from what he was

Brabham with Peter Revson in 1969. Brabham failed to finish the Indy 500 that season; Revson finished fifth. Courtesy Goodyear Tire

accustomed to and the track was an oval, which from his days as a midget driver he knew to be a completely different animal. Anyway, by 1961, the great 500 mile race had been removed from the championship for exactly those reasons.

But with some backing and a bit of prodding from a wealthy Englishman, Brabham retro-fitted a Cooper-Climax so it might run better at the Speedway. He re-bored and re-stroked the 2.5 liter engine to its limit and got just over 2.7 liters out of the same engine. The engine was mounted with a slight left hand bias so the car would turn into the corners better. And of course like any decent Grand Prix car, the engine was rear-mounted.

The move to rear engines had been established by John Cooper just a few years earlier. Cooper's success had been largely at the hands of Jack Brabham. The Grand Prix car weighed a little over a thousand pounds which was some forty percent less than most of the big front-engined roadsters. Although down in horsepower some 260 to 400 to the big Offenhauser fours, the weight would make up for the lack of power. The car was far more maneuverable.

In October of 1960 Brabham had tested at Indy and lapped at a respectable 144mph. The car was only able to achieve a top speed of about 150, but the car was able to negotiate the corners at an astounding 141mph, faster than any roadster had ever gone. He could actually keep his foot flat on the accelerator almost the entire way around the Speedway, where the roadster drivers had to use throttle and brake before the corners.

Brabham qualified on the fifth row for the 1961 race, which was expected by both Brabham and Cooper. They knew they were never going to win on outright speed, but hoped to outlast and stay away

At right
In the cockpit Brabham was as serious and committed as any driver in history. His tenacity gave him wins and his technical understanding gave him good cars. John Mahoney

Below
Brabham in 1970, in the new era. Aerodynamics had changed the look and feel of racing. Brabham retired soon after this season. Russ Lake

from the pits as their competition was re-fueling and changing tires all day long.

In one respect they were right. The little Cooper was fuel-frugal, and that proved to be an important facet of its success. But tire-wise, the team had mis-judged the situation. The Dunlop-shod Cooper wore tires far more rapidly than the Firestone-shod road-sters. The Firestones were developed, of course, for the Speedway and had considerable testing behind them. Dunlop engineers were just not as knowledgeable with what the tires would do in a five hundred mile, high-speed, left-turn-only race. Besides that, Brab-ham's crew was inexperienced in changing tires and spent almost twice the time the Americans did. Brab-ham found that by pacing himself just slightly he could divide the amount of stops in two. Rather than give the race away in the pits he dropped his speed. And finished ninth. A.J. Foyt won in a roadster.

The Brabham-Cooper proved that a race car could get around the corners of a super speedway quicker than a roadster by placing the engine mass over the rear wheels. It also tended to reduce under-steer. The engine was lighter and more fuel efficient and provided the car was set up right, it would out handle any roadster. With Brabham's patented stub-bornness, the car remained in the race — albeit not as competitive as Brabham would have liked. At any rate, the revolution that started at Indianapolis was as a result of Brabham.

The first direct result of Brabham's tepid success was that Grand Prix designers and drivers realized that a top finish at Indy was worth in cash about the same as running an entire F1 season. In addition, producing a car that was technically superior to the roadster was like falling off a log for the Europeans. The roadsters were bulky, unsophisticated things that had little tech-nical merit to their designs. They had always been designed that way, American racers thought, and there was no reason to change them.

Brabham inspired the much-needed change. After he arrived with the small Cooper, upgrades to the machinery came in revolutionary waves. Within just a few seasons the entire field had opted for the more maneuverable rear-engined car. Designers were at the forefront of American racing and a premium was on handling as opposed to just power.

In 1961 Brabham was becoming tired of the Cooper. He saw a better way to do it and formed Motor Racing Development with his hill climbing buddy Ron Taurnac who owned Replacement Parts Company Inc. Eventually they formed Brabham-Repco and in 1966 Jack Brabham won the World Championship in a Brabham-Repco. Rear engined of course. He would try the speedway again, but by then the entire world had caught on to his tricks. And like Sebring, Indianapolis is not always a place where the favorite or most skilled wins.

In 1964 at Indy. By this time Brabham's unique rear engined Indy Car had almost completely revolutionized the Indy field. Although he was not competitive his ideas were. Russ Lake

Chapter 4

Colin Chapman

By 1959, Anthony Colin Chapman, had discovered, as Porsche designers had years earlier, that although the past fifty years of development of the Grand Prix car had been in a front-engine rear-drive configuration, the layout was all wrong.

His 1958 Lotus 16, the last front-engined Lotus Grand Prix car, had been a disaster. The weight bias, he'd decided, had to change. The move in designing was to flip the engine to the rear, as Cooper had done so ably, capturing the Word Championship the first time out. But most manufacturers, however, were reluctant to do so. Ferrari hung on with its 246 Dino through 1960, but by the end of that season it was clear even to Ferrari that the future of Grand Prix racing was with the engine in the rear.

Clearer still to Colin Chapman was the irritating detail that if Ferrari and Porsche both were rear-engine his advantage was lost, for he had little of the horsepower either of those two had. So Chapman did what he did best: refined and reinvented.

The Lotus 16, as awful as it was, had some great ideas. For one, Chapman had moved many of the suspension components inboard. It made for a cramped cockpit, but it gave the car a less encumbered front end, making it inherently quicker than its bulkier counterparts. With the

Chapman with the classic cap. His critics said he was arrogant and unyielding; his supporters—men like Mario Andretti—called him a genius. John Mahoney

16, Chapman had taught himself how to master the art of how to stress a car—a skill that would come in handy later in the decade.

The ideas of the 16 found their way to the new 1959 Lotus 18. The 18 was a rear-engined car with all the same ideas of the 16. It was an extremely light car which—even before knowing it was a Lotus—one could tell just by looking at the magnesium wheels and aerodynamically slippery suspension and beautifully organized frame tubing. Chapman used his knowledge of suspension and springing to change the weight distribution of the 18. The car, which weighed less than a thousand pounds dry, now, with its engine in the rear, had four-percent more weight over the front wheels than with the front-engined 16! The understeer of the 16 had disappeared and the car now had a small hint of oversteer and the drivers marveled at its response. Innes Ireland finished fourth in the 1959 Drivers Championship.

Chapman capitalized on the successes of the 18, and as the formula for F1 changed in 1961 to a 1.5 liter engine displacement maximum, Lotus, and its new Type 21, found itself as the lightest car in the paddock by nearly 100 pounds. In two years Chapman had taken the tiny team out of F2 and into the hunt for the F1 World Championship. The 1961 World Championship went to Ferrari and Phil Hill, but driver Stirling Moss had won Lotus' first event at Monaco. Teamed with Moss was the impressive young Scotsman, Jimmy Clark, who was proving to be a very capable up-and-comer.

In 1962, the Type 25 appeared at Zandvoort in Holland. The sandy and cold track by the beach on the North Sea would be the place where Chapman would start at least two revolutions. The first was with the Type 25. The 25 was revolutionary in what it was not. It was not a car on which there was a main skeleton, which up until that point all cars obviously had to have. Chapman's design had eliminated the space frame, making it a seventy pound hull. The hull was

essentially an aluminum canoe which was about twelve inches deep, and which was formed of boxes that were torsional. All boxes were transversely braced and cross-membered. The car's torsional stiffness was three times greater than the Type 21, but the tub weighed just over half as much. In addition, the suspension components were mounted even more inboard than before, giving the car another 10 percent or so relief from drag.

Graham Hill won the World Championship in 1962 in a BRM, with Clark second. And by the end of the following year, Clark would capture the title.

It could easily be understood that Chapman, who was finally about to realize his dream of capturing a World Championship, would have no interest what-

Colin Chapman at the Indianapolis Motor Speedway in 1964. The car would be put out with a blown tire which ruined the suspension. Ford had been bankrolling Chapman in his first two seasons and he had failed to produce results. By the 1965 season, Chapman had a check and an ultimatum, win or else. He did. Russ Lake

soever in going to the United States to drive in the silly oval track race which had become the biggest race in the world. The Indy 500 could not have interested Chapman any less than it did at that point. He had a driver who was capable of winning the World Championship as long as he continued designing more technically superior cars. And Chapman had no shortage of ideas.

Dan Gurney, however, did.

Gurney, who had been driving for Ferrari, BRM and Porsche over the previous three and a half seasons, was keen on changing the direction of racing in his home country. The young American had never competed at the speedway, but he was scheduled to drive one of Mickey Thompson's lightweight aluminum rear-engined cars that season. But having been exposed to the analytical ways of designing of the Europeans, Gurney saw the future of American racing and it involved the enigmatic Englishman named Colin Chapman.

Driving for Porsche at the Dutch Grand Prix in 1962, he was absolutely stunned by the genius Chapman had shown in designing his Type 25. He immediately approached Chapman about preparing a car for Indianapolis.

Up until that point there was almost a contempt for Americans in European racing circles. Gurney convinced him to come to America, which was just a day before practice for the Monaco GP began in June of 1962. As the story goes, Gurney actually paid for Chapman's trip. Once there, Gurney introduced him to Ford people, who were trying at that point to return to racing. A deal was struck, and as Clark was being beaten in the last four races of the Grand Prix season by Hill for the championship, Colin Chapman was embarking upon a challenge that would change American racing forever.

Ford, which was enthusiastically throwing money at the idea of coming back to Indy, had purchased a Type 25 from Chapman and was testing the GP car at the Speedway with the 1.5 liter Climax engine. With that data they developed a bigger pushrod V-8 to be fitted in three specifically built Type 28s—called 29s for Indy—the latest version of Chapman's 25. They were rear-engined, monocoque-framed, fully independently suspended cars with slightly elongated wheelbases for speedway racing. With Ford's backing, they were the most highly financed cars ever to appear at Indy.

Chapman had been persuaded to field the cars by some arm-twisting by Gurney and Ford and with the reasoning that the well-handling cars, unlike the Cooper which had preceded it, would make it not just competitive but quicker than the almost archaic roadsters. Gurney had taken the first version of the Type 28 out in March of 1963 and lapped at 150mph right off the bat.

To say that the Indy fraternity was nervous is an understatement. Here was Chapman, a sort of icono-clastic, arrogant genius, not at all impressed with the traditions of Indianapolis, who'd hired Scotsman Clark to partner American Gurney at the Speedway in a British Racing green colored car—a long spurned color for the Speedway. And all was underwritten by Ford Motors, which was ready to spend whatever it took to win the race!

And more than a few were relieved when the team failed.

Clark qualified fifth fastest and Gurney qualified back on the fifth row. Although the Offenhausers were not making more horsepower, tire advancements over the past season had given Parnelli Jones a lift, vaulting him into the pole position for the race.

By the time the race had come around, this small British invasion had already started its first controversy. Determined not to make the same mistake Brabham had made in 1961, Chapman opted for Firestone tires. Firestone, of course, had a monopoly on speedway tires at that time. But the standard tires were 16s in the front and 18 inches in the rear. Chapman asked that 15 inchers be constructed, and Firestone acquiesced. Immediately, the other runners wanted the same 15 inchers and protested the fact that Firestone made them for Chapman but not for them (although they didn't say anything about Mickey Thompson asking for smaller tires the season earlier). Firestone first balked, but finally agreed to supply everyone with new 15 inch tires—if they wanted them. As it turned out, they did. And immediately, there was a run on fifteen inch Hallibrand *wheels* — which ultimately affected Chapman's team, since they were unable to get an extra set (hence the poor qualifying of Gurney who used Dunlop wheels). The irritation of the whole thing was so great on the part of A.J. Foyt that he approached Goodyear and asked that they create not just a tire but an entire racing program—which they did, ultimately knocking Firestone out of the winners circle within just a few years. But that's another story.

The race started with Chapman planning only one pit stop and lap speeds of 145 to 148mph, and all went as planned. The lead was held by Parnelli Jones with Clark just behind him. A few laps from the end, Jones began to leak oil. Badly. Cars were spinning out, but Jones was not black flagged. Although Chapman and J.C. Agajanian had heated words on pit lane, the marshalls never black-flagged Jones. He went on to win, as Clark decided not to risk a pass on this madman on an oil-slicked track. Lotus finished second. Some three months later, at Milwaukee, Clark led a wire-to-wire race to win with the Lotus, proving the car could do it on the right day. Chapman's rear-engined car made quite an impact. It forever changed the personality of Indy Car racing.

And Chapman now had a taste of the 500 and an understanding of victory. He was now ready to win the Indy 500. The lessons he had learned about the Speedway made an impression on him. By May of the

Andretti talks with Chapman prior to the 1969 race. Andretti was hired by Andy Granatelli to drive a Lotus, but was forced into the backup Hawk for the May race, which he won. Nevertheless, it was Chapman's first working experience with the charismatic young driver. John Mahoney

next season he had done several things to stack the deck in his favor. First, he had asked Ford to go back and make some more power, which they did, giving him an additional fifty or so horsepower. He also asked that the red line be adjusted upward to about 8,000. This was also done.

The car was fast enough to make pole, but unfortunately, Clark was still unable to put the car into the winner's circle in 1964. Ford had given the new engine to several other teams, and now armed with the new rear-engined chassis, the best were beating the Ford Factory team. Although Clark led near the end, a blown tire ruined his suspension and his chance for the victory. Oddly, however, it was A.J. Foyt in a front-engined roadster who took the victory. It would be the last ever for a front-engined car.

With Ford fingers pointing at him for his decision to use Dunlop tires for the 1964 race, Chapman's reputation was on the line. Clark and Gurney were busy trying to win the World Championship (where Clark trailed Graham Hill by several points), so both were relieved of their drives and Parnelli Jones and A.J. Foyt were hired to drive the Lotuses at Milwaukee (the same

weekend as the Austrian Grand Prix). Uncharacteristically, Chapman flew to the United States to be with his all-American team. Jones qualified better than Clark had the previous season, and won the race-wire to wire. He did the same thing at Trenton. Although not fully redeemed, Chapman had a Ford contract for the 1965 Indy 500—but just barely.

Ford was tired of Chapman's results—and of his budget. For the 1965 race, Ford did not give Chapman a blank check as they had in the past, but allowed him a chunk of money. They would pay no more than that single check and no bonus regardless if the job were done right or not. How Chapman spent the money was up to him, but the burden of success was now solely on his shoulders. And Chapman felt the pressure.

By 1965, of the 68 entries at the Speedway, 45 of them were rear-engined, and only four front-engined cars made the event. The Lotuses had been refined yet again, with longer noses to prevent lifting at high speed and slightly wider for more stability. Although Gurney had a Lotus, he was driving for himself, without Chapman behind him. Clark had the second car, and a third car went to Bobby Johns, a stock car driver. Clark, however, was second quickest on the first day of qualifying, officially posting the first four-lap run over 160, with an average speed of 160.729—being beaten by A.J. Foyt (not in a Lotus for this race, but Ford powered, nevertheless).

Although Foyt was in contention for almost half the race, an ill-timed fuel stop—which was actually necessitated by a completely empty tank—and then a transmission problem put Clark out front for good. He won by a two-lap margin.

Chapman had finally won himself a race at the silly little oval.

That might have been the end of the story except that in 1967 Chapman completely changed forever the way Indy and Grand Prix cars would be built. Up until the 1967 season, cars—monocoque or not—were designed as street cars were: with the structure of the car cradling the engine. It made perfect sense. Where else would one put an engine besides in a car?

But Chapman had found years earlier that a stressed member of the car is inherently stronger than a non-stressed member. His monocoque was weaker without the suspension and engine than it was with the components. The same could be said for an engine that was stressed, he'd reasoned. So why not build a stressed engine?

The difference between building engines and building chassis was the difference in making a firecracker and building an atomic device. Chapman had no experience in engine building. It was a specialized art. But he knew a couple of people who did and a factory that wanted to. With his contacts at Ford, Chapman commissioned a couple of Englishmen—Keith Duckworth and Michael Costin—to produce a new power plant. It was to be based on the engine that he'd used for both Indy wins, but was to be lighter, sturdier, and higher revving. It was also to be *a part of the frame.* What rolled out onto the grid at the Dutch Grand Prix in 1967 was the first Lotus-Cosworth—the world's first stressed engine.

The tub of the lotus stopped just aft of the driver's head. The car essentially was a tub that went from the drivers back forward. The engine bolted directly onto the back of the tub and the wheels were hung off the back of the transmission, which was bolted to the back of the engine.

It was a masterpiece of an idea, and one that is still used today. The Lotus was on pole nine times that season—more than any other year before or since—and won five times, just missing both Driver's and Constructor's Championships. In just a few seasons, just as Chapman had done with both monocoque and rear engine designs, the entire field would be using stressed engines—in fact, mostly Ford Cosworths.

Colin Chapman's next contribution to American revolts came in the following season in which he opted to remove the piston engine altogether, opting

Always a part of the day-to-day changes in the cars, Chapman oversees work being done on a Lotus. Chapman's strength was not just refining components but redesigning components so that they were stripped to their essence.
John Mahoney

instead for a turbine engine. The turbine engine concept was validated in 1976 with Andy Granatelli's entry in which Parnelli Jones nearly won the race before the car konked out with just a few lap laps to go. In the mean time, Chapman, who was interested in the idea, had redesigned his cars differently from the Granatelli entries so that the cars were symmetrical with the turbine engine just behind the drivers—and set off again to win the 500. Graham Hill, Joe Leonard and Art Pollard were competitive, but failed to win the race. Two dropped out with fuel problems and Hill crashed. That was the end of Chapman's direct participation at Indianapolis.

Yet Chapman's effect on Indy Cars after 1968 was less obvious but just as profound. When the aerodynamic revolution found its way to the Speedway in the early seventies, Chapman had a major realization: if a wing was used to create downforce on either the front or the rear tires, the effect of making the car a huge wing would create even more downforce.

He designed the car so that the bottom of the car was the bottom of the wing and the top side was the top of the wing. The Lotus 78, the car that took Mario

Chapman and Andy Granatelli in 1969. The two seemed an odd duo, but worked remarkably well together. Each man had his own unique ideas about racing. Unfortunately they never got a chance to race the Lotus together. The car was put out before it started. John Mahoney

Andretti to the 1978 World Championship was the culmination of those thoughts. The car was created so that air was forced through narrow channels at the front of the car—with almost no front wing—and tunnels beneath the car were swept upward at the back of the car. Air flowing over the top then pushed the car down. Because there was negative pressure at the back, the car sucked the ground. Side skirts were added to keep the undertray sealed and the effect was a total suction.

By 1983, the "ground effects" era had killed enough drivers who never quite came to grips with the handling characteristics of the cars. The F1 rule-making body banned the devices. But Indy Car simply restricted the venturis beneath the car. Indy cars still use variations of ground effects, although they are not nearly as radical as what evolved in 1982.

Mario Andretti, who credits his 1978 World Championship to Chapman, had this to say about his old boss: "Here was a man who could be a total magician when it came to motor racing as far as coming up with solutions and sort of plotting new ways to do things and looking for elusive advantage for his drivers. That was why he was such an innovator. We had some incredibly happy times together because of that. I always regarded Colin Chapman very highly. He was very high strung and so forth, but if he was on your side, you were going to do some big things."

Colin Chapman died in 1983. His sudden and unexpected death stunned and saddened the world of Grand Prix and Indy Car racing. His involvement with his team was so great that almost immediately Team Lotus found itself at the back of the grid. By 1995 the team had been through bankruptcy, and its future was uncertain.

Chapter 5

Jimmy Clark

For those of us too young or not lucid enough back then to remember Jimmy Clark during his contemporary days, we have to rely on words and pictures. And there is the photo taken of Jimmy Clark, face covered with grime and grit, goggle impressions still clear, when he is told that Alan Stacey has died. The look is of shock and disbelief, of sadness and grief. For some reason, that picture always seems as if it is Clark reacting to his own death.

What most of the current generation know of Jimmy Clark is sadness. There will always be a darkness to his images, to his career for this generation. Because in any editorial by anyone who knew him, the words "tragic," "horrible," "unnecessary," and "untimely" always pervade the text. For this generation, Clark was less a hero than a martyr for the new sport of auto racing.

In a book on Grand Prix drivers called *The Champions of Formula One*, author Keith Botsford wrote about champions from Jackie Stewart to the then-present champion Alain Prost. His demarcation in time, he'd said, was due to the complete change in attitude from Stewart to say, a Fangio, an Ascari, or even a Hawthorne. Those previous men were gentlemen, who raced for themselves, not for the masses. "Hawthorne," Botsford wrote, "a graduate of Kingston Technical College and then a student at the College of Aeronautical Engineering in Chelsea, London; in short a mechanical type who appeared at races in white overalls and a bow tie . . . When God called him to Maranello, Hawthorne hardly leaped at the chance: he wasn't sure he wanted to be a full-time racing driver and even less sure that he wanted to drive for a foreigner."

Jimmy Clark in 1963 in the first competitive rear-engined car. Clark qualified fifth fastest in this, his first 500. The race was planned with only one pit stop and lap speeds of 145 to 148mph. Sitting second behind Parnelli Jones, Clark settled for second. Courtesy Ford Racing

The point of the quote is not to spotlight Hawthorne but to spotlight the era of drivers in which Clark flourished. It was an age where drivers helped each other out, where they raced for personal reasons which hardly included fame or livelihood, but as Ernest Hemingway had said years earlier the "good fight"—the battle within more than the battle with one another.

That era definitely ended with the death of Jimmy Clark.

Clark was vulnerable. His strength and courage were all the more impressive when mixed with that vulnerable side. It was like watching a man like boxer Mike Tyson, with a passion and rage in his profession, who was then in his personal life a supreme pacifist (which Tyson obviously was not). Clark's rage was so much more powerful because in 'real life' he was so shy and quiet. Confident, but not cocky.

Jimmy Clark was born in Fife, Scotland on March 14, 1936. At the age of five he moved to a farm in Duns, a town of about 1,800 inhabitants east of Edinburgh. As drivers of his era did, Clark grew up loving mechanical devices. He was constantly tinkering with tractor engines and such utilitarian machines as he grew into adulthood. He was first introduced to racing by his brother-in-law who took him to Brands Hatch in 1948. It was not until 1956 that Clark would make his debut at the controls of a race car. At twenty-three he had signed with Lotus. Chapman, who had watched the Scot for a couple of seasons, was happy to get Clark on his team.

When the Lotus 18, the first rear-engined Lotus, made its debut, Clark was not at the wheel. Innes Ireland and Stirling Moss piloted the cars in Buenos Aires and Monaco in 1960 (Moss switched from Cooper to

Clark credits his Firestone tires for his win. Frankly, the tires probably were responsible for getting him to the winner's circle. Prior to 1965 Dunlops were used intermittently and Clark had had trouble. Courtesy Firestone

Lotus after Argentina). Moss won in the car at Monaco, proving its competitiveness. So it was in this atmosphere that Clark was stuck in the car at Zandvoort, Holland. He finished an admirable fifth in his first race. The next, in Belgium, saw Moss crash and suffer a severe injury which was to keep him out of the car for several months. Clark finished third in Portugal that season and found another fifth in France. He had no wins and no poles, but finished eighth in the World Championship—not bad for a first attempt and running only six of ten races.

The following season, with a better understanding of what the GP circuit was about, Clark ran all eight races in the new Type 21, putting the Lotus on the front row once at Monaco and taking two third place finishes and a fourth. He also managed to set fastest lap at Zandvoort. He finished seventh in the championship with eleven points.

In 1962, in the new Type 25 monocoque car, Clark hit stride finally. The season opened in Holland and Clark put the 25 on the front row. Clark set off and led the race early, but was sidelined with transmission woes by the 12th lap. He stole pole for the next race at Monaco and was again put out. But clearly, he was the quickest in the field by almost a second-and-a-half. The next stop left him off the front row for the only time that entire season, but he was finally to win a race.

His first ever Grand Prix was now in the books, and as other drivers have done, the first was only one in a long string that began right after the long wait. At Aintree in Britain two races later he pulled his first hat-trick, taking pole, setting fastest lap and winning the race—a feat he was to repeat at Watkins Glen two months later. Alas, the waning events of the championship were to fall to Graham Hill and the BRM. With the exception of the German Grand Prix where he finished fourth, he would score no other points except

for those in his three wins. Hill, on the other hand, won four times, finished second twice, fourth once and sixth once. The string of Hill successes came just as Clark was failing to finish.

It was a crushing blow, considering the performance of the car and driver. But it was to serve an ultimate purpose. The following season there was nobody who could beat Clark, and he won his first championship, winning seven of ten races and finishing third in three others. He sat on pole seven times and set fastest lap at six outings. Of his seventy-three points collected (of which only 54 counted; the best six finishes of ten races), the next closest was Richie Ginther who had 34 (of which only 29 actually counted). Clark was now considered, as some had assumed earlier, the best in the world. He was to prove that fact again in 1965, with a World Championship in six wins in nine races. And in 1968, with the unstoppable Lotus 49, probably could have captured the championship again. Clark died after his first win at the opening race at South Africa. Hill, who had proven slower than Clark in similar machinery, won the World Championship hands-down.

Meanwhile, in the states, Clark's reputation was nearly unknown. Racing had been insulted from outside influences for many decades. The last true attempt at capturing the Greatest Spectacle in Sport was by Fiat in 1924. Before that, of course, the Indy 500 was as international a race as the 24 Hours of Le Mans. But in 1963, it was truly an all-American race.

With Jack Brabham and the Cooper, the door had suddenly been opened to the idea that perhaps there were other ways to do things. A meaty football player who spends his life solely in that sport doesn't see the wisdom in being unencumbered by bulk like the soccer player until, that is, the advantage is made clear in head-to-head competition. Brabham's Cooper was that fleet footed runner. And although it didn't have the strength to get the job done, it had sounded a wake-up call to the Speedway. Theirs was not the only way to construct a car for the Indy 500.

Dan Gurney, unlike either Mickey Thompson or Jack Brabham, was to understand this completely. Unlike Brabham, Gurney was an All-American boy. He'd grown up with the race; unlike Thompson, he was also sophisticated enough to have seen the superiority in European machinery. That he was involved with Clark was purely coincidence. Gurney liked Chapman's 25 and talked Chapman into producing a car for The 500; Clark was a Chapman driver and was the first person Chapman wanted to head the effort.

And, in fact, Clark disliked the Speedway. More to the point, he disliked the way he was treated at the Speedway: ". . . Just to see that I was a good little boy the officials had invited a number of drivers along just to watch me go round and see that I did the correct thing at the correct time," Clark wrote in his autobiography, *Clark At The Wheel*. "This is one thing that really annoyed me. They treated me like a kid who had never raced before. On this occasion, I took things easily and tried to get the hang of driving round left hand corners all the time . . I did about a hundred laps on that occasion and I remember thinking that it was a bit dull. My fastest lap of 143mph average made most people sit up and take notice, but what made them even more interested was the speed at which I was taking the turns . . . Our Lotus was doing over 140 in the corners."

As Leo Levine said in his definitive book, Ford: The Dust And The Glory, "At first he knew little and cared less about Indianapolis, but as he became more and more involved in the event, it became of prime importance to him. Within a few years, he was not only to become the dominant driver at the speedway, but he would also revise many American opinions about the abilities of European pilots."

Clark qualified fifth fastest in his first 500. The race was planned with only one pit stop and lap speeds of 145 to 148mph. All went as planned. The lead was held by Parnelli Jones with Clark just behind him. A few laps from the end, Jones began to leak oil and the cars of both Eddie Sachs and Roger McClusky spun out, but Jones was not black flagged. Clark decided to risk a pass on the oil-slicked track and Jones won. Clark finished second. Some three months later, at Milwaukee, Clark led a wire-to-wire race to win with the Lotus.

By May of the next season Clark was fast enough to make pole, but unable to put the car into the winner's circle. He led, and victory looked certain until a blown tire ruined his suspension and his chance for the victory. In 1965 Clark was second quickest to A.J. Foyt. But although Foyt was in contention for almost half the race, a transmission problem put Foyt out and put Clark up front for good. He won the race, his one and only victory at the Brickyard, by a two-lap margin.

He would return to the Speedway the next season, driving a BRM-Lotus sponsored by Andy Grantelli and

Three of the greatest British drivers ever. The two Scots, Jackie Stewart (right), Jim Clark (center) and the Englishman Graham Hill (left). All three drove for Lotus at Indy; all three became Formula One World Champions and two of the three won the May race. Stewart was the only one of the three not to—although he came very close. Russ Lake

Clark Passes tech. Here he sits in the 1963 Lotus at this, the first attempt at Indy for both Clark and team boss Colin Chapman. As his face shows, he was not all that smitten with the track or the Indy fraternity, who often treated him as if he were an inexperienced driver. Russ Lake

STP. The Lotus was leading, followed by Al Unser, the second driver, when Unser crashed. The cars, painted alike in day-glo orange, except for the numbers "18" and "19" were mistaken for one another. Clark was said to have been leading, but after a moment, the scoreboard blinked and the order was changed; Hill first, Clark second. The race ended in that order, with Granatelli, of course, blowing his stack.

The following season Clark raced one final time at Indy, with Granatelli's STP Sponsorship on the car (Clark also raced at Rockingham in 1967 in a NASCAR Ford Fairlane), qualifying 16th and finishing 31st in 1967.

"Jimmy was the greatest there ever was," Andy Granatelli said. "He was a super guy. He was a gentleman on the track as well as off the track. He was the most learned driver I ever worked with. He was just cool, calm and collected. Put him in the turbine car,

he could just start it up the first time and drive it as if he had always driven it. Like he was an airplane pilot. He was super."

On April 7th, 1968, on an overcast day in the Black Forest of Germany, Hockenheim Ring took Jimmy Clark's life. In an insignificant F2 race, Clark slid off the track and plowed into a clump of trees, crushing himself to death almost instantly. A blown tire has been blamed as the cause of the crash. Pilot error was never considered. Not even remotely.

Grantelli, a close friend and huge admirer of Clark was more blunt: "He was killed by Colin Chapman's greed," Granatelli said in 1995. "Because he was too good a driver to lose control of the car. Colin built cars light and only when they broke, he'd make them heavier. He flat out cost Jimmy his life."

Whether that's even close to the truth is only a

matter of sad conjecture now. What is true is that Jimmy Clark was a tragic hero. Those who were too young to have seen him race are haunted by the memory of this man whose life was cut short. Those Americans who watched him race from this side of the Atlantic as he was winning first had resentment toward him; then begrudging respect; and then, finally, outright affinity for the young Scot.

That support was betrayed when he lost his life, as if an entire comradeship had grown only to be crushed in his death; as if he had betrayed his fans by dying. Drivers who had allowed themselves a modicum of humility and generosity during his life shut themselves off. That, fans and drivers alike assured ourselves, would never happen again.

After Jimmy Clark, we all saw racing differently.

Clark at speed in the winning Lotus in 1965. Two previous times he came up short, but in 1965 he brought the little car home. At that point Clark ceased being an outsider. Russ Lake

Chapter 6

Mark Donohue

On a hot summer afternoon in Sonoma, California, Bob Bondurant, in one of his impromptu court sessions at Sears Point Raceway, was talking about driving and drivers, giving his impressions of the latest and of the greatest, reminiscing, as he often does, with people he doesn't know. When the subject turned to Mark Donohue Bondurant became somber.

Donohue was a true friend, he'd said. They had begun racing at the same time and had followed each other in retirement: Bondurant involuntarily as he crashed heavily at the Belgian Grand Prix (he woke up, he said, sitting in a puddle looking at his broken feet, and decided there must to be a better way to make a living; and opened one of America's first race car driving schools, The Bob Bondurant School of High Performance Driving); and Donohue, voluntarily, in 1973.

"I asked him why he had returned," Bondurant said, "especially after what he'd said about driving—with all the headaches. He said he needed the money. I remember thinking then that that was the wrong reason to race. I still believe it."

Mark grew up around Pennsylvania, where his longtime partner Roger Penske also was based. In 1960, at an SCCA driving school, Donohue met Penske, who was an instructor at the school. The two formed a loose association which would eventually blossom into one of the strongest partnerships in

Donohue circa 1970. Donohue was not just a great driver, he was also a great engineer. With his graduate degree in engineering, he was a great asset to Roger Penske not just on the track, but in the shop as well. Judy Stropus

American racing, rivalling the partnership Penske had with later find, Rick Mears. It can truly be said that Donohue was "Penske's boy."

In 1961 Donohue, who was twenty-three at the time, won an SCCA amateur championship. Within two years he was driving in the pro classes, but had not yet turned professional. But that was how American road racing was in the mid-sixties: a hobby, but nothing more really. So, the money was a source of worry for Donohue, who had received his masters in engineering just recently.

Although he had done well with co-driver Walt Hangston (who was also an instructor at the school where Donohue met Penske), finishing third at the 24 Hours of Daytona and the Sebring 12 Hours, it wasn't until later in that season that he would become a full-time race car driver. He finished second in the SCCA Can-Am Championship behind John Surtees, winning one round of the six-race championship in his Lola.

Penske hired Donohue to drive an SCCA Trans-Am Camaro in the 1967 season as well as to follow up the second season in Can-Am. The SCCA had been Penske's major stomping grounds and he wanted to prove his point as a car owner. Donohue posted two second place finishes that year and a fourth in the first five races of Trans-Am, and on the sixth try at the Marlboro Speedway, he captured his first Trans-Am

Mark Donohue in 1972, passing his teammate Gary Bettenhausen. The McLaren, prepared by Penske Racing, was good enough to win at the Indianapolis 500 that year. Donohue would finish fifth in points that season, his best finish in Indy Cars. Russ Lake, Milwaukee Mile

win for Penske, having taken over the driver from teammate Craig Fisher. It was the first win for Chevy in Trans-Am and established both Donohue and Penske as a firm Chevy team. Donohue was to win twice more in the twelve-race championship, finishing second in the year-end standings. He would also finish third in Can-Am behind Denis Hulme and Bruce McLaren. Hulme would also become Grand Prix World Champion that season.

This was a time in American road racing when there were no lucrative driving contracts. The sport was an esoteric creature which was followed by few fans in comparison to speedway racing. Most of those interested in sports car racing were wealthy, affluent types who were competitors, not paid drivers. The racers tended to know one another and drove for the

love of it, certainly not for the money. But Donohue, was not from a wealthy family. He was being paid to drive, but was not making himself wealthy in the process. Inevitably, it would be his downfall.

In 1968, Donohue utterly dominated the Trans-Am series. He won ten of thirteen races, finishing third and fourth in two of the other three. The eight straight wins and ten in the season would be a record that would stand through at least 1995. He would also manage to finish third again behind Hulme and McLaren again with one win at Bridgehampton in Can-Am. After years as an amateur, his career as a pro driver had begun. He was making a living at what he had considered a hobby.

In 1969 Donohue repeated the previous season's success in Trans-Am, capturing six wins in twelve races

Mark Donohue talks with Penske-Ferrari co-driver David Hobbes as Roger Penske looks on. Hobbes and Donohue co-drove at the 24 hours at Daytona where they finished third. Judy Stropus

and outclassing drivers like Parnelli Jones, Peter Revson and George Follmer. He was also to take Penske's Chevy-Lola to victory at the 24 Hours of Daytona and to start his first Indy 500.

"Mark was a very talented driver," Parnelli Jones, who finished second to Donohue said. "I credited

Baby-faced Mark Donohue in a Chevy Can-Am car in 1967. Although he had retired, by the end of the 1974 season Donohue was back at the wheel of an F1 car, driving the final two Grands Prix of the season. Judy Stropus

myself in a lot of ways in Trans-Am for making him a better driver because I pushed him so hard in Trans-Am. I was with Firestone and they were with Goodyear."

Donohue and Penske moved to American Motors and the AMC Javelin, taking second behind Parnelli Jones, with three wins in eleven races in 1970. If 1967 were the learning season for Trans-Am, 1970 was the learning season for the Indy Car championship. The first year was a learning experience for both men—the first effort of Penske and Donohue. Donohue would finish second in an impressive showing.

In 1971, Donohue captured the Trans-Am Championship for AMC, winning seven of ten races that season. The Indy Car season was also part of Donohue's repertoire, with Donohue winning his first race at Pocono, then following up two weeks later with a victory at Michigan. At the Brickyard, Donohue, who was one of the favorites going into the race, had a transmission failure and had to drop out.

But by 1972, Donohue was back at The Brickyard with experience and impatience. He sat on the front row, out qualified by Bobby Unser and Peter Revson. His Penske teammate, Gary Bettenhausen, took the lead in the late stages of the race and looked like a lock for the victory when, on lap 188, with Donohue in third spot, Bettenhausen lost power and rolled into the pits. Donohue was then second, catching Jerry Grant's Eagle. As Grant had to pit, Donohue sped past. He won by a full lap. The win at Indy was the only one for Donohue that season. He would finish fifth in the championship.

But the win at the Speedway would give Donohue a long-awaited taste of financial success. And he liked it. Although he qualified third quick again the following season, he would not repeat his win. The Indy start would be his last. Instead of concentrating on the Indy car championship, he preferred instead to contest the Can-Am series, which he dominated by winning six of eight races in his Porsche 917, the most of any driver in history.

"He was a great competitor," Gordon Johncock remembered. "He was a guy you could run wheel to wheel with and be confident that he wasn't going to put you in the fence or spin you out. He was the kind of guy you wanted to race with."

At Road Atlanta, heading down the back straight at the dip, his Porsche got airborne. He crashed the car and injured his leg.

"He went to the hospital in Gainesville, Georgia," Judy Stropus, long-time Donohue friend and legendary PR and timing whiz said. "They kind of told him to keep walking on it. But it was killing him. I remember I flew in and picked him up and took him to the Atlanta Falcons doctor, who knew about all those kind of injuries. The tendons were separated. They were making him walk on something that wasn't together."

After the accident and the recovery he just decided he wanted to change his life. He retired. He had been racing when racing was a pastime less than a career. It pleased him to race, but he had never dreamed it would take him as far as it had. He was slightly insecure of his position as a professional driver and decided to make a break.

"Unfortunately, "Stropus said, "he wasn't a very good businessman. He needed work. He tried to get a dealership but you can't just get a dealership based on your name. You have to show them some businesses sense, and he really didn't have any. He was really only good at the driving.

"I talked to him about it (and) what he told me he was coming back. I thought it was a mistake and I told him that. He kind of semi-agreed, but he had no choice. He had to go to work. He couldn't make it as a team manager. He was a race car driver."

But by the end of the season, he was driving the final two Grands Prix of the season—right there on home turf at Mosport and then at Watkins Glen. He had raced a McLaren F1 car in 1971 and had enjoyed the experience, finishing third in Canada. Now it was his chance to get back into racing in the big time with his old partner, Roger Penske.

In 1975 he was racing for Penske again in the full F1 World Championship. In Austria, the twelfth race of the fourteen-race season, Donohue's front tire failed on race morning in pre-race practice. He had hit a light post and it had given him what was first report-

Donohue in an Indy Practice session in 1969 as USAC technical inspectors and Roger Penske look on. Within a few years they would be the team to beat. Courtesy Goodyear Tire

With the Borg-Warner Trophy in 1972. The win would be Donohue's only at the Indianapolis Motor Speedway and one of his last in Indy Cars. Donohue won by a full lap over Al Unser. He would finish fifth in the championship. Judy Stropus

ed as a light concussion. He was taken to the hospital and by the afternoon of August 17, 1975 he was dead.

Unfortunately, that was not the end of Donohue's story. The crash was blamed on Goodyear's tire, and Donohue's family sued. Ironically, Donohue had often spoken about the nature of the business and fully understood the consequences of his choice to be a race car driver. The suit affected the sport significantly, and Goodyear, as well as some other companies, reportedly settled with Donohue's heirs, in effect bequeathing them the money Donohue didn't make as an engineer or car dealer or whatever. It was an even sadder ending than what had originally been scripted.

In a book written in 1972 by racing journalist, Jerry Miller, a few paragraphs of the recent Indy 500 winner would be prophetic:

"Asked then about the recurring suggestions that he could find happiness in the luxurious Grand Prix circuit overseas," Miller wrote, "Donohue answered, 'I'm not independently wealthy like some race car drivers. I just couldn't pack up and go over there and announce I was ready to take over racing in Europe. There's plenty of good racing over here and I don't see why I should give that up and go over where I can't make a living.' "

No amount of money was worth what Donohue paid.

Chapter 7

Fred Duesenberg

Nearly a century later the word "Duesey" still has a meaning. Big. Wild. Incredible. The man who was the namesake for the word's origin, Fred Duesenberg, was himself a real "Doosey". He was at once a genius and a model of disorganization. He was revered and he was dismissed. But he was rarely unspectacular.

Fred Duesenberg was born in 1874 in Lippe Germany; his brother, August-Samul, or Augie, was born five year later, also in Lippe. With five siblings in the family, the death of their father at a young age was to have a profound affect on the Duesenberg boys. The eldest son, Henry, moved to the United States, land of opportunity, then sent for his mother and four brothers and sisters. Almost immediately, Augie and Fred worked to support the family. As one might expect, neither had any formal education. Both, however, were lifelong students of machinery.

From a very early age, Fred was making a living off fixing broken farm machinery in rural Iowa, where the family had settled outside Des Moines. By the time he was twenty-one he had created his own manufacturing business, making bicycles, which years earlier had created a sort of new freedom in pre-millenium America. Fred was drawn to the bicycle originally from mechanical interest, but as he began to ride bicycles himself, he found himself racing as he was in building, and by 1898 he had established world records for two and three mile distances.

By 1900, he had bolted a small motor to a bicycle of his own design and the quest for motorized transportation overrode any goals of improving man-

The brothers: Augie (left) and Fred. Looks are not deceiving; the brothers were as friendly as they appear here. They worked hard, expected miracles, but had a faithful group of followers. Fred was the technician of the pair, able to take Augie's creative ideas from paper to reality. Courtesy Auburn-Cord Duesenberg Museum

powered vehicles. Two years later he decided he needed more understanding of how the automobile functioned and he began working for the Rambler Motorcar Company in Wisconsin. At the same time, he was attracted to early flight technology and studied this in his spare time. With that knowledge and understanding under his belt, he returned to Des Moines and opened up The Iowa Automobile and Supply Company, which, with the help of his bother Augie, modified and raced automobiles.

In 1907 an entrepreneurial attorney named Mason saw the talent the Duesenberg brothers possessed and provided them seed capital to start an auto manufacturing company, called Mason Motor Company. The brothers produced a small, rugged little two-cylinder car which could withstand the beatings of the mostly rural Mid-western country. The car was reliable—odd for its day—and eventually the entire business was bought up by Frank Maytag, the washing machine tycoon. Without the direction of Duesenberg, the company, Maytag-Mason, closed in 1916, six years after it was purchased.

During his stint at the Mason plant, Mason compelled Fred Duesenberg to use his knowledge of racing to produce an engine for Mason to use in racing applications. Duesenberg agreed but asked that he retain the rights to his inventions. To the Duesenberg good fortune, Mason coalesced. The result was the walking-beam engine, so called because of a huge rocker assembly that operated the valves directly and simply. The system was so efficient and sturdy that it was adopted by several manufacturers and lasted well into the 1930s. It was to become one of Duesenberg's trademarks.

When the Maytag deal went through, the company moved out of Des Moines, leaving the Duesenberg brothers behind. They returned to their original business of preparing and racing cars, and used that little engine in some of the leftover Masons, which they renamed, appropriately, Duesenberg.

By 1912, they had created a 350 cubic inch straight eight walking-beam engine that produced a then prodigious 100 horsepower, with which they quickly found success. By the following season they had entered the Indianapolis 500 with five cars. Although the rules allowed for 450ci engine displacement, they did well enough in their first outing producing a ninth and an eleventh place finish. By 1914, they had Eddie Rickenbacker (not yet the flying ace he would become) driving for them, and they scored their first major win at Sioux City on the Fourth of July.

In 1914, with the outbreak of war, they had turned their attention to marine engines. They had created a straight twelve on commission for a wealthy boat racer and had set up shop in that arena as well, cranking out pairs of pistons that could be connected easily enough to produce two, four, six, eight, ten or twelve cylinder marine powerplants. They were selling like proverbial hotcakes.

By 1916, Duesenberg was experimenting with a V-16 aircraft engine for use in the war. The engine was actually developed by Bugatti, based on Duesenberg's straight eights and manufactured in Paris by Duesenberg. In fact, an odd footnote appears at this time. While Duesenberg was first testing the engine in Paris, an American soldier was stationed there with him, overseeing production on behalf of the U.S. Army. While testing the propeller equipped engine, the soldier accidentally walked into the prop and was killed. The first U.S. soldier killed in Europe was therefore killed in the Duesenberg plant. After that disaster, the manufacturing for the Bugatti was moved back to the United States, to Duesenberg's plant.

The U.S. Government used the Duesenberg plant as a sort of test bed. While Fred Duesenberg created and tested his own ideas, the U.S. government, which had bought and installed a 1,000 horsepower capacity dyno in the plant, was testing every possible creation of U.S. inventors right there in the Duesenberg plant. The information available to Duesenberg first-hand was incredible.

After the war, the success of the 16-cylinder aircraft engine—which was essentially two walking beam eights fused together—took the Duesenbergs back to the track where they began winning again in 1920. Although racing had never completely shut down as it would do in the 1940s with the advent of WWII, it had slowed for Duesenberg personally because of his commitments to the aircraft engine project. In fact, the Duesenberg had compiled an impressive record. From

1917 to the end of 1919 (the Indy 500 was run only once during those years) it was used as an aircraft repair depot in 1917 and 1918. Duesenbergs had won thirteen races of the fifty-four in the championship over those three seasons, and seven of eighteen in 1919 alone. Developed for their passenger touring cars, the Duesenberg engine, which debuted in 1919 and was a throwback to more reliable and simplistic engines of years earlier, had forsaken the dual overhead designs of the 1910s to a SOHC design racing engine. Although originally a pushrod engine, the engine was cast as a single unit, incorporating crankcase, cylinders and combustion chambers. The Duesenberg's guts were easily accessible and the compression low, thereby keeping gasket failure to a minimum. With it, Duesenberg made history.

In 1920, Duesenberg inaugurated the new Beverly Hills board track with a convincing win at the hands of Jimmy Murphy. Although Murphy and Tommy Milton would win eight of eleven races in the championship that season, and Milton would take the championship, the Indianapolis 500 would remain unconquerable for Duesenberg. In 1921 also, a Duesenberg would win fifteen of twenty races, but fail again to win the prestigious Indy 500.

Duesenberg's creations, although beautifully thought out, were often poorly executed. Where, as you will find in the chapter on Miller, contemporary Millers were technically perfect and parts were interchangeable from one engine to the next, Duesenbergs were made with one-off parts, which if they failed, needed to be re-machined to that specific engine.

The Duesenberg engine had been technically superior—so much so that Harry Miller had copied many of the design innovations. But the Duesenberg execution had been poor. Jimmy Murphy purchased the Duesenberg in which he had won the 1922 Le Mans race and junked the Duesenberg engine, replacing it with a Miller copy of a Duesenberg. With that creation, Duesenberg officially won their first Indianapolis 500. Of course, Duesenberg was sorely disappointed that it had not been in his own car, under his own management.

From that time on, Duesenberg was on the defensive. In 1923, Duesenberg would win no races, the first time since 1914 that that would happen. All eight would be swept by Miller cars powered by Miller engines.

It was the Duesenberg straight eight that Miller copied and eventually perfected to beat Duesenberg. It was ironic that the engine was successful at the hands of Harry Miller, who had experimented with straight eight and sixteen cylinder engines with little success.

But the following season, 1924, with a 121ci, DOHC engine, Duesenberg would finally win at Indy, with Pete de Paulo at the helm; then repeat the effort next season with Joe Boyer. The Duesenberg would

Fred Duesenberg in his office at Duesenberg Inc. in Indianapolis. The clutter seen here is nothing compared to what drivers like Eddie Rickenbacker and Wilbur Shaw described. But despite his disorganization, he was revered and respected. Drivers of the time yearned to drive for Duesenberg. Courtesy Auburn-Cord Duesenberg Museum

win twice more before racing's Golden Age would slide into oblivion at the end of 1929, with Miller taking the other three 500s. The 1930s and the era of frugality at Indy changed the emphasis from a high-tech spectacle to a run-what-you-brung show. In that climate, Duesenberg and Miller's cars were essentially obsolete.

But as Millers were winning on the track, Duesenbergs were winning on the street. Duesenberg passenger cars were selling well, and try as they might, Miller was not as romantic an image as a Duesey had become in all those years.

As obsessed with the racing as Fred Duesenberg had become, his original raison d'etre had already been accomplished. He was in racing to sell street cars and to that end he was extremely successful. The Duesenberg reputation was sterling and the customers ranged from entertainers to dignitaries. There were few street cars that had the workmanship and the attention to detail that the Dueseys had. Nor were there any passenger cars that had the performance of the Duesenbergs.

Fred Duesenberg died on July 26, 1932, when his Model J skidded off the road in Pennsylvania. His injuries were critical, but it was pneumonia which ultimately killed him. With Fred gone, it was difficult for Augie, who excelled at taking Fred's ideas and making them work, to carry on with the overall marketing and management of the racing and production lines. The line was eventually incorporated into Auburn-Cord-Duesenberg.

In the end, unlike Harry Miller, Duesenberg's critics were few. He had a childlike trust that made him a poor businessman and a gregarious and overwhelming warmth that made him like a brother—or later a father—to his employees and his peers. He was said to have had energy that was unbounded and ideas would keep him up days at a time until he got them down on paper.

The name Duesey came to mean something fantastic, out of the ordinary, and ultimately unbeatable. In fact, it was beatable. But for three decades, there was nothing that evoked the kind of emotion like the name of Fred Duesenberg.

Chapter 8

Emerson Fittipaldi

When race fans think of Emerson Fittipaldi, they think of an eternally smiling, ultra-competitive Brazilian, blessed with that flair specific to Latins. That sort of zest for life that is often characterized in movies, but that rarely moves from the screen to the street. Or at least not where mere mortals can easily see it. Fittipaldi has it in spades.

But while he was in F1, while he was winning, and even worse, while he was losing for all those subsequent years, he was not the man we know now as an Indy Car driver. In the mid-seventies, when Emerson Fittipaldi was the hottest driver in F1 racing, there was a different demeanor. He had become a sort of dour young man on a mission. That mission was to win World Championships; to be the best ever.

To see him now is akin to seeing an alcoholic who has found religion. He has changed dramatically. Lightened up tremendously. And his performance on the track has improved to where it was before he felt the weight of the racing world upon his shoulders.

Take a look at him. Born in December of 1946, in 1996, he is now the oldest active driver in Indy Car racing. Ironically, he was the youngest World Champion in history when he captured the Grand Prix title in 1972. But as he ages, he seems to get younger, more vital. Yet he is just as quick as when he started driving nearly thirty years earlier.

In 1996 Fittipaldi was the oldest active driver in Indy Car racing. He began racing in the mid-sixties in Brazil and ironically, he was the youngest World Champion in history when he captured the Grand Prix title in 1972 with five victories. Courtesy Marlboro Racing

Fittipaldi began racing in the mid-sixties in Brazil. Inspired by his father, a famous Brazilian motorsports broadcaster, Fittipaldi won his first championship—in Brazilian Formula Vee—by the time he was twenty-one years old. He quickly moved to England and by the middle of the 1970 season found himself in a Lotus F2 car, which became a Lotus F1 car by season's end. It was to yield him his first Grand Prix victory, with a win at Watkins Glen in October of 1970. By the end of 1972, Fittipaldi had his first Grand Prix World Championship, with five victories. In 1974, Fittipaldi won his second title—this time with McLaren, whom he joined at the end of the previous year. He took three wins that season, then two in 1975 and was never to win again in a Grand Prix car as he struggled with his own Grand Prix team.

If the funk had started in those days following his first championship with the demands put upon him by sponsors and the team, by the time he went from McLaren to his own team, he was in a major fog.

The team, called appropriately Fittipaldi, was a disaster almost from the start. It was originally a single-car team, and so development was much slower. And because Fittipaldi was relegated to being the team manager as well as the driver, his concentration in the cockpit was less than optimum. His brother Wilson was responsible for administrative and fiscal decisions of the team, but was not adept at either. The team was poorly funded and regarded as mostly noncompetitive.

Fittipaldi's results were horrible: he scored three points in 1976 in the Copersucar Ford (sponsored then by Brazil's largest sugar manufacturer); eleven points in 1977, seventeen in 1978 (his best season on his own, finishing seventh in the championship); three in 1979; and eleven in 1980.

By 1981 he was done with driving. He'd hired Keke Rosberg and Chico Serra to drive, but they fared worse than he had, posting no points at all in 1981 and a lone point from Serra in 1982. Fittipaldi disbanded the team. The end had come—until he rediscovered Indy Cars .

"The first time I watched Indy I was about seven or eight years old and I watched a documentary about Indianapolis back home in Sao Paulo," a happier Fittipaldi said more recently. "That was the first time I saw it. Then when I joined Lotus and Colin Chapman, it was the first time I saw that it was possible I could go race at Indianapolis. That started my real interest at Indianapolis. I was asking anyone who knew, 'How was the experience? What did you think about it?' You know the European people are very strange when they talk about Indianapolis. They like Indianapolis, but at the same time they are very jealous of Indianapolis, being the number one motor race. Even talking to not just Colin Chapman, but different people who tried Indianapolis different drivers, European drivers. I talked to Denny

"Off the racetrack he's just a super person. We work really well together and share information," said Penske teammate Al Unser Jr. Here Unser Jr. leads Fittipaldi. Courtesy IndyCar

Hulme, Jackie Stewart, Jack Brabham, Jochen Rindt. They all drove Indianapolis. They all had that feeling."

Fittipaldi eventually had his chance. It was not just the 500 he came to do, but the entire series. It would take him five years to win the race, but eventually, when he did it, it was a tremendous victory. For anyone watching it was obviously a very emotional and special occasion. The Brazilian, who eventually became only one of two people to have won the F1 World Championship, the Indy Car Championship and the Indy 500

"The first time I watched Indy. I was about seven or eight years old," Fittipaldi said, "Then when I joined Lotus and Colin Chapman it was the first time I saw that it was possible I could go race at Indianapolis." Here, Fittipaldi leads his fellow countryman, Mauricio Gugelmin, another huge fan of the hoopla—the Indianapolis 500. Courtesy IndyCar

(Mario Andretti was the other), had won the 'Greatest Spectacle in Sports.'

"It's very, very special," Fittipaldi said about the success at Indy. "It will always be very special. Of all my racing victories throughout my career, those two wins at Indy were the two most important, no doubt about it."

And there were many. He won 14 World Championship Grands Prix; captured two World Championships, becoming the youngest man to ever win a championship at the age of 24. But for sure, the most enjoyable were the times after 1982.

"I enjoy much more here than Formula One. Race to race, the ambiance is much nicer, it is much more fun," he said.

Ironically, when Fittipaldi had his first chance to test an Indy Car, he drove around, got out and proclaimed he would never drive one of these. He did indeed drive an Indy Car and became a two time Indy Car Champion.

Fittipaldi's first season in Indy Cars, 1984—as well

as his second, third, fourth and fifth—was inauspicious. Driving for Pat Patrick, his best finish, was a fourth place and he finished 13th in the PPG Indy Car Championship, finishing runner-up in Rookie-of-the-Year standings behind Roberto Guerrero.

In 1985, although he won at the Michigan 500, he finished sixth in points. The following season he won once at Road America, but still managed to finish only seventh in the year-end standings. The 1987 season gave him two wins and tenth in the championship. And in 1988 he won twice and finished seventh again in the championship.

If you had looked at the man in 1988 and then again in 1989, you would have noticed a remarkable change. In the off season, Fittipaldi had adopted a strict diet and emotional regimen. The food went from being normal pit food to very healthy, very calculated meals. As an adjunct to the diet, Fittipaldi was doing more physical exercise. Most important, he was concentrating on racing. Odd to say, but Fittipaldi had not completely returned to racing. Not really.

With his World Championships came fame and lots of money. With the money came investments. The 500,000-plus acre orange groves in Brazil, the Hugo Boss sportswear franchises in Brazil, the Mercedes-Benz

Emerson Fittipaldi in 1993 with his second Borg Warner Trophy. If the milk looks slightly odd, that's because it isn't milk. Fittipaldi, the owner of some of the most expansive orange groves in Brazil, chose to buck tradition for his second victory and drink orange juice instead while accepting the accolades. Rick Dole

Now that it's all over, he still looks as fresh as if he just woke up. Fittipaldi's physical regimen, which he started in the late eighties, gave his racing career a renaissance. He looked younger and admitted feeling better than he had in years. His results showed it. Rick Dole

dealerships, and the Fittipaldi race gear. And the would-be champion was always on the phone. It was his bane when he was in F1 and it was his bane in Indy Cars.

"Even after he got out of the race car he was working. He was on his cellular phone talking to Brazil and then he would get in his race car and go qualify it," Gary Smith, one of his personal trainers, said. "He never took a break. And it was affecting him."

So Fittipaldi came to the 1989 season with a new attitude and a new outlook. Racing was racing, and during a race weekend he did nothing but concentrate on his driving. It proved to be his biggest year. He captured the PPG Indy Car World Series Title, winning at Detroit, Portland, Cleveland, Nazareth and the Indy 500, beating Al Unser Jr. in a race that put Unser out of the event. Fittipaldi became the first foreign-born driver to win at the Brickyard since Graham Hill did it in 1966. The season also proved to be the most lucrative in the history of American racing, with Fittipaldi becoming the first driver to surpass the $2 million mark.

In 1990, He joined Penske and teammates Rick Mears and Danny Sullivan. He finished well off the next two seasons, winning only once each year, but was bitten by the victory bug. By the 1992 season, he was back in winning form, taking five victories and finishing fourth in the series. In 1993, he won three times and finished second in the championship. And in 1994, he finished runner-up yet again in the series.

Pictured here in 1992, Fittipaldi's World Championships gave him fame and money—plus the added workload which came with managing his new business interests. The multi-directional tug-of war for his attention was affecting his performance on the track. In 1989 Fittipaldi came to work with a new attitude and a new outlook. Racing was racing, and during a race weekend he did nothing but concentrate on his driving. Eva Vega

If he has moved back into his element, it surprises few people. Fittipaldi, even during his bad days has been known as a giving man. Even in the off times, Fittipaldi was always ready to lend a hand.

Emerson Fittipaldi rounds a corner in his Penske, the famous psychedelic helmet visible from a distance. When it appeared in Formula one almost two decades earlier, it made quite an impression. Even today it's still one of the more wild designs on the track, toned down as it now is. Rick Dole

Long Beach. The street circuit had never been good to the Brazilian. Although teammates Al Unser Jr. and Paul Tracy had won at the Southern California venue, Fittipaldi, who raced here even during the days when the race was a Grand Prix, never managed to ascend farther than second place. Rick Dole

"Off the racetrack he's just a super person. We work really well together and share information. It was one of those things that kind of clicked to begin with. But Emerson is just a super human being," Al Unser Jr., Fittipaldi's Penske teammate, said.

Unser Jr., who was involved in one of the most dramatic moments of Indy 500 history, should know. While grappling for the lead with Fittipaldi, Fittipaldi tapped Unser and he spun up into the wall. Unser was out; Fittipaldi went on to the lead and to the win—his first. As he came by for the victory lap, Unser, who was not his teammate at the time, applauded his victory.

"That '89 deal, had I thought he did it intentionally or maliciously, it would have been a different deal. But Emerson's not that kind of a man, so I knew it was an accident, a racing deal. Even though it hurt really bad, he deserved it. He had driven well all day. Emerson really just cares about his fellow competitors.

"He was the one who stopped his race car and jumped on top of Niki's car while it was full of flames into the fire and pulled Lauda out of there," Unser said. "He's been the first one at a number of different accidents and as a race car driver, that's very tough to do."

Fittipaldi may or may not have been involved in Lauda's rescue. Lauda was unconscious and claims to having three men come to his rescue—none being Fittipaldi. But what is certain is that Fittipaldi dispatched his own doctor to Lauda during that critical time. Regardless, the paddock at any Indy Car race would trust their lives to the man they call simply "Emmo."

In 1996, he was still as enthusiastic as ever to get back for the new season. Having come off a horrible 1995 season, Fittipaldi was confident, smiling. Happy.

"It had been a very tough year for us. It was my most difficult year in Indy Car racing. When you don't go to Indianapolis (because the Penskes were unable to qualify) it's very tough. But you have to find motivation from race to race. Sometimes that's very tough," Fittipaldi said. "(But) I still enjoy it here as much as I did five or ten years ago. It's very enjoyable when the car's going well. I still love it. I don't think there's much difference."

And when is it time to stop?

Fittipaldi, in 1995 smiled with that twinkle in his eyes and said slowly, "No Idea. No Plans." Then he said again, "If you love the sport you have the motivation to carry on and you have the dedication to be quick. That comes with love and dedication. You have to dedicate yourself to the sport."

Certainly a change from how he felt in 1982.

Chapter 9

A.J. Foyt

The man is an enigma. A damnable enigma. Every time you want to like A.J. Foyt, he does something that makes you hope he never succeeds again, ever, as long as he lives. And every time you find yourself grinning because of his misfortune, he'll do something that makes your heart break.

You'll find no A.J. quotes within these next few pages. A.J. Foyt doesn't do interviews for books. His public relations person, Anne Fornoro, will tell you: he just doesn't. So don't ask.

He is tough. More often than not, he's fuming about something. More specifically, it usually has to do with someone, a person, and not an inanimate object. But right as you're ready to believe he hates everybody on the planet, you get another jolt.

The eyes are unmistakable: A.J. Foyt, in the orange helmet which marked his later days in racing. And he looks like something's bothering him. Again. Rick Dole

In 1991, in what was supposed to be A.J. Foyt's final season, Foyt appeared on ESPN's Speedweek. Along with him were Al Unser Sr. and Johnny Rutherford. The discussion with host Bob Jenkins revolved around Foyt and his contribution to the sport. As you might expect, it was a fawning tribute to the driver many have called America's greatest; and yes, Foyt was suitably humble.

There they were, the four of them talking about how wonderful Foyt was and there was Foyt, blushing like a thirteen year old girl, looking so uncomfortable and so human you just had to love him.

Of course, he promptly went out and decided, no, he wasn't going to retire after all, slapping the face of any journalist who had fawned over him.

That was A.J. Foyt.

"A.J. can be tough, and he is tough," Johnny

Rutherford said. "But to his friends and to the people he knows he's very soft-hearted and a very nice guy. We've been friends for a long time."

If Foyt has a soft side to him, it's usually well hidden. One year at Indy, Foyt came screaming into the pits with an ill-handling car. While the crew changed tires, Foyt gestured wildly. The radio was apparently not working—either that, or he was screaming so loud the words were unintelligible. The crew had not the slightest idea what he was gesturing about.

As they leaned toward him trying to determine what was so important, Foyt became desperate. Arms flailing outside the cockpit, he looked as if he might burst a ventricle. The crew, now plainly frightened of this maniac in the Copenhagen helmet, still had no idea what he wanted.

So he unbuckled the belts. And got out.

In the middle of the race, with cars whizzing past, Foyt was admonishing the crew. He led them to the front of the car, and could we have read lips through the full face helmet, he might have been saying, "Wing! Idiots! Wing. Adjust the Goddamned thing!"

Just to make his point he even kicked it.

After a few minutes, presumably once his blood pressure got back down to triple digits again, Foyt got back in the car and raced off to finish somewhere down in the field.

After qualifying for the Indy 500 in 1985, Foyt was asked about his run. Foyt replied, in front of 350,000 fans, "It ran like a tub of shit." All stood up and applauded. Only A.J. could get away with something like this.

Then there was the time late in his career when Foyt

was racing a GTP in the Camel GT series. The Texan was doing well in the race until Argentine driver Oscar Larrauri drove into him. It wasn't very nice, and not all that professional, but it was obviously not deliberate.

Foyt's 962 Porsche's suspension was disabled—but the car still had power. He restarted it and waited for Larrauri to come 'round again. When Foyt spotted him, he shoved the car into gear, dropped the clutch and tried to sideswipe the Argentinian. Then, afterward, he said a few choice words to the TV crew covering the event.

A few weeks later, at the Canadian Grand Prix, Larrauri was still shaken. When asked about the incident with Foyt the normally calm and cool Argentine began rambling about racing and Foyt, fame and Grand Prix driving. That's what kind of affect Foyt had on people. He scared the crap out of them.

He usually seemed like he would just as soon run you over as talk to you. But as you'd suppose, there's more to it than that.

"One time in Phoenix there was a crash and I got my hand burned very severely," Rutherford said. "A.J. had dropped out of the race with engine problems early, I think, and as a result he was standing down in the fourth turn when we slid to a stop in that area. He

came running over to the scene and of course was very concerned about my hand being burned third degree.

"He really kind of took charge. He went to the hospital with me, made sure that the doctor got there and took care of me. He called my wife and told her about the injury and told her I was okay, but my hand was burned. He and his wife Lucy, who was at the race that day, took care of me overnight and made sure everything was okay, got me on the plane the next morning. A.J. has got a soft side to him. He's a good guy."

But, Christ, he keeps it hidden.

Rutherford nodded his head assertively, "I don't think (he wants people to know it). I'm not sure that he doesn't like people to know it, it's just that he's . . . I don't know . . . maybe it's that he just doesn't do it for everybody."

But when he does, he makes a friend for life. In 1965, A.J. Foyt was solidly in the field and newcomer Al Unser was struggling to find a car to make the race. Unser was driving for Al Arciero in a car that really wasn't competitive. Foyt somehow saw the potential of this kid from Albuquerque and got him into his first 500. Foyt took him aside and asked him if he'd like to drive his backup car. Unser said of course, and Foyt

A.J. Foyt in 1967. He would win five of twenty-one events and capture his third Indy 500, and his fifth Indy Car title. The following season he would win an unprecedented fourth Indy 500 victory. Courtesy Goodyear

gave Unser Sr. his first ride. Unser went on to race in Foyt's backup car, finishing ninth in his first event.

"A.J. gave Al his backup car and got him into the race," Rutherford recalls. "Al and I both have a special fondness in our hearts for old Ironhead Foyt," he said.

Foyt's idiosyncrasies would not be so tolerable and his generosity seem so remarkable if he was not the driver he was. In his prime, Foyt was the best.

In his thirty-five seasons as a race car driver, Foyt won some sixty-seven championship races. He has won fifteen races more than second place man Mario Andretti, and more than twice as many as any active driver in Indy Cars.

Foyt was born in Houston, Texas on January 16, 1935. The son of a racing enthusiast, Foyt's father was responsible in getting him into racing in the first place, as he prepared midgets for him in the early fifties, and was instrumental in his later successes in championship racing, building his cars and acting as crew chief until 1982.

Foyt began his career in Championship cars in 1958 with the Dean Van Lines Special Roadster. He finished tenth in the championship and sixteenth at Indy. In 1959, he was fifth in the championship and finished the Indy 500 without incident, managing a tenth.

His fortunes changed in 1960 forever, as he won his first race on the dirt at DuQuoin, then won three times in the next five races, capturing the championship. He repeated the championship in 1961 with four victories, and took home his first Borg-Warner Trophy with a success at the Indianapolis Motor Speedway as well—his first victory at Indy.

In 1962 he won five of thirteen races and was runner-up to Rodger Ward. He won the championship in 1963 and 1964, capturing five of twelve in 1963 and an astounding ten of thirteen in 1964, including seven in a row, his second Indy 500 among them. In 1965 he was second to Mario Andretti. 1966, his worst season in his early years, failed to bring a single win. His best finishing position was a lone second place. He came back in 1967 to win five of twenty-one events and captured his third Indy 500, and his fifth Indy Car title. It would be ten years before his fourth and final 500 victory, but the wins at other tracks would keep coming. That season, he also partnered Dan Gurney to win the 24 Hours of Le Mans, becoming the only driver in history to accomplish such a feat.

In 1968, he tried his hand at stock cars, driving the USAC Stock Car championship, then driving some NASCAR events. He won three times in Indy Cars in 1968; once in 1969; and none in 1970, but won five of nine stock car races he entered, becoming runner up in the stock car series. He won once in 1971 while winning one race in stock cars and finishing fifth in the championship.

In 1972, he won the Daytona 500. In 1974, he won twice in Indy cars and once in his only start in stock cars. In 1975, he won the national championship with seven wins in thirteen races, contested

Always a winner. In 1967 Foyt would win the Indy 500, then go to Europe a week later to partner with Dan Gurney to win the 24 Hours of Le Mans, becoming the only driver in history to accomplish such a feat. Courtesy Goodyear

A Firestone endorsement, with Foyt crediting his Firestones for the win at The Speedway. When Firestone constructed 15-inch tires for Colin Chapman, A.J. Foyt was so irritated by the whole thing that he went to Goodyear and asked that they create not just a tire but an entire racing program—which they did, ultimately knocking Firestone out of the winners circle within just a few years. Courtesy Firestone

several stock car and dirt track races, and finished second in the first IROC championship. In 1976, he won twice in Indy Cars, and three of four USAC stock car races. In 1977, he won his fourth and final Indy 500 as well as the championship. In 1978, he won three times. And in 1979, he won the tainted USAC championship as the major players had moved to CART.

By 1979, Foyt's world had changed. It didn't seem to matter anymore that Foyt knew how to drive a roadster at full lock on the dirt. Nobody raced on dirt anymore. Foyt won one more Indy Car race—at a non-points race at Pocono in 1981—but as the eighties came and went, it was clear that the world's greatest was no longer such.

A.J. Foyt is still out there in a manner of speaking. He is now a team owner and has had the same kind of frenetic relationships with his drivers as he had before as a driver with his mechanics. He seems to love them as he starts, nurtures them as they grow and then, when they fail to do what he feels they should do, he launches them.

It is unfair to try to sum up this complex man in just a few pages. He has far more content and experience than even a full book could possibly describe. Journalists like to make things easy. We take a person's memorable experiences and, like tea, try to elicit the valuable byproducts of a personality in just a few minutes and spill it forth onto a page or two or, in this case, five.

Foyt was nothing if not adaptable. Here, at Milwaukee, his car was for whatever reason not ready for the race. He rolled out his sprint car, qualified it on the pole and is seen here racing the car against a field of mostly rear-engined, state-of-the-art cars. Russ Lake, Milwaukee Mile

Robby Gordon, seen here in 1992, had a temperament similar to Foyt's, which doomed the working relationship. At the end of the season, Gordon left for Walker racing even though Foyt said he wanted Gordon to stay. Gordon said he worked for Michael Kranefuss and Ford, not A.J. Foyt. Foyt ended up with Eddie Cheever, which was just as ill-fated a relationship, with Cheever leaving before the season ended in 1995. Courtesy Copenhagen Racing, US Tobacco

Having a good time here, Foyt was not always so much fun in the pits. He tended to keep not only his mechanics on their toes, but other drivers as well. Foyt was as respected as he was feared. Rutherford called him "Old Ironhead Foyt." Courtesy Copenhagen Racing, US Tobacco

A.J. Foyt can not be pigeonholed. He is not what you have just read in these past few pages. And he is not what you have read elsewhere. Every time you think you have him figured out, he will throw you a curve; every time you figure him to zig he'll zag; when you're positive he'll zag, he'll double zag.

But through it all, he has remained consistent about one thing: his desire to win. Not at all costs, nor for mere glory. He does it because it is a part of him, and because he finds personal satisfaction in it. And for that he makes no apologies. To anyone.

The two greatest drivers in the history of American racing, together for the final time as competitors in 1993. At Andretti's first professional race at Langhorne, Foyt won; at Andretti's first appearance at Indy in 1964 Foyt won. Mario's been catching up ever since. As of 1995, Andretti had still not won at Le Mans. Foyt won in 1967 with Dan Gurney as co-driver. Rick Dole

Chapter 10

Leo Goossen & Fred Offenhauser

One of the most amazing histories in Indy Car racing concerns the little engine that refused to die—the Offenhauser, or Offy for short.

The story of the Offy could fill the pages of an entire book all by itself. The evolution and unbelievable fifty-year run is incredible in any context. The engine won nearly 350 championship races and countless sprint car races. At one point, from the middle of 1947 to the middle of 1964, the Offy had won all but three races (one was Louis Unser's Pike's Peak win in a Maserati, one by Jimmy Clark in his Lotus Ford and one by Bob Finney in a Lincoln)—219 in all and 99 straight.

Although this chapter is on both Offenhauser and Goossen, the latter, not the former, is really to be credited with the "Offy" engine, for it was he who took Offenhauser's project over when Offenhauser thought that the engine was obsolete. Goossen sustained it for decades longer.

But the fact that this powerplant survived for so long in the highly competitive racing arena says a great deal about its hardiness and sound design to begin with. The engine, an alternative to the Frontenac Fords that were so dominant on the dirt tracks of the early thirties, was essentially a converted Miller four cylinder marine racing engine. A west coast dri-

*At left,
Leo Goossen worked together with Fred Offenhauser to create the little engine that refused to die—the Offy. Goossen was actually responsible for the longevity of the engine, sustaining it for decades longer when Offenhauser thought the engine was obsolete. Courtesy Bruce Craig*

*At right,
Offenhauser hired Goossen to work for a company owned by Harry Miller. Offenhauser was the shop manager at the time. Miller and Offenhauser were producing racing carburetors and were working on manufacturing racing engines. Courtesy Bruce Craig*

ver lit on the idea of transforming the Miller marine into a lightweight, low-cost alternative to the Fronty-Ford. The engine, made for either 151ci or 183ci hydroplane racing, only cost about a thousand dollars. It was truly a thing of beauty and Leo Goossen was mostly responsible.

Goossen, born of Dutch parents living in Michigan, was out working before he was sixteen years old. Always a visual person, Goossen wanted more than anything to become a draftsman. He worked for Buick for some time before he showed his potential as a draftsman, but what was more impressive were his ideas in design.

Although his career was developing quickly, he had, in 1919, a cancerous growth develop in his lungs. He immediately moved from the East to New Mexico, where the dry heat was prescribed by his doctor for his affliction. In the weather, Goossen did well, and the cancer subsided. He was, however, a prisoner in New Mexico. And there was not much automotive designing going on in Silver City, New Mexico. But there was Harry Miller.

Miller, along with his shop manager, Offenhauser, were producing racing carburetors at the time and had been trying to get deeper into the manufacturing of racing engines. Offenhauser, born in 1888 in Los

Together the two began developing an engine for sprint car racing. Although Miller, who had extensive knowledge of racing engines, saw no future in that particular project, he financed it as a way to keep his men happy. Goossen is shown on the far left. Courtesy Bruce Craig

Angeles and of German extraction, saw Goossen's expertise and hired him immediately, putting him to work as a team leader on a sports prototype project. Although the project was scrapped, it served as a springboard for Goossen.

Goossen quickly was caught up along with Offenhauser in the day-to-day operations of the Miller company. When the 122s and 91s were built, he helped retrofit them with superchargers.

Offenhauser and Goossen became interested in the idea of building and developing an engine for sprint car racing. Miller, as intelligent as he was, saw no future in either grassroots racing nor in replacement parts. He could have cared less if Goossen and Offenhauser wanted to waste their time on it, as long as it didn't affect their input in their main jobs, working on championship race car design. The creation was not independent, but financed by Miller himself more as a way to keep his men happy than anything else.

The engine was developed with a preoccupation toward both sturdiness and adaptability. Although it

Goossen quickly was caught up in the day-to-day operations of the Miller company. When the 122s and 91s were built, he helped retrofit them with superchargers. Courtesy Bruce Craig

was based on an old marine engine, with the new frugality rules of the speedways of the thirties, the engine could be used not only at Indy but on the banks of the dirt or board tracks around the nation. It was powerful, producing perhaps 200 horsepower with 10 to 1 compression ratios to run on pump fuel and benzol. It was cheap—$2,000 dollars for a race-ready unit. It fit the Depression era perfectly.

The engine began winning and, with the right transmission, was capable of some very high speeds. In 1930, Bill Cantlon qualified the car on the front row and finished in the top three at the Speedway, finishing second in the championship that season to Billy Arnold. In a few short weeks, Millers were being snapped up and Miller's shop was deluged with orders for replacement and aftermarket parts. Offenhauser and Goossen had struck upon a cheap racing engine for the privateer.

The marine engine already had some important characteristics from the beginning. It was powerful, but it was also compact and relatively lightweight, meaning it was efficient and, mounted in a sprint car, nice and unobtrusive. The design was eventually changed slightly, incorporating bigger, tougher parts with some very important design characteristics that gave it its long life.

The block and head were designed as a single unit, the crankcase and crank bolted onto the bottom. It was fitted with four valves per cylinder and the bore/stroke was nearly squared, at 4.64x4.25. Everything—except the four valve engine, which was designed during Miller's reign, but not produced until his departure—was provided for the grassroots racer.

By 1933, Miller's business was suffering a complete meltdown. He had almost no interest in continuing the low-budget operations with the little four cylinder, or with any engine as unsophisticated as the rules had specified for that matter. He filed for bankruptcy in 1933, and Fred Offenhauser purchased the tooling from Miller, forming the Offenhauser Engineering Company and rehiring the genius at Miller, Leo Goossen.

From the middle of 1947 to the middle of 1964, the Offy had won all but three races—219 in all and 99 straight. The engine won 350 championship races and countless sprint car races. Courtesy Bruce Craig

When Harry Miller filed for bankruptcy in 1933, Fred Offenhauser purchased the tooling from Miller, and formed the Offenhauser Engineering Company. He rehired the genius at Miller, Leo Goossen. Offenhauser is pictured here at the plant in 1946. Courtesy Bruce Craig

In the late 1930s, Offenhauser Engineering increased the size of the engine to 270ci with a 4.36x4.63 bore/stroke combination. The compression ratio was raised to about 13 to 1, giving the engine nearly 300 horsepower.

The threat from the new formula which allowed supercharging forced Offenhauser to look at re-inventing the Offy. Instead, he sold the company to Indy Winner Louie Meyer and Dale Drake in 1946, and they promptly hired Goossen again.

The recently supercharged competition was more powerful, but still had enough design flaws to allow the Offy more wins than losses. In fact, in Championship racing, the Offy had not been beaten since Louis Unser did it with his Supercharged Maserati. Even though the Offy was still competitive, both Goossen and Offenhauser knew it couldn't last unless the engine was refurbished.

So it was generally strengthened, then fuel injected and by 1950 Meyer and Drake had introduced their supercharged engine—a 177ci, eight-to-one compression engine. The engine now developed a prodigious 480 horsepower at 6,500rpm, or within a few percent of the same figure of the larger supercharged engines.

The Offy, blessed with the same inherent compactness of when it was created in the 1920s, lasted through the roadster age due to its ability to be laid on its side, thereby lowering both the center of gravity as well as the silhouette of the cowling.

When the engines were moved to the rear in the mid-sixties, Ford created a V-8 to challenge the establishment. Drake and Goossen (Meyer had departed for Ford) stepped up to the challenge and revised the supercharged engine, then actually offered a turbocharged version of it, thereby getting more than 600 horsepower out of it. Although it would take some time to get any reliability, the engine, either supercharged or turbocharged, was back on top. Bobby Unser won the first race on behalf of the turbo Offy, and given the jump they had on Ford, the Offenhauser stayed dominant another several seasons.

Finally, the Cosworth, which made its way from Europe to the U.S., knocked the little engine off its perch. In 1975, the de-stroked turbo Cosworth made its debut, and its first win came a year later with Al Unser at the wheel. The Cosworth, which would revolutionize racing engines in its own right, would eventually be the powerplant of choice. Twenty-one months later, the Offenhauser was obsolete, winning its last race at Trenton, New Jersey at the hands of Gordon Johncock—after nearly fifty years of successful boat and automobile racing.

Goossen died in 1973 of a heart attack. He worked up until his death at the age of 71. His last project was to re-design the combustion chambers for the 1974 season for Drake Engineering and Pat Patrick to compete with the new Cosworths. It was half finished by Goossen and then turned over to the Drake company at his death. The engine was renovated one more time by George Bignotti and was as quick as it had ever been, but was not to be pushed any further into racing history. Who knows what would have happened had Goossen been around to have overseen the final product.

Chapter 11

Andy Granatelli

Andy Granatelli arrived at the speedway for the first time in 1946, unconventionally, as he was apt to do for the next twenty seasons.

He'd recently purchased an old 1936 Miller-Ford from the Ford Museum in Dearborn for $5,000 and fully expected not just to race the thing, but perhaps to win in it.

The fact that the car was gummed up, creaky, unsophisticated and outright noncompetitive didn't seem to phase Granatelli in the least. He swapped engines with the flathead in his street rod, fabricated some cams and manifolds through his budding company, Grancor, and got ready to go to Indianapolis.

When he was finished he realized he had a slight problem. There was no money left—not even enough to get the car to the Speedway. Granatelli had no trailer, and worse still, if he had managed to find a trailer, he had no way to tow the car to Indy since his engine was now in the Miller.

Simple enough: he'd *drive* the Miller to Indianapolis.

So Andy and his brother Joe hung a set of Illinois plates, fitted a set of headlights to the Miller and drove the city streets and highways to the Indianapolis Motor Speedway from Illinois.

Grantelli wrote in his autobiography, "It had run like a watch all the way from Chicago, just howling along. When we parked it at Gasoline Alley, it just sat

Andy Granatelli at the Indy 500 in 1973. His lone win at the hands of Mario Andretti in 1969 crowned his car owner campaign which spanned three decades, but for the charismatic Italian, just being there was reward enough.
Bob Tronolone

there, sort of humming quietly to itself while we checked in.

"'Where's yer race car?' the guy said. He had glanced at the Miller Ford and raised his eyebrows. 'You mean you . . . ?'

"'Certainly. We drove it here. Ye Gods, if it's supposed to go 500 miles in a race, don't you think it would last down here from Chicago?'"

And of course, the Granatellis were the talk of the garage. Since it was their only car, they drove it everywhere: to eat, around town or anywhere else they needed to be (they slept in the garage that first year, except for their driver, Danny Kladis, who had a room), which made the establishment green with contempt.

The car qualified on the last row on the final day and a fuel delivery problem put the car out of the race (even after Granatelli fixed it and made it raceworthy again, it was disqualified). An unspectacular finish to an eventful start—which was the story of Granatelli's run at Indy.

At almost every one of Granatelli's many Indy 500s there would be something just not quite right. If they were not unlicensed, then they were four-wheel-drives, if not four-wheel-drives, then jet cars, or something.

From the very beginning Granatelli was controversial. Even when he finally won the race in 1969

Andy Granatelli with Lotus designer, Colin Chapman, looking like the Granatelli most would remember. Later that month he finally won the May 1969 classic with Mario Andretti at the wheel. John Mahoney

with Mario Andretti, Granatelli had successfully pissed enough folks off so that he had almost no friends at the two-and-a-half mile oval.

Granatelli also said this: "We were sort of mini-celebrities. People would come around and stick their heads into our garage and look at the old car. Some of them would chuckle a little; some of them would laugh out loud. Some who were more kind than others came around and introduced themselves and wished us all the best of luck; those where the drivers and owners with a sense of class—which is rare in racing."

Simultaneously seeking acceptance from and repelling the Indy fraternity, his lasting legacy was that of a trouble-maker, a showman, and kind of a clown. His autobiography from which the preceding quotes were extracted was as controversial as anything the man brought to the Speedway. Not actually its contents, which were filled with self-righteous adulation, but more the title: "They Call Me Mr. 500."

With the possible exception of himself and possibly his brothers, *nobody* called him Mr. 500. When the book was written just after the 1968 season, Mr. 500 had not won a race at the Brickyard in 23 years of trying. He only drove the speedway once—but crashed before the car ever qualified.

What Grantelli was, was not a great car owner or a great mechanic, but a great promoter. He promoted Grancor and STP, his companies, shamelessly and very, very successfully. But to the end, Granatelli was always a fan of the Indianapolis 500, ultimately bringing the race even more publicity than it already had.

"All the races in world combined don't have the prestige and the aura of the Indianapolis 500," Granatelli said in 1995. "Seven hundred thousand people attend that race, and it's the largest single gathering of people in the world anywhere, that's something. It's the track. It's magic, that's all."

"And actually, not winning the race was the best thing that ever happened to me. When I didn't win in 1967 with the turbine car I became even more of a crowd pleaser than ever before. Every time I ran and didn't win I was always the underdog, always loved by the crowd, and always got more publicity. I used to garner more publicity than the guy who won the race. You'd open the paper and the first five pages would be about me and my company. It didn't hurt me to lose the race, except for my feelings."

As scorned as he was at the Speedway his antics sold a lot of STP oil treatment. It made him richer than he had ever believed possible and famous, which he would have been anyway. But of his promotions, which spanned the gamut from STP uniforms that looked exactly like pajamas to kissing Mario Andretti sloppily on the cheek in his first and only win at Indy in 1969, Granatelli would become known for two things more than anything else: Novis and jet cars.

The Novi experience began back in 1946 when he saw Ralph Hephburn in the powerful Novi turn a lap at 134.449 mph. That car, with its roaring supercharged, single-planed crank which would up to 8,000 revs, had captured the imagination of the crowds at Indy. It was able to get up to 170 on the straights before braking down to make the turn. The sound it made was unlike anything ever heard at The Speedway. And it was unlike anything Grantelli had ever seen.

The front-wheel-drive, Leo-Goossen designed car had horrible balance problems. The Novi engine was a thirsty monster, which while dry tended to have an awful tendency to understeer. The fuel needed to keep the car running—all eighty-five gallons of it—tended to take the car's weight bias more to the front, which caused terrible oversteer. As the car lost its fuel load it would be neutral for a few laps and then settle into push again. It was so heavy that it wore tires at an astounding rate and was a brute to drive. It didn't do very well, even during its heyday.

In fact, the cars were almost jinxed. Drivers were as respectful of the awesome power of the Novi as if it was a hurricane. Ralph Hephburn had the throttle linkage tied so that he could only use part of the power that was available, and was later killed in the car in qualifying for the 1946 race. Chet Miller was killed in the car in practice in 1953. In 1958, Paul Russio crashed in the first turn of the race and eliminated seven cars.

The cars went through various metamorphoses during the years and lived—although just barely—all through the fifties, often failing to even qualify. Grantelli paid $111,000 for two cars and all the spares that went with them and set off again to the Speedway.

In the course of his business as an aftermarket parts retailer and supplier, Grantelli was making superchargers. He immediately found that he could elicit more power from the car if he tuned the supercharger. When it finally ended its unsuccessful reign at Indy it was producing 837 horsepower!

Plastered with STP stickers all over creation, the car failed to get into the field. He eventually realized that the best way to run the car was neither with front drive nor rear but with four-wheel-drive, which is what he did. By 1965, he had not only a Ferguson four-wheel-drive system, but also Bobby Unser controlling the monster. In 1964, Unser qualified the Novi, but was taken out in the now-infamous crash with Eddie Sachs. In 1965 he had an oil leak and was forced out. The bad luck of the Novi had continued, ultimately dooming the car.

"I still have a completely assembled old high-tailed Novi sitting in the STP Corporation main offices

. . . And occasionally, in a nostalgic mood, I will go out into the garage and sit in that fabled old Novi and relive its days of glory—hearing that high-pitched wail all over again, feeling that burst of power that was like no other. I suppose the legend is over now. The Novi days will never come back. But I can say this: no matter how glamorous the turbines—even if they were to win the 500 for three years in a row—I would rather win just once with the Novi," Granatelli wrote.

In fact, he wasn't to win with the turbines either.

But first came 1966 and the Lotus. Granatelli had partnered Colin Chapman that year for a combined Lotus effort, sponsored, of course, by STP. With Jim Clark and Al Unser driving, Clark led in the late stages of the 1966 race, and Unser crashed. The cars, painted alike in day-glo orange, except for the numbers "18" and "19" were mistaken for one another. Clark was said to have been leading, but after a moment, the scoreboard blinked and the order was changed; Hill first, Clark second. The race ended in that order, with Granatelli, of course, blowing his stack.

"We should have won the race before. In 1966, we *did* win the race and we got screwed out of it. Ironically, two years ago, the scoring man from Indianapolis brought me the documentation which con-

Ever the showman, Granatelli makes sure fans know who he represents. His company, STP, was one of the companies most closely related to racing. "The Racer's Edge," STP's slogan, became synonymous with Indianapolis.
Jack Mackenzie

Granatelli with Indy 500 winner, Gordon Johncock in his STP Double Oil Filter Special. This was Granatelli's final win at The Speedway. Jack Mackenzie

bine engines, effectively cutting his output by some 30 percent. And Granatelli sued, a mistake which would haunt him forever.

While the suit was pending, he hired Colin Chapman to design a Lotus around the engine. Chapman did, and the result—even with the restriction in intake—put driver Joe Leonard on the pole. The cars were even faster with the restriction than before. Two of the three cars dropped out and the final car, driven by Leonard, failed to win again. The following season the turbine was all but completely banned. So was four-wheel-drive.

For 1969, Grantelli, without a plan for the race, bought a young sprint car team, with now-legendary mechanic Jim McGee and Clint Brawner. Grantelli bought the latest Lotus for Andretti, but the young Italian crashed the car. In a year-old Hawk-Ford—a fairly simple and straightforward car—Grantelli finally won the race he had been trying for all his adult life. The now famous wet kiss on the cheek is part of Speedway legend.

"I'm obviously Italian, so I can't control myself," Granatelli laughed. "But it was a combination of things. The world thinks I just grabbed him and hugged him and kissed him. Sure I hugged him and kissed him, but I also whispered in his ear to tell the press there, the world, that he had more STP in his Ford than the other guys.

"Those were the words that came out of his mouth. It made my sales skyrocket. Here's a guy who gets out of the car after three hours and he makes that statement: "I had more STP in my Ford than the other guys." It was the greatest plug in the history for the company. So I kissed him, then I kissed him again. There's no question about it. I'm Italian, you know?"

Granatelli stopped racing in the early seventies when the horrific accident and fire at the Speedway at once killed one of his crewmen and his driver, Swede Savage. "When my driver, Swede Savage got killed, and my mechanic got killed at the same time, I decided I had to campaign for safety, and by doing that I alienated the track and the drivers and the car owners and the officials and everybody else. Since I did do that, hardly anybody's been killed—or burned to death, I should say—like they used to be. They just needed to make those rule changes and they made them because I campaigned for them.

"The fire was in turn four and when the fire occurred and my mechanic started running down towards the car and a stupid tow truck driver rolled backwards down the track—which you're never supposed to do and just ran the kid over. The kid was running and he was so excited that the guy drove right over him like he wasn't there. That was enough to get me out. I came back with my son in 1989, but that's why I actually quit."

But out of the action or not, Granatelli's presence will always be felt in Indianapolis during the month of May.

firmed that we did win the race. But that's the way it goes."

By next year, Granatelli was looking for other ways to make a splash for the 1967 race. What he found was a jet engine. Granatelli had seen a turbine engined car come to the speedway in 1963 when Norm Demler's car was producing nearly 260mph with a turbine. It was just the gimmick Grantelli needed. He created the now famous GTP Turbine Car, a center-spined lopsided machine that had the driver sit on one side of the machine and the engine—a Pratt & Whitney helicopter turbine on the other.

With Parnelli Jones at the wheel the car qualified on the second row. There had been loud protests from the field about the noisy car and Jones had reportedly been coached on how *not* to show off. When the race started, the car literally jetted off into the distance—only to fail two laps from the end due to the now fabled six dollar transmission bearing.

The Speedway promptly cut the inlet size for tur-

Chapter 12

Dan Gurney

Dan Gurney always has time. No matter what, no matter when, and no matter with whom, he always has a moment for a smile and a chat. After all, diplomats have to be tolerant.

The three great all-around drivers of the twentieth century—not counting specialists like Johnny Rutherford or Richard Petty—should be listed as thus: Mario Andretti, A.J. Foyt, and Dan Gurney.

If Andretti is great for his ability to win and charm masses from Maranello to Milwaukee, and Foyt's anger and domination put the U.S. on the map as far as racing was concerned, then Dan Gurney pulled it all together. Gurney will be remembered not so much as being the best driver in the U.S., for he was not, but he was the best spokesperson, the most perfect ambassador for motor sports on both sides of the Atlantic.

Gurney's win record is slightly less than sterling. He never won Indy; he never won a World Championship, a USAC Championship, a NASCAR Championship or a Sports Car title. He started 86 Grands Prix, won four times, finished in the top six thirty-one times. He started racing Indy Cars full time in 1967, won seven times and quit by the middle of 1970. He was fast and he was always in the hunt, but he was not a Mark Donohue, not a Jackie Stewart and not a Mario or A.J. Then again, neither were they Dan Gurney.

Gurney in 1962. Gurney's expertise behind the wheel ranged from Grand Prix cars to Grand National cars. But as a born leader, he will be remembered most for his ability to create a team. Bob Tronolone

What Gurney did was to integrate racing. He brought Lotus to America and Ford to France. He brought European design to Indy and American initiative to Europe. He took the first American-made car and put it in the winner's circle on the Grand Prix circuit and then went out and showed the NASCAR drivers that there were more people than "good ol' boys" who could drive an oval.

"I happened to be interested in things that were going on over there. Too bad we don't have one formula that is the pinnacle around the world," Gurney said, still hopeful, still arbitrating, still being the intermediary. "Everybody calls themselves World Champion this and World Champion that. There's a kind of cross-pollenization that is sort of counterproductive. I mean, everybody puts their pants on one leg at a time. Once you get beyond prejudice, I think you get a mutual respect from each side."

Gurney has been a manufacturer for the past thirty years, becoming successful enough that by 1973, twenty-one of the thirty-three cars in the Indianapolis 500 field were Eagles, constructed and built by Dan Gurney.

In the early nineties, his facilities in Southern California included an autoclave for fabricating carbon fiber parts, a wind tunnel, and lots of employees. Gurney brought Toyota into American racing circles in a

Gurney on the main straightaway at Indianapolis on Race Day, 1968. Although he never won the May classic himself, Gurney's cars won the 500 three times. Bob Tronolone

way no one had ever done before. He tolerated fuel protests and back-biting, played by the rules and became a voice of reason, ultimately coming to dominate the GTP class in the International Motorsports prototype division.

When you ask him a question, he smiles politely, listens attentively and answers honestly. He doesn't play you; doesn't try to use you. He gives you an opinion. The thing is, his opinion is always what's good for the sport—not what's good for Dan Gurney.

In the nineteen-nineties, and into his sixties, Dan Gurney doesn't cut quite the same picture he did back when he was winning at Le Mans, when he was taking the Lotus and Eagles around Indy and driving the Porsche and Ferrari Grand Prix cars. He looks slightly like somebody's Grandfather. Still handsome, he has a bit of a paunch these days. And he wears reading glass-

es—the little half glasses—which make him look slightly vulnerable. So it's hard to imagine the man with enough hostility to drive a race car as he did, cranking his Ferrari around European circuits in anger. It's hard to imagine because he looks so . . . passive. So friendly.

At this writing, Gurney was preparing to bring Toyota to the Indy Car championship in 1996. In 1993, he had captured the last of the great sports car championships. The wins were, of course, in cars of his own creation, in Eagle chassis.

Daniel Sexton Gurney didn't have the actual flair of Andretti, nor did he have the staying power as a driver like Foyt did, but he was as impressive because he was not only a quick driver but a great engineer. More importantly, he was a phenomenal listener.

Gurney was born in April 1930 in Long Island, New York. Had his life been slightly different, Gurney might have been a opera star as his father had been. The family had tried to groom the young man for the singing world, but he had shown no interest. What he was interested in of course, was racing. Before his father retired and moved west, Gurney had discovered a variety of forms of racing.

And in California, like every other male youth in the early fifties, he fell in love with drag racing. Although he did some amateur drag racing, he would give it up. It was not in him. Where he would ultimately make his mark was in road racing.

Gurney's first sports car was a used Triumph, which, in 1955, he road raced in California. By the time he was 27 he had impressed a great many of the domestic drivers. He had beaten Carroll Shelby, amazed Phil Hill and had proven his worth in almost anything that drove around corners. In 1959, he got his big break and was signed to drive on the works Ferrari team at the 1959 Le Mans 24 Hours.

By 1962, Gurney, who had been driving for Ferrari, BRM and Porsche over the previous three and a half seasons, was keen in changing the direction of racing in his home country. The young American was scheduled to drive one of Mickey Thompson's lightweight aluminum rear engined cars that season. But having been exposed to the analytical ways of designing of the Europeans, Gurney saw the future of American racing. Up until that point there was almost a contempt by Americans for foreign competition. Driving for Porsche at the Dutch Grand Prix in 1962, he was absolutely stunned by the genius Chapman had shown in designing his Type 25. He immediately approached Chapman about preparing a car for Indianapolis.

Chapman balked, but Gurney convinced him to come to America just a day before practice began for the Monaco GP in June of 1962. As the story goes, Gurney actually paid for Chapman's trip, and introduced him to Ford people, who struck a deal with Gurney, Chapman and Lotus. Gurney would pilot a factory Lotus at Indy with a Ford engine. It was a revolutionary association.

Gurney drove that first season with Lotus and dropped out due to tire problems. The following season, he returned, but took the Lotus on his own. It was the beginning of what would ultimately become the founding of his own team, the Gurney All-American Eagle team. But in the mean time, A.J. Foyt made history by becoming the first man to ever win the 24 Hours of Le Mans and the Indy 500 in the same year. The races were back to back and within a week of one another. The incredible feat is only rivaled by what Dan Gurney, who partnered Foyt in the Le Mans-winning Ford that year, did the following weekend. Gurney not only won the Belgian Grand Prix, he did it in a car of his own construction, becoming the only American to ever win a modern Grand Prix in his own car.

The effort had started in 1965. Gurney's move to running his own team started as a proxy for Goodyear

The 1975 Indianapolis 500 winning Eagle. This car won the 1974 national championship at the hands of Bobby Unser, who drove the car to victory in four races that season, beating Johnny Rutherford for the title. Bobby's only win in 1975 was at Indy. Courtesy Dan Gurney's All American Eagles

Tire. Set up originally by Carroll Shelby, the Eagle team was created. They initially used a Lotus and a pair of Shrikes for the 1965 race and in 1966 competed in the F1 World Championship.

Gurney hired Len Terry, who had designed the Indy-winning Lotus of the 1965 season. The car was designed essentially like the Lotus 38—except that it had a Coventry-Climax four cylinder engine in it as the Weslake V-12 were being prepared. The Climaxes vibrated so badly that at the first race at Spa in Belgium, Gurney had to stop the car in order to urinate, propping a rock against the tire while the car idled and he relieved himself. He said the vibration had gotten to him.

He would win no races that season, but would finish fifth twice. By the next season, however, the car had proven its worth. At a prestigious but non-championship event at Brands Hatch in Britain, Gurney and teammate Richie Ginther had run first and second until Ginther was put out with a bad brake pad. Gurney brought it home for the win over Ferrari. Although the win at Spa capped a delicious season for Gurney, the Weslake proved to be unreliable. Gurney decided to stay at home and devote his time to the managing and racing of his home country. Within a few seasons the incredible record of wins began.

"The Eagle had been done before," Gurney said. "Bruce McLaren and Jack Brabham built and drove their own cars. Design and engineering groups mostly fabricated and guys who mostly just loved racing took them and created their own cars. They were almost kit cars. These things were available. It didn't seem so unusual back then as it does now."

In 1968, with Bobby Unser at the helm, Gurney's Eagles finished one-two at Indy. Gurney was second behind Unser. The season was a complete success in his first outing as team owner. Gurney, through Unser (who was still a privateer with Bob Wilke's turbocharged-Offy team, and not yet driving for Gurney's team), had won the USAC championship, and eight of twenty-eight races in 1968.

In 1969, Gurney was to develop the Ford engine to his own specs and the car would be raced as an Eagle-Gurney-Ford. It was to win only twice in that configuration—both times in his own hands. Bobby Unser drove the Eagle from 1971 until 1976, winning the Indy 500 for Gurney in 1975. Gordon Johncock also managed to win in the Eagle at Indy in 1973 with Pat Patrick.

"We had a pretty good run there," Gurney said with a smile. "When seventy-two came and it was a quantum leap to the prior cars and what it was was to come up against the McLaren, which was a great car. The McLaren brought up the (speed) record 12 to 13 mph. And we brought it up 11 or 12 mph."

In the next five seasons, including seventy-two, the eagle chassis would win twenty-six of sixty-six races. Its main competition would be from the Parnelli, the McLaren and, occasionally, A.J. Foyt's Coyote.

In the mid-eighties Gurney tried unsuccessfully to repeat his run in Indy Cars. He then campaigned an IMSA GTU team, then GTO and finally GTP, where they won the championship three times for Toyota. The screaming turbo engines took their time to get going. They had teething problems in the first seasons, and looked sick in comparison to the Nissans and the Jaguars.

But even while they were being beaten, even while Gurney should have been upset, somber or vindictive, when you talked to Gurney he was good for a smile and a knowing nod. Five years later, they had

In 1995, Dan Gurney stands next to his most recent Eagle, the 1996 Toyota Indy Car. Gurney's Eagles have been some of the most successful cars to run at speedways over the years, regardless of which manufacturer backed his projects. Courtesy Dan Gurney's All American Eagles

dominated so much that the series was cancelled.

But in those days, prior to where the fronts of the starting grids were shared by Juan Fangio II and P.J. Jones, and the podiums were filled with Toyota orange and yellow, Gurney was always ready to give a quote or explain something to the press.

"It's just the way I feel about life," he smiled. "In the end, this is not a dress rehearsal. I like to treat people the way I want people to treat me. You get wall-eyed sometimes, but in the end it usually works out. Maintaining integrity is the most important thing I think. That's the way I go through life," he said.

Three old hands talk tires. Here (left to right), Richard Petty AJ Foyt and Gurney (far right) talk to Leo Mehl, Goodyear's worldwide director of racing in 1981 during a tire test. All three men were critical in Goodyear's eventual dominance in racing. Of the three, Gurney had the most varied career. Courtesy Goodyear Tire

In 1964, Gurney won Le Mans in a GT car, finishing fourth overall. The Cobra Daytona Team included a few very famous people. Arm-in-arm, left to right is Carroll Shelby, Gurney, Bob Bondurant and actor Peter Ustinov. Courtesy Goodyear Tire

Chapter 13

Janet Guthrie

Strictly in terms of statistical results perhaps, Janet Guthrie achieved few things in Indy Car racing. She competed for only three and a half seasons. Her career best finish was a fifth place at Milwaukee, and she only got as high as ninth at Indy. She won no championships, and she posted no poles.

But she broke through barriers like no other driver, ever.

Guthrie was Indianapolis' first woman. Her accomplishments, based on what additional hurdles she had to overcome, are right up there with Roger Bannister and Jesse Owens— or perhaps even men like Mario Andretti or Parnelli Jones. More concisely, her career would certainly have been chocked full of more impressive results had she been in better machinery.

That, in auto racing, is an old story. But Guthrie was in sub-standard equipment not just because of her financial backing— which is not only acceptable but expected—but because of her sex.

"Back in the late sixties," she said in 1995, as a fifty-two-year-old, "I was talking with a guy who really thought I was quite good, but I remember him saying, 'You will never be a winning driver because no one will ever give you a winning car because you are a woman.' And I believe that's still true."

Guthrie was born in Iowa in 1938 and grew up in Miami. Her family was a supportive base for whatever

Janet Guthrie on Race Day, 1978. Guthrie, who was Indianapolis' first woman, had to overcome major hurdles to gain a spot on the male-dominated race track.
Bob Tronolone

challenges awaited her, encouraging her in whatever endeavor she chose. She began her love with machinery when she was thirteen, flying airplanes. By the time she was sixteen she had soloed, and at seventeen, she had a private pilot's license.

Out of college in the early sixties, she bought a Jaguar XJ120 "because it was such a beautiful car," she said. "Basically, one thing led to another, and I started running at gymkhanas, field trials, hillclimbs and found out that sports car racing existed. After two years, I bought another Jaguar, an XK140 this time, that was set up for sports car racing. That was really the beginning."

In 1964 she entered her Jaguar XK140 in the first ever 500 mile race at Watkins Glen and had a co-driver—a guy who she'd gone through drivers school with. She campaigned the Jaguar for five years and got to the runoffs—which was a more significant event back then. She quickly made a name for herself in amateur racing.

"I spent thirteen years racing sports cars of one sort or another, at the end of which time I was in rather desperate financial straights. I had a used-up race car that I had spent a year of my life building. What I did have was a reputation. Out of the clear blue sky I got a call from an established Indy Car team owner and car builder who asked if I would like to take a shot at Indianapolis. This was the late seventies, and things were

Guthrie on the main straightaway at the Indianapolis 500 in 1978. Guthrie ran her own team this year and had her best finish at Indianapolis at ninth place. Bob Tronolone

just opening up for women. He thought that he would like to be the first car owner to bring a woman to Indianapolis. His name was Rolla Vollstedt.

"When I got the phone call, I had no idea who he was. I called up Chris Economaki and said, 'Who's Rolla Vollstedt?' because there had been some non-productive situations involving the possibility of women going to Indianapolis, and some women who ended up looking a little bit silly. I didn't want to end up like that. Because from my part, are you kidding, any racing car driver would have jumped at the opportunity. But I do remember that for a good chunk of my time in sports car racing, I would hear from time to time about a woman setting her cap for Indianapolis and nothing ever came of it. I just didn't want to have that happen with me."

Economaki told her who Rolla Vollstedt was, and that, yes, he was a serious team owner. Good, Economaki said, but not great; talented, but not rich. But there were doubts on Guthrie's part about the offer. She did not want to look stupid. So she set ground rules.

"When I returned his call I said, 'Here is my condition: we have a private test with your cars and if the cars go fast enough, and I can make them go fast enough, and if I like you, and you like me you can go ahead and make whatever noise you feel like you need to, but until then this is our secret.'"

He agreed. And in secret, a test took place at Ontario, California. And it did in fact go on from there.

The first race she drove was Trenton, New Jersey. It was first scheduled for late April of 1976, but was rained out and ran the first weekend of May. In that race, she was successful enough that she was accepted at Indianapolis for the rookie test and, once accomplished, practice—both of which she did well in.

Of course, when she got to Indianapolis, it wasn't quite that easy. There was a small matter of her gender. This was a first, a woman at Indianapolis. And the establishment—all male—wasn't going to just sit down and take a woman invading their race track.

"It was a major, major fracas," she said, voice filled with irony. "I still have all the clippings. It made

In the Texaco Indy Car in 1978, Janet Guthrie pulls the car into the pits at the Indianapolis Motor Speedway. With her start in 1977, she became the first woman to ever race at Indianapolis. Although she broke new ground, only Lyn St. James has since followed. The sport is still a male-dominated fraternity. Courtesy Janet Guthrie

the full page of the *New York Times*, and you know how extensively the *New York Times* covers auto racing, then and now. Bobby Unser delivered himself of the opinion that he could take a hitchhiker and teach him to drive better than Janet Guthrie, even though he had never seen me drive *anything*. There were guys going into the USAC offices in Indiana, saying, 'You must keep her out.' Oh, it was a *big* deal."

In 1976, she passed her rookie test. Vollstedt was one of the last of the shoestring operators, and Guthrie knew that everything had to go right. Unfortunately, everything didn't go right. The car failed to make the field. On the last day of practice A.J. Foyt let her take his back up car out. But the commitment to let her race didn't come. She was out of the Indy 500 even before she'd started.

"I did run that car fast enough to make the field, but then he changed his mind. In the meanwhile, with all that hullabaloo going on, Humpy Wheeler (General manager of Charlotte Motor Speedway) decided it would be a good thing if I came and drove at his race. So he got in touch with a few people and the day after practice ended I had the offer of a ride at the World Six-Hundred at Charlotte.

" . . . And it was the same thing all over again: 'She'll never make the field; if she makes the field, she'll never be able to go more than forty laps.' I did make the field and finished somewhere around fourteenth. It was physically more taxing than Indy Cars, but, jeez, I had a good time."

With all the attention around Guthrie in 1976, Vollstedt was able to get more sponsorship money and a better car for 1977. With that car she made the field. For the first time ever, the starter's orders for the Indy 500 were "*Lady* and gentlemen, start your engines." It was a historic day in Indiana.

Her best finish at Indianapolis was the next season, when she actually ran her own team. The best Indy car finish she had was fifth at Milwaukee in 1979. Her best qualifying position was fourth at the Pocono 500—also in 1979. She was fourth to A.J. Foyt, Danny Ongias, and Johnny Parsons Jr.

When Guthrie received her car in 1979 from Sherman Armstrong, there were broken teeth in the gears. Crew Chief Bay Darnell labored over the car to make it driveable. That is the way it was with Guthrie—always a glitch.

That first season she drove Trenton, Indianapolis, Michigan, Ontario, and Pocono in 1976. She drove with Vollstedt all of 1977. And also in 1977, she went for Rookie-Of-The-Year in NASCAR, contesting nineteen of the possible thirty-one races that season. Her best finish in NASCAR was a sixth and she finished an extremely close third to Ricky Rudd and Sam Summers, a champion sports car driver. She drove one final season of Indy Cars, in 1979, but dismisses it as a wasted year with an owner she would just as soon forget. By 1980, she was out of racing.

"I deeply regret that I was not able to continue racing," she said with a note of sadness, "and accomplish what was clear that I was capable of accomplishing. I miss racing dreadfully. But, hey, that's life."

Guthrie knows full well that auto racing is one of the few sports where women can compete with men on an equal footing. There is no physical advantage. It doesn't take big muscles and broad shoulders and twenty-one inch biceps. A woman does have the facilities, both physical and mental to compete equally in one of the most complex and difficult sports on the planet. But, just as men have to find the funds to race, so do women. But, she says, it is as hard or harder for women because of the arena in which the sponsors exist.

"For many many years I have said that what the sport needs is a woman with not only what it takes

When she failed to make the Indy 500 her first try, Charlotte Motor Speedway arranged for her to drive a NASCAR Winston Cup car at the World 600 on the same weekend. The following season she was a NASCAR regular and had earned the respect of the stock car fraternity. Courtesy Janet Guthrie

but with a fortune as well. And that when we see that woman . . . they might find victory circle. Corporate funding is not available for women. If someone in the corporate world came to me and said, 'Look we want to make it possible for a woman to be truly competitive in the business, find her.' Believe me, I could find enough candidates that at any given year or time some woman out there has those capabilities."

"There is a certain element of it never having gotten fashionable," she says. "But I believe it has changed, is changing as the perception of racing changes. But in the past it was always thought of as a totally redneck activity. And it is cultural to the extent that even in the entry level, there aren't as many women as men. Why women don't look at auto racing as they do like say horse jumping—equestrian classes and so on are—that's not really clear to me. As you know, (that sport) is dominated now by women. But I do know that the domination by women in equestrian sports is quite recent. Even though women had always been extremely good, no matter how good they were they could not get on the Olympic team. And that was the case in the late 1970s. I believe that if the opportunity to fit more glamour to the sport (of auto racing) comes, it will change also—at the entry level. Now as I say, at the top level that's another question.

Janet Guthrie was not an activist in the traditional sense of the word. She was forced into the position because she was an oddity, but she drove for the same reason any driver worth his weight in mud dri-

Janet Guthrie in the nineties. Due to financial difficulties, she was forced to give up racing in the late seventies. She still misses it, but figured it as a fact of life. She does her best, however, to inspire other young women to follow their dreams—despite what their male counterparts advise.
Courtesy Janet Guthrie

ves: to satisfy the urge for the feeling one gets from moving a machine around a narrow band of asphalt at its limits.

"The competition is the essential element," Guthrie said. "Speed and the access to that marvelous machinery was certainly part of it, but the essence of what a driver does is in the turns. If you go through a turn as fast as that particular car will go through that particular turn and you pass somebody in traffic, that really was what made it such a compelling activity."

Unlike Shirley Muldowney, three time National Hot Rod Association Top Fuel Dragster Champion, Guthrie did all of her own work. The years in sports cars, not being rich, she built all her own engines and did all her own work. There was no husband until January of 1989. And, unfortunately, few friends in the field.

Vollstedt was a staunch supporter. Says Guthrie, "I don't think I could have driven for a better team owner than Rolla Vollstedt. He was passionate about the sport and what he lacked in dollars, he made up in passion. So I'll always be grateful to him." And in stock car racing her team owner was a woman who initially got involved through Humpy Wheeler of Charlotte (and who eventually ran a team in NASCAR) by the name of Linda Ferreri, who was an ally of sorts.

But for the most part, she was on her own. Ultimately, she did become a sort of political folk hero. At first unwitting, and then perhaps embracing the role. But it was the racing that got her there in the first place. As it did every other male driver. Racing was her avocation as well as, for a short time, her vocation.

Her driving suit and helmet now sit in the Smithsonian. And in the *Philadelphia Inquirer Magazine* just as Guthrie was to end her career in Indy Cars, Bobby Unser finally said in May of 1979, "She's done a good job. I gotta admit that I had my doubts about her. But she's proven her point . . . she can be up there in the top ten. There are a lotta guys who can't say that."

It took until her retirement before she had become one of the guys. But for the most part, Indianapolis was a cold and lonely place for Janet Guthrie.

Chapter 14

Jim Hall

The first sixty years of the aerodynamics in Indy Cars evolved on a simple basis of reason: If it looked fast it must *be* fast.

Science had little to do with how Indy Cars plowed through the wall of air. Advances made from the late 1950s to the late 1960s were done as a result of trial and error. It was far from an exact science.

In Texas, however, while working with sports cars, independent racer and oil man Jim Hall happened on a discovery that would change the sport of motor racing. The tall soft-spoken Texan, fresh from a degree in engineering, had found an odd way of increasing performance. Hall, who was in no way a great driver, became one of the great innovators.

"What happened," Hall said in his quiet southern self-effacing manner, "is that I decided to build a mid-engined Chaparral in Texas. We got the car finished and we decided to go out and test it. We didn't have the bodywork done, so we just ran it without bodywork. We'd run them without the bodywork before and we didn't think it was that dumb an idea. Anyway, we could watch everything work and everything. So we started out pretty slow, but we found that with a little windscreen on it we could run it pretty hard. And we did that."

Jim Hall in 1994 with the Hall VDS project. Hall was an independent racer and car builder from Texas. Although he wasn't a great driver, he became one of the great innovators, changing the sport of motor racing forever.
Courtesy Pennzoil Racing, Deke Houlgate

When the bodywork was finally finished Hall fitted it and found that for some strange reason he was substantially slower *with* the bodywork.

"That was surprising to us at the time," Hall smiled. "So I started to instrument it. I found that when I went down the high speed straightaway—there was a slight bend in the test track—I found that I had absolutely no grip at all. It was real obvious that we had a bad body. It was real detrimental to the car which meant we had to fix it. The lap times when we ran the car with no body was two or three seconds faster than when we ran it with the bodywork on it! So that's how I got interested in aerodynamics. I said, 'Gee wiz, if the forces are that great on the car that it could screw up the handling of the car,' my first thought was to fix it. But then I realized I could help the car with aerodynamics.

"I think up until that time people tended to think of (aerodynamics) as a negative. They said, 'Well, lets reduce the amount of drag or the amount of lift on the car. Some engineer said it's round on the top and flat on the bottom so it must lift. So everybody said, 'well lets reduce the lift by reducing the drag.' It just occurred to me: 'Well, I've got all that force to deal with, why don't I use it to

Jim Hall with Johnny Rutherford in 1980. JR would win five of twelve races in the Chaparral, capturing the championship as well as the Indy 500. This, Hall's first reincarnation of the 1979 car, was the first ground effects car to compete in Indy Cars. Courtesy Pennzoil Racing, Deke Houlgate

help me?'. That was probably my contribution right there. That idea."

Hall started changing the front of the car to change the lift. That ended up being the snowplow device on it. His first task, as he saw it, was to stop the car from lifting. Which he did. The car didn't lift at all. But it occurred to him as he was campaigning that car that there might be more to aerodynamics than just reducing lift. Hell, he realized, he might be able to actually produce downforce.

The wings came in 1966—the full wing. Hall had used a little slap wing in 1965 and had started putting more and more downforce on the cars in 1964. His cars' lap times kept dropping every time he did something to the body. Eventually, the cars had a lot of drag. They had a lot of download but a lot of drag. They weren't very fast on the straightaway.

"We had put a little flap on the back. So instead of a fixed flap we put a moveable flap on it, which increased our straightway speed and gave us the same braking force and download in the corners. That was the first thing we did in 1965. What happens is that you put so much downforce the car squishes to the ground and you lose your springing. So I thought why don't we get it off the sprung mass and get it

onto the unsprung weight. So I stuck it onto the wheels. That's what we ran the first time. It was really quite a nice car. It was a good way to do it."

Wings had appeared on sports cars as early as 1964, and on Grand Prix cars by 1968. The wings tended to break, however, and horrible accidents took place. In addition, they looked ridiculous. Although they inevitably returned, moves were on to renew the ban on wings, or at least reduce the swept area and height, so they didn't work effectively. USAC said that the highest part of the car could not be any taller than 28 inches. USAC had been keeping an eye on Europe, and limited front wings to nine inches on either side of the body, without exceeding the center line of the tire.

In the meantime, Hall had built his now legendary Chaparral Fan Car. "Really the first ground effects car was the fan car we built back in 1970—with the skirts around it and the evacuated air. That was the original idea. Then Colin Chapman took that idea and said, 'Well, gosh maybe I can do that without the fan'. So he used the skirt part of it and shaped the underside of the car until he produced a low pressure under it and, bang, he had a new idea. We originated the thought but he developed it in a good way.

But in 1971, the new McLaren was designed around the new regulations. Rather than making the devices a separate part of the car, the McLaren designers made the *body itself* a part of the aero package. The McLaren M16 used twin low-mounted nose radiators to reduce drag and allow the creation of a wedge shaped front end. The dampers and springs were mounted inside the bodywork and the rear wing was designed to more contribute 500-600lbs to the rear wheels at speed. Where previous wings were aimed at redirecting air and reducing drag, the McLaren's wing was designed to reduce drag and produce downforce — a revolutionary concept at Indy.

So in the 1970s the buzzwords were "downforce" and "aerodynamics." And subsequently, Colin Chapman, the little Brit who watched one of his drivers take a Lotus-Ford to victory in 1965, had made another breakthrough—and it was coming to Indy Cars. Using Hall's ideas, Chapman discovered in 1977, while looking for another place to concentrate on the effects of the wind, that the entire bottom of the car had never been addressed. Here was this huge area that could help the downforce of the car, and it had never been studied—at least not by anyone who raced open-wheeled cars. Hall had already invented it and raced it in his Chaparral Fan Car, but it hadn't been done on an open-wheeled car. The concept, in F1, was as revolutionary as the Lotus 49s had been in 1967. The Lotus 77 didn't win races as convincingly in its first season in 1977 as the 1978 did the following season. But the car would come to dominate GP competition.

Chapman introduced the concept to American open-wheeled cars. Two years after they were intro-

Jim Hall congratulates Al Unser for putting the Chaparral on the front row of the Indianapolis 500 for the 1979 race. Courtesy Pennzoil Racing, Deke Houlgate

duced to Europe and Grand Prix racing, ground effects came to the United States. Ground effects was at Indy.

"I only built one Indy Car, that was in 1979. Wings were already well established. We did the first ground effects car at Indy. It was probably the quickest car in 1979. Al Unser Sr. just drove away from everybody in the race until he had a transmission failure. But by the next year that car was dominant. Johhny Rutherford drove for us and won the championship and won Indy. That was the first ground effects car at Indy."

If there is anything that is certain about Jim Hall, it is that he is sure to keep thinking about doing things a new way. His latest focus has been with other people's cars and his team, but there is likely to be a change just around the corner.

Says Hall: "I think anytime you do something like racing—I mean, it could be anything else—but people work toward the optimum setup, don't they? So

you get closer and closer. So the chunks of development that change the design are going to be smaller. I don't think there's any question about it. The more people who look at it—the more people who spend their time effort and money at it—it will be refined. I think the cars are more optimized now—at least until the next revolution.

"People seem to think they've got a good idea of where it ought to be. The weight distribution of the parts—we did a lot of that work in the sixties. The radiator location and some other things. But somebody will come along with a different idea and it will be a better one. That's what happens. The competition is a wonderful thing. Everything gravitates toward the best, and until somebody comes along with a new idea they all look alike for a while. When there's a new idea everybody moves that direction."

For example? "I think you could run at Indianapolis with no wing at all now," Hall said thoughtfully. "But the nice thing about the wing is that it's easily adjustable. The driver needs to have a trimming device that allows him an easy way to adjust the center pressure on the car so that it does things he'd like it to do on the race track. If you take it away it makes it difficult to do that. You can reduce the size so that the effect is almost nonexistent, but I don't think you need to eliminate it altogether."

And for the future?

Jim Hall looked at the floor of his motorhome which serves as a moving office and retreat from the nerve racking business of racing, then he smiled broadly, with great interest. "To start over with a clean sheet of paper you really ought to take a look at the other possibilities." Like what? With a bit of prodding Hall rubbed his face and grinned again. Perhaps there was something. "At the speedway maybe you could run a front drive car," he smiled. "It doesn't sound like the thing you'd want to do, but you ought to take a look at it to see. They've eliminated four wheel drive cars, but you can still drive front drive cars. It's not obvious that on a speedway that that would be the wrong set up. I think on a road circuit it probably is because you need the traction control in the corners but on a superspeedway I guess it's a possibility. I wouldn't want to say that it's the way to go for certain, but I think you ought to look at it anyway.

"If it's going to be front," he said, more animated, "I think you have the major part of the car near that area and it would be teardrop shaped. Less drag. The wheels I think still have to stick out don't they. I think you have to do a lot of work to see if its worth trying something radically different from what they're running today. But I think you could do it. I mean today you've got a simulation program now so that you could see how it would work without actually doing it. Or you could make a model and bring it to a wind tunnel. In a few hours you could have a big laugh and say no, we're going to go back like we thought we should."

Or maybe not. Hall is still overflowing with ideas.

Unser in the first Chaparral, Hall's first Indy Car. The car was designed in cooperation with John Barnard, legendary Formula One designer. From this photo it's easy to see Hall's size wasn't ideal for racing, which is why he remained a builder for most of his racing career. Courtesy Pennzoil Racing, Deke Houlgate

Chapter 15

Gordon Johncock

Gordon Johncock made some mistakes. He knows that; but so, he says, did the other guys. If Johncock, who quit racing Indy Cars in 1985, had it to do all over again, he wouldn't have retired when he did. At nearly sixty years old as this book is being penned, Johncock still hasn't quiet found the means to retire. Not that he needs the money; in fact, he's living the life of a gentleman farmer in Michigan. But, God, does he ever crave the racing.

"It was a big mistake," Johncock said with a solemnity that could make you weep. "I was upset with the team and Jim McGee—he's a back stabber—and things weren't going well. We were running pretty decent at The Speedway and, well, were second quick overall, but really having to strain to do it. The car wasn't working that well and McGee, he's around looking at other teams and cars, and he comes back and comments that we've got to lower the car and do this and that, and I just got tired of all of it and said, 'I've had enough of this,' and I quit."

Oops.

"That was a mistake. I shouldn't have done that. I should have went to another team. I really wasn't ready to quit. But I got upset. I went back a few times and I drove for Ron Hemelgarn. It's just so hard to get

Gordon Johncock at the Indianapolis 500 in 1967. Johncock won the Indianapolis 500 in 1973 and 1982, driving for Pat Patrick. He retired from Indy racing in 1975, much to his regret, even today. Bob Tronolone

it out of your system." Then he paused for a moment, and when he spoke once again his voice had a different sound to it: happy. Or *trying* to sound happy, at any rate. "I'm trying to put a deal together now to run that new oval series that Tony's going to run," he said. "I'm trying to put a deal together with Dick Simon. If you know of any sponsors . . . "

His successes notwithstanding, Gordon Johncock was as far from his prime in January, 1996 as Mohammed Ali was from his prime on the same date. As any rookie can tell you: it's not enough to want to be the best, you have to be *prepared* to be the best. A pro athlete simply can't be away from his sport for ten years and keep up with his peers any longer. It is physically impossible.

And unfortunately for Johncock, his career will always be footnoted by the retirement that dragged on like a Michael Cimino movie.

Johncock was born in Hastings, Michigan, on August 25, 1936. Nineteen years later he was driving modifieds in and around the Great Lakes area. He worked on his family farm and as a contractor after he left school. Then a cousin who was four years older got him involved in modified cars, and soon enough he was driving the car competitively—and winning.

As it is with many pro drivers, it was not initially a profession they saw themselves a part of. Johncock just did it for fun.

"I was driving a supermodified and working as a contractor and working on the farm and I never really paid much attention to racing. I didn't really even know about Indianapolis.

"I think a race driver's career is like that of a baseball player or football player or something. You go to high school and do well, and you've got the college scouts looking at you and then you do well there and you go to college and if you do well there you go to the pros. In racing, if you do well in one class, your name's in Speed-Sport and your picture's in there, and first thing you know, somebody up the line wants you to drive for him."

His prowess in modifieds earned him a ride in a USAC sprint car for the 1964 season, running his first race at Springfield in August of that year. By September he had set a World's Record for the half-mile at 17.18 seconds at 104.773mph, quite an achievement in 1964. He finished twentieth in the USAC standings that first season.

By the following year he was at the Indianapolis Motor Speedway. In the Weinberger Homes roadster, Johncock started in the 14th spot on the grid and finished in an admirable fifth place, then went on to win at Milwaukee in August. It was his first Indy Car win—in a rear engined Offenhauser. He would go on to finish fifth in the championship.

In 1966, Johncock won no races on the USAC Trail, but still managed to finish third in the USAC Championship with several top five finishes. In 1967 Johncock won twice—at Milwaukee and Hanford—and finished fourth in points. Then he followed up in 1968 with a win at Hanford again, ending the season with twelfth spot in the series. In 1969, he won twice and finished fifth again.

In 1970, the scouts were watching so to speak, and Johncock moved into the McLaren, one of the

Johncock rounding turn three in the Indianapolis 500 in 1973—the year of his first victory at Indianapolis. Bob Tronolone

best cars to ever hit the Speedway. In that car he won once and finished seventh in the championship, then was involved in an accident in turn three of the following Indianapolis 500 and was eliminated. He competed in nine of the other eleven races of the series championship, but finished a dismal 27th in the standings.

By then, Johncock's focus had shifted slightly and he was running more stock car races. He ran ten stock car races to his six Indy Car races, winning once in stock cars and nothing in the open-wheeled class. He finished ninth in points in the stock car series.

The 1973 season was the beginning of a long and fruitful relationship with car owner Pat Patrick. Johncock won his first Indy 500 in the rain in a shortened race, then went on to win twice more at Phoenix and Milwaukee, finishing seventh again in series points. He also won in stock cars that season. Although in 1995—ten years after he left the team—Johncock had a hostility toward the oilman, the relationship was one of the few which lasted over the years and brought both Johncock and Patrick success.

Before leaving, Johncock ran every one of the fourteen races in the USAC championship in 1974, Driving an Eagle-Offenhauser, he won twice that season and finished third in the championship. In 1975, he was fastest qualifier in the Indy 500. He won at Trenton and finished twelfth in the standings. He also ran four Formula 5000 races, his best finish being a sixth at Road Atlanta. He won at Phoenix and Trenton and then finished second six times, third three times and fifth once. He captured the championship from Johnny Rutherford in 1976 by a mere 20 points—4,240 to 4220. Then he followed up in 1977 by finishing fifth in the championship with two wins, and finished third in 1978 with another pair of victories.

Then came the 1979 season.

That season was a season of strife within American racing ranks. The schism between CART and USAC ripped into the heart of racing—into the Indy 500 itself. The main players had jumped ship and had gone to CART, and Patrick was part of the mutiny's leadership. In cooperation with Roger Penske, Championship Auto Racing Teams was formed to take the place of the moribund USAC championship. The new series was to incorporate more road courses into the championship. Road racing was far from Johncock's forte, and the season marked the beginning of the end for Johncock.

Johncock ironically won CART's first race at Phoenix on March 11, 1979, ultimately finishing third in the CART Championship. In 1980, Johncock suffered a fractured ankle in a crash at the Brickyard, just two days prior to qualifying. He courageously qualified in seventeenth spot and raced the 500 with a cast on his foot, finishing fourth and even leading eleven laps. He won no races that season, but managed to string together several top finishes, and took a sixth place in year-end results.

In eleven races of 1981, he finished the year with no wins, but a fourth in the CART championship. Although he won his second Indy 500 in 1982 in the famous battle with Rick Mears, unfortunately, it did not count toward the championship and Johncock was not credited with points. He finished fourteenth in series totals.

In 1983, he won at Atlanta in what looked like it would be a good season. But he crashed in Michigan and severely injured his legs. The crash put him out of the rest of the season. That first win of the season at Atlanta marked Johncock's last success in an Indy Car. He never won another race. He started the 1984 Indianapolis 500, but was forced out after a wreck at the Speedway.

He looks back on 1982 with fond memories. It was, he felt, his best and most satisfying race at The Speedway. If the first win was slightly bittersweet, the second was a knock-down, drag-out fight with one of the best up-and-comers in American racing. "The 1982 race when I beat Rick Mears by sixteen hundredths of a second (was special). The first one was marred by a lot of accidents, and it was rain-shortened. It was a race that they never even had a victory banquet for. It was a race that just everybody wanted to have over and get home."

At the end of the 1984 season, Johncock announced his retirement. Having been with Patrick for an astounding eleven straight seasons, he said he had had enough. By the following season, he was rethinking the move. In 1987 he raced at the Speedway again, starting 28th and finishing 28th. In 1988 he raced twice—at Michigan and Pocono, finishing sixth twice. In 1989, he ran Indy, Michigan and Pocono, with fifteenth his best finish of the three. He

Gordon Johncock in the mid-nineties, still sporting the 1970s blue and red on his helmet. His latest Indy trials have not been so successful. Rick Dole

GORDON JOHNCOCK
INDIANAPOLIS MOTOR SPEEDWAY 1971

A youthful Johncock sits atop the cockpit of his car, sponsored by Norris Industries. He was to crash the car after just 11 laps at The Speedway. Even so, he was just coming to the top of his game at this point. Jack Mackenzie

raced no events in 1990, but drove at Indianapolis in 1991 and 1992, finishing sixth the first race and twenty-ninth the second. The 1992 race was his last.

By 1992, his performance even in ovals had waned. But what ultimately got to him—especially in the early eighties—was his inability on road courses. Even in Johncock's prime, he was not a great road racer. Patrick knew that as early as 1979, but kept him on, choosing instead to hire other drivers to augment the team at road courses.

"Well," Johncock said eleven seasons later, still angry about the ordeal, "I don't have any good words to say about Pat Patrick. It was all right at first, and I guess I should have realized that I was getting used. He doesn't care about anybody but himself.

"In a way it was my own fault. I wasn't hardly getting paid anything. They kind of had me buffaloed. They had a guy that worked for them and did his dirty work for him and he said, 'Well, Patrick thinks of you just like one of his sons.' It didn't end up that way. Really never was. If I'd have been smart enough I guess to

really have guessed what was going on, I'd have went and drove for somebody like Roger Penske or Jim Hall at the time. But I was loyal. I should have left."

When talking to Gordon Johncock, one gets the impression that his whole life revolves around that retirement. His past victories and almost domination on ovals are not important, it is what he *might* have achieved that counts. And he would have achieved a hell of a lot more, he insists.

Some see it differently.

"Gordon doesn't realize what Pat did for him," Jim McGee said in 1995 without malice. "He wouldn't be Gordon Johncock if it wasn't for Pat Patrick. Gordy was really his favorite. When Gordy got to a point in his career where he should have got out, he couldn't accept that fact. I think Pat did so much for Gordon, its a shame he feels that way because certainly without Pat, Johncock wouldn't have had the reputation, won Indy or done the things that he did. You have to look at the whole picture. If you look at the whole picture, Pat was very good to

Gordy . . . "

". . . Maybe toward the end of his career Gordy couldn't understand the fact that Pat Patrick was (running a business)," McGee said. "You know, some race car drivers can't see it themselves when they're losing their edge and when they should move on and when they should step back. I think maybe Johncock thought that Pat should have stayed with him even when he wasn't competitive in certain areas. Certainly, he was still competitive on the ovals. But that was in the era where we were changing and getting more road courses. Actually Pat—and it was my decision too—decided that we would just run Gordy on the ovals and hire somebody else to come in and do the road courses. He was just not competitive on the road courses and I think that probably ticked him off."

Johncock doesn't wish to hear that. In his mind he was still competitive; still ready to take on anybody—on the ovals. Not the road course, since road courses were not what America was founded upon anyway.

"That's one trouble with the sport right now is that there's too many guys who've got money that are there that don't belong there. Too much road racing. Those foreigners are coming over and taking over because that's what they were brought up on was road courses. And the race fans are kind of getting tired of it. If you talk to them and listen to them. They're getting so they don't like it. They don't even know these guys anymore. Where do they come from? Who are they? It's a shame."

Regardless of what kind of racer or what kind of man he is today, Gordon Johncock amassed a great record in his sport. He won at Indy twice and was an absolute master on an oval. If he had a failing, it was that he loved racing so much he couldn't find a way to give it up.

With the prospect of racing an all-oval series beginning in January of 1996, Johncock was at it

Still smiling, Johncock, even as this book was going to press in 1996, was still trying to remain in racing—some four decades after he had begun. Jack Mackenzie

again, trying to find a way back to The Speedway. It mattered not that he would be nearly twice as old as the average Indy Car driver, nor that he hadn't had any decent competition for several seasons. He was still ready to race.

"If you find me a ride," Johncock said, "we'll be there."

One can only wonder.

Chapter 16

Parnelli Jones

If it wasn't for his size, Parnelli Jones might have been a pro football player. Maybe a boxer. He's got the attitude, and he's got the look. Hell, with the haircut, he could even be a lineman, Art Donovan's brother.

Although to talk with him now, you'd never know that Parnelli Jones was one of the fastest men on a racetrack. Today, he just looks like any other guy with a bad haircut. But during his prime, Jones was a formidable opponent both in and out of his race car.

"I guess I got that reputation from that Eddie Sachs thing . . . when I poked Eddie . . . ?" Jones says, kind of hoping you haven't heard the story.

It's a good story.

When he knows he's too far in to stop, he tells it again: "What happened is that the year I won Indy the track was oily all day and the Novi and the Vita-Fresh Orange Juice car both ran completely out of oil. My car broke an oil tank and it started dropping a little bit of oil out, but it only did it for one of two laps and then it quit.

Parnelli Jones as he usually appears in the 1990s—with a big smile. Although Jones was known for being a fierce competitor in the sixties, he is still one of the more personable ex-Indy Car drivers. Courtesy Ford Motors

And Sachs, after making a pit stop, went back out and spun in the first turn. And then later he got going and a few laps later one of the wheels came off and I think he spun because of the wheel coming off. The track was consistently oily all day," Jones says again for emphasis.

"So he jumps on the bandwagon that it was my car that oiled the track down. So the next day after I won at the hotel, Autolite had a little luncheon and I was there and he came up to me and congratulated me for winning the race and then he says, 'But they should have black-flagged you 'cause of all the oil you dropped.'

"I said, 'Sachs, it wasn't me, I think your wheel came loose.' I said, 'And besides, that the track was oily all day and two or three cars ran completely out of oil,' and I said, 'I don't know how you can blame me.'

"And he said, 'Well, your car was throwing most of it.' I said, 'You're full of shit.' And he says, 'You are.' I say, 'You're a liar,' and he says, 'You're a liar.' And we started arguing like that and I said, 'I ought to bust you in the mouth.' And he said, 'Go ahead.'"

So he did. Jones busted him in the mouth. Right there at the Autolite reception.

"He had a little blood coming out of his mouth, and so he ran upstairs and had a black flag coming out of his mouth for the publicity. And then he didn't show up at the banquet that night, and made a big deal out of it."

It's hard to imagine the Parnelli Jones of the 1990s doing what the Parnelli Jones of the 1950s and 1960s actually did. The latest version of Jones is a soft-spoken balding guy who you'd see at a ball game somewhere. He smiles more than most people and seems to have a good time. You could see him getting riled.

Jones in the STP turbine car. He led the race easily and looked like a certain winner when a bearing failed with just a few miles to go. After this season he retired from Indy racing. He raced a few seasons in SCCA Trans-Am and then stopped driving altogether, choosing instead to focus on running a team. The Vels-Parnelli team was one of the most technically advanced ever seen.
Russ Lake

But punch a guy at a luncheon? Nah. Too hard to imagine.

Rufus Parnelli Jones became interested in racing when his cousin made a jalopy stock car out of his wife's old car. Jones was working in a garage after school, cleaning parts, and keeping his own car running. Although only sixteen years old, due to his mechanical knowledge his cousin wanted Parnelli to help with the car. So Jones used to help get the car ready to race and would go watch him run it. After about a year, his cousin blew the engine. The car sat for a while until Jones and a friend bought the hulk from his cousin.

"I drove the first race—he wasn't too enthused about driving—and so I kept on driving it. We did-

n't do very well, but at that time it gave us the bug and later he got drafted during the Korean War, and we were kind of out of it for a couple years. And then he came back and were in a position financially for us to support a stock car. So we went back and started doing that. Of course, I had just enough experience from the time before I thought nobody could beat me.

"Well, after wrecking my car week after week, I finally realized it took a little talent. I blew the engine up and another friend came up and said, 'Look, I'll build an engine for your car if you'll just listen to me.' He must have seen something in me. All he said was, 'Just slow down.'

Parnelli Jones in 1970 watching his driver Joe Leonard. Beside him is Al Unser Sr. Jones had moved from his role as a driver to the role as a team manager by this time and the team was flourishing under his control. The longtime Ford/Firestone partnership helped all three interests. Russ Lake

"So I started winning right away. All I did was listen to him and back off and not get too aggressive. Once you get a taste of winning it got a lot easier for me. I won a lot of races and was running two or three times a week. I wasn't making a lot of money, but I was living at home with my family, so it wasn't costing me a great deal, and pretty soon people were inviting me to drive different types of cars. And people started saying, 'Boy, you're Indianapolis material.' But that wasn't my goal to begin with. I had no real intentions of doing anything like that. But I kind of grew into it. I jumped into different divisions and won races right away and kept pushing me forward so to speak."

Backing off slightly didn't mean slowing down or giving in. And because of his aggressiveness on the track, he earned the right to race at Indy for the first time in 1961. He was voted co-rookie of the year and qualified fifth fastest. He led the race for 27 laps. "Knowing what I know now," he said, "I could have easily won that race. I think I finished twelfth." That season he won his first race at Phoenix.

He came back the next year and turned a 150.370mph run at the Indianapolis Motor Speedway, becoming the first man in the history of the Speedway to run over 150mph. "I was leading the race and long gone—really long gone—and lost the brakes," he said. He managed one win later that season.

Even with his famous aggression and outright talent, he seemed to be able to finesse a car. "I came

back in 1963 and won," he said.

Convincingly, too. He sat on pole and led most of the race, winning against Jimmy Clark. Dripping oil. So much so in fact that Clark didn't want to try to pass him and risk crashing. Nevertheless, it was a great victory for a man who had only been at The Speedway twice before.

In 1964, he was leading the race and made a pit stop and his Lotus caught on fire. He only drove the Lotus at Milwaukee and Trenton—where he won both races. At the end of the year in 1964 Ford gave him Jimmy Clark's car. In 1965, he came back in that car and finished second. In 1966, he began building his own cars. He qualified fifth and was running second in the Indy 500, when he lost a wheel bearing. He won no other races that season. In 1967, he drove the famous Turbine car of Andy Granatelli. And by next year he had quit racing Indy Cars.

"I quit doing Indy Cars after the Turbine in 1967," Jones said. "Frankly there was a couple of things: I had a friend who was always worried about me, and I told him, 'Hey, if I ever win Indy, I'll quit.' He kept saying, 'You're going to kill yourself, you know.' So after I won in 1963 the doors opened in so many different ways that I almost couldn't afford to quit. I almost didn't want to anyway. So I pacified him by saying, I've got to capitalize on what I'm doing.

"But when I drove that Turbine car in 1967, it was in the back of my mind. And when I was leading the race, almost a lap ahead of Foyt, I said to myself, 'You know, winning itself is not going to be as thrilling as it was the first time. Of course, a few laps later the car quit. But later it helped me make a decision. Because, jeez, if it's not *that* thrilling and the financial future was already taking off in my tire business, I thought gee, 'Everything's kind of coming together.' And I thought—and also I got married about that time and I wanted kids—it just seemed like everything was set for me to do that.

"On top of that, the Turbine that I was going to drive that next year—1968—for Granatelli would have been the car to beat, but on the other hand, I didn't think it was going to be very safe. It was a Lotus, but I just wasn't very enthused about it. I'm enough of a practical engineer that I just didn't think the car was safe. I knew it was going to be quicker than the year before, too.

"So it all kind of came together. I said, 'Hey, you ought to just quit.' I made that choice, but I always felt that I could come back. That's why I kept driving all kinds of things. I always felt that I could turn the corner and come back. I came close in 1969. Al Unser broke his foot, and we didn't have a driver. So I was seriously thinking about it. But I knew that if I did that, if I didn't (drive the race) then I could stay away."

Racing didn't actually stop with that decision; just racing Indy Cars. He ran Trans-Am for Ford and did some stock car racing. In Trans-Am he won six races in his two-and-a-half seasons. He finished second in

Jones in 1963 at Milwaukee, head up and fast. Jones was capable of driving just about anything fast. He went from sprint cars to jet cars with relative ease and was always out front. Russ Lake

the championship to Mark Donohue in 1969 and won the championship in 1970, beating Donohue. He raced stock cars with success, winning four races in his time in Grand Nationals. He also raced Baja, before quitting completely, and moving toward the next stage of his life as a car builder.

With the first Lotuses in 1966, Jones got the taste of being a car owner. So with long-time partner Vel Militich, Parnelli began his career as a car builder. The first several seasons Jones worked with Joe Leonard and Al Unser. Jones, whose specialty was chassis adjustment, worked on the cars as well as oversaw the team.

In 1969, with Unser out, Leonard was leading the Indy 500 with nine laps to go when the car quit. But the team came back in 1970 and led 190 laps, giving Unser his first victory at the Speedway and Jones' first as a car owner in the Johnny Lightning car. To top it off, they returned in 1971 and won it again, with Unser at the helm once more.

In 1972 the "superteam" was formed. The superteam, with Leonard, Unser and Mario Andretti was one of the most technically superior teams to have ever raced at Indianapolis. Joe Leonard won the championship that season for Jones. Vel's Parnelli Jones, the name of the team, had spared no expense to create the best and most technologically superior machines. Teamed with the drivers, the team seemed unstoppable. They were in fact stoppable. Unfortunately, it was by their own hands. By 1974, they were to win no races.

"What happened was after we won in 1971 we ran another car with Joe Leonard with Firestone. In 1972 we came back and Firestone wanted us to take on Mario. So we had Mario, Al and Joe. That was when people like the press and so forth labeled us the "Superteam."

"Running three cars, see, is more difficult than running two. They don't support each other. Pretty soon they start hoarding parts and they aren't working together. And when you aren't winning either it's tough. When you win it breeds success, and losing breeds failure. I don't think we were a failure, but we had our struggles.

At Indy in 1965, Jones smiles for the cameras. He had won in 1963 and was riding the wave of publicity, turning a hobby into a very serious business by this time. He would eventually retire with several dozen tire stores and large real estate holdings. Russ Lake

"In 1972, we didn't qualify all that well. Penske sat on the pole with Donohue. They couldn't keep an engine together. They kept on blowing them up for whatever reason. So at the last minute we sold them an engine. And they won the race and our cars won second and third." Jones laughed. "We designed a belt that goes around your waist with loops on it so you could kick your own butt. We should have never done that I guess."

Jim McGee, who worked as team manager for Mario Andretti, recalls the organizational and design problems of the team: "It was a big team at the time," McGee said. "It was meant to compete with the Dan Gurney operation, which was the Goodyear backed program. There was a lot of talent assembled there—probably too much talent.

" . . . George Bignotti was more or less the team manager, and then you had three chief mechanics and then you had a group of engineers and really highly experienced people. I think the concept was good, but looking back on it, the concept was too far ahead of its time. It was kind of like a Mickey Thompson deal. We were trying to progress too far, trying to do too many new things. And part of the reason it was unsuccessful was that fact. We lost track of the basics."

It didn't help either that the team was also sponsoring a Formula One team in Europe. The team, called simply Parnelli, was campaigning a Grand Prix car with Andretti while the Indy team was buzzing around the ovals of the U.S. And in 1974, U.S. Firestone "pulled the plug" says Jones.

"When Firestone got out of racing their support was a great deal of our subsidy. That's what really broke up the superteam. We kept running one car until Mario left and went to (Lotus) Formula One. We developed the Cosworth engine and won the first race at Pocono. We should have won Indy that year, we were very quick.

"But we just didn't have the financial backing. Vel and I were spending too much of our own money. And after a couple years of that you kind of look in the mirror and say, 'I could be in the Bahamas.'"

So Jones got out of racing altogether. He continued opening Firestone stores—ending up with a total of about forty-five, which he sold in the early 1990s. By 1995, Jones was still doing public relations for Firestone and, over the years, he's accumulated commercial real estate which he develops and trades. He writes an article in FYI magazine four times a year and he still does personal appearances for Ford. "I keep plenty busy," he says.

And as far as the aggressiveness? He says it isn't a problem. In fact, he says, it really never was. Except that one time with Sachs. And then that other time . . .

"In all the years I've been in racing I've never been in a fight . . . except for one time and that was in the years of stock car racing. That was the only fight I ever had in all the years of racing. I've had guys come up and want to fight me after a race or something, and I've always said, take your best shot. Nobody's ever challenged me yet."

Probably for good reason, too.

Chapter 17

Nigel Mansell

Nigel Mansell's career was over in 1985. Or should have been, at any rate. The young Brit had had as many chances as any young driver should have had, failing on each occasion. Driving for Lotus and Colin Chapman for four seasons, he had done absolutely nothing with the opportunity.

But Mansell, like a wounded pit bull, did not give up. And perhaps what Nigel Mansell is, most of all, is a tremendous survivor. His true grit was probably never illustrated as dramatically as it was in 1984 at the Dallas Grand Prix. After having captured pole and running at the top of the field, he ran out of fuel just a quarter of a mile from the finish line. Instead of tossing his helmet and walking back to the pits, Mansell did the unthinkable: he got out and pushed the Lotus-Renault in 110 degree Dallas heat to the finish line, where just feet from the stripe, he collapsed onto the pavement. For the effort, he received a single point for sixth place. The man had heart. But, regrettably, no talent. So most thought.

And perhaps that past, that tenuous future in the sport he loved, was the reason he says what he says and does what he does. Perhaps he still feels his place in racing history is in jeopardy.

Because, in 1985, he got a reprieve from retirement. Frank Williams offered him a job as driver alongside ex-champ Keke Rosberg. It was literally his last chance. Mansell was already thirty-two years old when Williams gave him the call.

He had started serious racing quite late in life. He was twenty-five when he began racing Formula three in Europe after utterly dominating Formula Ford for the previous several seasons. He won thirty-two of forty-two races. He sold his home in 1978 to finance four drives in a March F3 car and caught the attention of Lotus boss Colin Chapman, who hired him as a test driver. His first race was in Austria in 1980, and by the following season, he had earned himself a place on the team as a regular driver.

In 1981, he finished fourteenth in the championship. His teammate, Elio De Angelis, also a relative rookie, finished eighth. In 1982, Mansell was twelfth while De Angelis was ninth; in 1983, Mansell was twelfth and De Angelis was seventeenth; and in 1984, De Angelis finished third in the championship. Mansell was ninth and had crashed out or left the track five times.

In the instances he had the wherewithal to capture victories, he made mistakes. At Monaco, where

One can not underestimate what Nigel Mansell did for American racing internationally. Never before had a reigning champion left Formula One as World Champion to compete in another series—and certainly not in Indy Cars, which most F1 pundits saw as a minor formula. In 1993, Mansell won five races and seven poles to become the first rookie to win the Indy Car championship. Bob Tronolone

Red Five. Nigel Mansell in 1993 on his way to a championship win. Mansell's number corresponded to his number at Williams in F1, where he retained the nickname, "Red Five." In both instances, he took the number to the championship, where it was changed to number one the following season. Courtesy IndyCar

he started on the front row and inherited the lead mid-race in the rain in 1984, Mansell simply threw it away, crashing heavily in Mirabeau and putting himself out of the race. Pictures the next day of Mansell sitting on the guardrail pounding his helmet with clenched fists said it all. Too many failures.

If Mansell paled in comparison to his own teammate, put up against relative same-generation drivers such as his new teammate Rosberg, Nelson Piquet or Alain Prost, Mansell was truly no match. Clearly not an Alain Prost, thought pundits.

And for the first few races of the 1985 season, he once again seemed to be headed toward unemployment. His first points were from a fifth place in Portugal. Then, although he qualified on pole for Monaco, he failed to finish in the points again. In Canada he posted a sixth, and at Detroit he was on the front row, but again failed to capitalize, having an accident. In France, he injured himself and was unable to start the race. Although he captured a sixth and a front line starting position in the next four races at Germany, Austria, Holland, and Italy, he still seemed on the way out. Until Belgium.

At Belgium Mansell finally showed something, some small spark of brilliance. He finished second to

Ayrton Senna, some 28 seconds behind the Brazilian, but made no unforced errors which had been so common while running in points-paying positions.

The following race secured his future. At the European Grand Prix held at Brands Hatch in Great Britain, Mansell took his first win. In a race with Senna, Mansell took the lead on his own, drove away for 67 of 75 laps and won the race hands-down. He crossed the finish line half out of the cockpit and with tears streaming down his face. Dying of thirst, he had finally opened the floodgate.

At the next race at South Africa Mansell was on pole—only the second time in his career—and won the race, leading 74 of 75 laps. He then came back at the last race of the season, and again put the Williams on the front row of the grid for Australia, but failed to finish. By that time, it didn't matter. Mansell was now a hot commodity.

In 1986, he was lead driver for Williams, with Rosberg having left for McLaren. His co-driver was Piquet, and Mansell was consistently as quick as the Brazilian, taking the front line on the grid seven times (as did Piquet) and matching poles with Piquet with two each. But where Piquet won four times, Mansell won five times.

Unfortunately, the Mansell bad luck now had a different twist to it. It was no longer specific to losing just individual races, but to championships. Although Williams had the lion's share of the wins and was unbeatable in the Manufacturer's championship, it was Alain Prost in a TAG-Porsche who took the drivers Championship by two points over Mansell in the final race of the season. Mansell was put out in the last stages of the race.

In 1987, he lost the championship to Piquet, who won only three races to Mansell's six. Again, as the season wore down, Mansell made unforced errors. Piquet finished in the points when he didn't win. Mansell didn't. Mansell injured himself in practice at the Japanese Grand Prix and Piquet capitalized, winning the event and moving himself into the lead due to more top six finishes. Mansell finished second in the title fight again.

In 1988, without Frank Williams (who had been paralyzed in a road car accident), the team lost Honda engines and faired poorly. Mansell only managed a pair of second place finishes. In 1989 and 1990, Mansell was paired with Ferrari and won several times in a noncompetitive car, finishing fourth in the 1989 championship and fifth in the 1990 title. The Italian fans called him "Il Leone," the lion, for his courage and amazing heart.

In 1991, after announcing his retirement, he returned to Williams and once again just lost the championship in the late stages of the season when a wheel nut came loose (he was disqualified for a crewman pushing his wheel-less car back to the pits). He finished second to Senna.

In 1992, Mansell finally did it. He took nine victories in sixteen races and captured an incredible fourteen poles. The season was magical for Mansell, who was for sure the sentimental favorite. Finally, finally, he was World Champion.

But with success and victory fresh in his mind, Mansell felt he was not getting the respect he deserved at Williams. Having just won the championship in grand fashion for Williams, he expected some respect—perhaps some sort of concession from Williams on his contract. He did not get it. And when Williams tried to negotiate Mansell's salary, he fled the team, landing in the United States.

Indy Car fans can not underestimate what Mansell did for American racing when he did that. Immediately, exposure to Indy Car racing increased threefold. International exposure was incredible. Never before had a reigning champion left the sport as World Champion to compete in another series— and certainly not in Indy Cars, which most F1 pundits saw as a minor formula.

But Mansell had, and he put Indy Car racing on the map. Sure, Emerson Fittipaldi and Eddie Cheever and Danny Sullivan and a number of others had come to Indy Cars. But their success not withstanding, those men were not as competitive when they came to Indy

Mansell in 1986, after the long spell of failures had ended. The confidence in Mansell was palpable by this time. He was quickest in practice for this race, the Canadian Grand Prix, and won easily over Alain Prost, with over twenty seconds to spare. Tony Sakkis

Cars as Mansell was. With Mansell, the world saw the level of competition in the U.S. In 1993, Mansell won five races and seven poles to become the first "rookie" to win the Indy Car championship.

But although the exterior of Mansell's reign in Indy Cars seemed harmonious, he created tension within both the team and the series. Mansell's normal *motis operendi*, as with Piquet, then Prost, and finally with Mario Andretti, was Mansell tended to divisiveness when it was unnecessary. Andretti, who was teamed with Mansell during his two seasons in Indy Cars, was less than impressed with him. Although Andretti ultimately saw Mansell as a fantastic racer, as

The year before his successful move to Williams. He looks whipped and beaten. It seemed to be the end of the road for Mansell who even at this race, was to make another of his patented mistakes; he blasted through the pack and caused a crash before the first corner. This photo was shot in Detroit in 1984. Tony Sakkis

a teammate Mansell commanded less than respect from the elder statesman of racing.

"Our situation with Nigel sort of didn't work out," Andretti said in 1995, then retired from the sport. "I had known Nigel for many years. As a matter of fact he was a test driver when I was at Lotus. And we had been friends over the years, but we had never really worked closely together.

"But somehow, he's a man who, when he comes into a team—especially when he came in on this side—he just wanted to trash everything and everyone else around him. And he certainly wanted no competition and tried to draw all of the attention to his side. And he succeeded in doing that. They all rallied totally behind him. I mean you sit there and you've been part of the team for so long and you're totally left on the side, like in the middle of the lake with no oars. So I figured, 'What gives?'

"It's not all his fault. I think the team kind of abandoned me to some degree. While we were teammates, we did not communicate. We always used to have all of our after-practice meetings together and whenever I had a teammate that's what we used to do, try to share everything. But when we got to the first race in Australia, I thought that's what we'd do, but he flat refused. He just divided the team at that point. And the team, to my dismay, went along with it. All because if they didn't do what he wanted, he would throw a tantrum. And because of that, obviously we couldn't continue as teammates and the whole thing divided. It's unfortunate because I have a lot of respect for him as a driver, but as a human being there was just like zero communication."

If Mansell's relationship with Andretti was less than perfect, his relationship with the press and Indy Car regulars was met with even less enthusiasm. Much of that criticism was unfounded.

Monaco, 1987. Mansell was quickest in practice, but lost to Ayrton Senna after leading 29 laps. Senna, who was almost unbeatable in Monte Carlo, was an arch-enemy of Mansell's, with the two nearly coming to blows on many occasions. Tony Sakkis

Mansell, like any other driver, tended to have his bad moods when something or someone let him down. At Indy, when he was put out of the race in 1994, he refused to see the doctor and left the track, not commenting to the press. The press, at that point and in other instances, called him childish. At the same time, Indy Car regulars resented the attention Mansell received. He hoarded the spotlight and they took the opportunity whenever possible to make it known that Mansell was not their favorite competitor. In both cases, it was probably a case of intolerance or selfishness. And Mansell did have his fans. In the team, Mansell and Jim McGee, the team manager, were inseparable. They even appeared on TV commercials together for Texaco.

"We're still very good friends," McGee said after he left his stint with Newman-Haas for Patrick Racing again in 1995. "Nigel is a great person. He's very difficult to deal with as far as if you confront Nigel. You have to know how to work with Nigel. If you give him an inch and he'll give you two. Sometimes, maybe, if you don't know the circumstances you might take (his temper) the wrong way. But knowing Nigel from a personal standpoint and the family standpoint and as a race driver, he's great.

"He's very serious and motivated. With his position with everybody pulling on him from different directions, it's not easy for him to be nice to everybody. He tells it like it is and a lot of times you can't tell it like it is. He does speak up when he doesn't think things are right. There's a lot of guys who don't say anything. They just sort of trudge off.

"You confront these guys—I mean I don't care if it's (Pat) Patrick, (Roger) Penske, Mansell or Andretti, you got to turn them the direction you want to turn them without confronting them all the time. Because all you do in a confrontation with those guys, because they want to win, is do more harm. They want to win in every confrontation. You want to avoid confrontation and get everyone pulling in the same direction."

If engineers and crew chiefs have a soft spot in their hearts for drivers who perform up to the standards of the machinery, then the crew must have worshipped Mansell. For whatever his failings, when it came to personalities, he had almost none when it came to his relationships with his machinery.

At Newman-Haas, the relationship with his car was not very apparent, but while at Williams, designer Patrick Head claimed that Mansell's confidence in his traction control was so total that he would leave his foot practically planted at every opportunity, letting the wheels take care of themselves as he steered the thing. That total faith in his machinery was mind-boggling even to Head.

"He would ask me what's going to happen and what should I do and he believed me," McGee said. "I didn't tell him if I didn't absolutely know that was the truth for sure. We established a good relationship because of that point. I didn't bullshit him and I didn't tell him something that was going to get him in trouble. I let him know the facts."

In the final analysis, Mansell was surely a temperamental man with which to work on a regular basis. For teammates, competitors or regular beat media, Mansell was eccentric. He was quirky, he was selfish, and he was sometimes ruthless. But nobody would ever say that he was slow. Not since 1985, anyway.

"He's a performer," McGee said. "That's probably why he gets himself in so much trouble, because when he gets on that race track it's a performance. If his performance is ruined by something else, he has to let the public know why he didn't win or that this guy did that. To me, where a lot of other drivers would take it as part of the business and take it down the road."

In the end, Mansell did take it down the road. But he did it the only way he knew how: with a snip and a jab. He made it seem as if his two years in Indy Cars was only little more than passing time; that it was easy; that it was beneath him. As if trying, for some odd reason to convince us that he was *that* good. But he needn't have bothered. We already knew.

A team switch? Nigel Mansell talks with team boss Roger Penske at Laguna Seca, Monterey in 1992, prior to his first season in Indy Cars. Mansell would increase exposure to the series almost threefold with his defection from Formula One after winning the Grand Prix World Championship. Eva Vega

Chapter 18

Jim McGee

Jim McGee is a pragmatist. In what he does, being practical is the only method there was to keep him from becoming a nervous wreck.

"I never got burned out on racing because I never took the highs too high or the lows too low," McGee said. "I just liked to do it. People who get burned out are the ones who take the victories and make such big things out of them and by the same token the same with their defeats."

And in 1996, after forty years of preparing successful race cars for other people, Jim McGee should know. McGee is one of the winningest team managers in the history of Indy Car racing. Since he started working as a car builder and mechanic for Indy Car teams back in 1956, McGee has had eighty championship wins, four Indianapolis 500 victories, nine National Championships, thirteen 500 mile race wins (including Indianapolis), six poles at Indianapolis, and numerous pit and mechanic awards.

Quite simply: he is the best.

"It's been fun," he says. "I enjoy the changes. So many people get trapped in this not wanting to change and, 'it was better in the old days' and, 'I wish it would get back to what it was.' Well, you can't look back on that stuff.

Jim McGee back at home with Pat Patrick. Most of McGee's career has been spent with Pat Patrick, although he did stints for Roger Penske, Parnelli Jones, Andy Granatelli, Bobby Rahal and Carl Haas. Patrick allows McGee to do whatever he feels is right, and in that atmosphere McGee has produced some of his greatest work. Courtesy Jim McGee, Patrick Racing

Today's racing is better than it's ever been. It's changed, naturally. You're part of a big team, not an individual. I get a lot of pride and a lot of comfort from seeing my guys do well and seeing them work together.

"When I was working for Clint Brawner, he was a great guy and a great mechanic, but he was miserable. All he could think about were things he could have done or the races he should have won and he'd keep those memories.

"One of the things I've always tried to do through my career is try to forget things—bad things—quick. The minute we crash a car or blow and engine, that's the end of it as far as I'm concerned. I don't even care [why] it happened."

McGee, who began his career as a driver and who is now one of the most successful mechanics ever, has also had a lot of time to forget. He started racing modifieds in New England, and then decided he was ill-equipped to drive. He turned his efforts to wrenching and tuning, working as an apprentice for Dick Carman, a mechanical engineer who was building an Indy road-ster. The relationship—as well as the project—was sidetracked as McGee was inducted into the Army, as a mechanical specialist, to work on trucks and heavy equipment. He spent six months in active duty and two years in the reserves.

In 1961, he formed a friendship with Clint Brawner, the man who discovered Mario Andretti. Working on the Dean Van Lines Special, McGee worked with several drivers from Andretti to Eddie Sachs. He became the co-chief mechanic with Brawner until 1969, when Granatelli bought the team. That was the first year McGee had a hand in winning the Indy 500. It was also Granatelli's only win. Sort of.

"That wasn't really the truth," McGee said. "What happened was that Mario had driven for Clint Brawner and myself—who were mechanics on the car. He started driving for us in 1964. The team was owned by Al Dean, of Dean Van Lines, which was a moving company out of Long Beach, California. Dean died in 1967 and his widow ended up with the race team. Mario actually bought the team from Dean with some help from Firestone and Ford. He actually ran the team in 1968. In 1969, he sold the team to the Granatellis.

"One of the stipulations of the sale was that if we were going to stay on and run the car in 1969, the Granatellis could have absolutely no part of it in any way. In other words it would not be run with any of them involved. They were actually banned from our garages. As far as having anything to do with the winning car, they had absolutely nothing to do with it except Andy was the sponsor with the car."

Mario won his one and only Indianapolis 500 that season and Granatelli gave him the kiss that was seen around the world, taking credit for the win after twenty years of trying.

In 1970, Mario moved on from Granatelli and Brawner and McGee, citing philosophical differences. He went with Hayhoe Racing and Roger McClusky. McClusky would win no races, but finished sixth in the championship. In 1972, the famous partnership of Brawner and McGee broke up. It was an amicable split.

"Clint Brawner and I stayed together actually after Mario left, and what happened was that the funding in 1971 wasn't available to let us both stay together. Mario had called me, and I had an opportunity to go back with him. Clint could then stay and run a smaller operation by himself. So we parted. But we parted as far as working together, but we never did as far as our friendship. We were always close throughout his life, and then when he died. I hated to leave, really, but he kind of kicked me out. He said, 'Hey, it's time you went out and did your own thing. There's not enough sponsorship here that would justify us working together. Go do your own thing.'"

So in 1971, McGee went back to work for the STP Group for one year, watching from pit wall as Mario finished a dismal ninth in the championship. He then went to work for Parnelli Jones in California, in the "Superteams operation." For a short time afterward, McGee worked for Parnelli Jones as Mario's chief mechanic.

A young McGee with a young Mario Andretti. McGee, along with Clint Brawner, took Andretti to the Winner's Circle at Indianapolis. It was Andretti's only win there and the first for McGee. John Mahoney

"The basic successes in racing come from getting something that's reliable, dependable, and practical. You work on the details. Very few innovators ever win. It took a group that more or less worked on something that had a history and had reliability and you worked on details and that's what won you races. The cars that we built there were more like Formula One. They were very unreliable. All new concepts. At the time, probably we should have had a development program that worked on that side of the racing and we probably should have run cars that were more practical, more state of the art rather than advanced as the cars that were being built."

In his two seasons with Vels Parnelli, the team had only one win with driver Mario Andretti (although the team won more than that single race at the hands of the two others drivers). McGee departed in 1974 for Fletcher Racing, taking Pancho Carter to Rookie of the Year honors at Indianapolis. And in 1975, McGee was able to turn his genius into results. He moved to Penske.

"I ran Penske's operation from 1975 to 1980, with Mears and Unser and Mario and Tom Sneva. We won twenty-two races and three championships and won Indy. When Firestone was getting out of racing, that's when Penske came to me. Mark Donohue had just been killed in Formula One. (Penske) didn't have an Indy team at that time. He had let his Indy team kind of lapse. We started an Indy team in 1975 and hired Tom Sneva. The second year we hired Mario and ran a two-car team. Actually the last year I was there we ran a three-car team, with Mears, Unser and Andretti. Then I went to work for Patrick in 1981."

Although the Penske years were successful and put Jim McGee on most team owner's short list of capable chief mechanics, the Patrick days were his most enjoyable. Under Penske, McGee was still effectively leashed as to what he could do. With Patrick, McGee was able to make all the decisions and all the calls. In that atmosphere, he flourished.

"Pat and I had talked, and we had actually made deal the year before I went to work for him. Pat was the kind of a guy where when I went to work for him he hired me to do a job and then he'd stand back and let you do the job. He'd make suggestions, but the reason he'd hired you was to do the job, and whatever decision you made that was it, you lived with it. To me it was refreshing because with Roger Penske you never knew or not whether what you decided

Jim McGee keeping an eye out. Here at Newman Haas, he was seen as the engineer of Nigel Mansell's 1993 IndyCar championship. He has seen a great deal of success in his career. Jim Mahoney

Looking intense, McGee, who is normally amiable, isn't inviting conversation. At the track McGee is all business, and his results in racing prove just how serious he is. Courtesy Jim McGee, Patrick Racing

was what he was going to go with or not. Roger also was a great guy to work for, but you never really felt that you had control and you were always second guessing because you were never sure whether or not he was going to change (the car). But with Pat, he told you, 'I hired you to do this job, and you're going to do it; I'm not going to interfere.' To me that was a lot easier. We went through a lot of tough times and a lot of great times, but we have rarely had disagreements," he said of Patrick.

In 1990, Patrick changed McGee's title and job from team manager to owner, letting McGee buy into the team. Unfortunately, the team folded in 1991, when Bobby Rahal bought it, lock, stock, and barrel. McGee stayed on and ran the team to a national championship in 1992, its first season.

In 1992, McGee moved on to Newman-Haas racing and helped Nigel Mansell capture the championship in 1993. In 1995, he was back at Patrick, back where he was with an old friend in Patrick and a title as general manager. Back where he knew the surroundings and knew the game. Pragmatically, he was back home again.

At this writing, McGee was heading forward with Patrick, Scott Pruett and Firestone. Unlike drivers, crew chiefs do not have a finite number of seasons, and McGee seems prepared, both emotionally and physically, to take on all comers. Pruett broke the ice in 1995 and won his first event for himself and for Patrick Racing. As always, McGee takes the wins as they come.

Chapter 19

Rick Mears

Rick Mears is an actor. He admits as much, saying what you see is not usually what you get. But unlike a lot of professional drivers, Mears is not an actor in front of the microphone or camera, but away from it, behind the wheel of his Indy Car.

Speed and aggression is very unlike the 5'10" Californian. When in most drivers you see a kind of wound-up neurosis that make them similar to predators, always on the hunt for food, Mears always looks as if he were a part of the landscape. Just hanging out. You asked him a question, and he responded naturally, unforced. Fans wanted autographs, and he obliged happily.

But strapped into the Penske Racing cars, Mears became the proverbial Mr. Hyde. He would chop your nose off in a corner as soon as look at you. No amount of intimidation could slow him and no modicum of performance was overlooked.

Which is the real Rick Mears?

"They both seem natural to me," he said, chuckling. "In the car, that was what I was out there to do. I was seeing how fast I could go and compete against the other guys. Out of the car the way you see me is the way I am.

"I talked to (TV commentator) Paul Page about it," He continued. "I've had other people ask me

about it, so it's made me start thinking about it. It's kind of like acting I guess. I could do things in the car and do it legal. I could get aggressive and it was fair. That's what you were supposed to do. In acting you get to play a part or a role that's not really you. I think that's the way the racing was. I've been able to lean on guys maybe a little bit and force my hand so to speak, which I wouldn't do in person."

Mears has been successfully leaning on guys for a long time.

Born in Wichita, Kansas, on December 3, 1951, Mears began racing motorcycles when he was sixteen, winning more than 60 times in his short career. Worried about his racing, his mother lobbied for him to quit racing motorcycles. Mears acquiesced somewhat and agreed to race dune buggies instead. By 1973 Mears was an established off-roader and was beginning to campaign stock cars at local tracks in and around Bakersfield where the family had moved.

Racing against his brother, Mears would learn a skill that would be instrumental in his later success: he would discover team work.

"I understood how a team works—and teamwork has always been a very big part of the (Penske) team. It's like a chain: no matter who it is, if there's one weak link you can't get the job done. I've always under-

Mears in 1994, as Team Advisor. His expertise helped Al Unser Jr. win both Indy as well as the championship in 1994. Courtesy Marlboro Racing

Long Beach, 1991. After his accident at Sanair, Mears would only win one more road race in his career—the final race of the 1980s at Laguna Seca in October of 1989. Known for his prowess on ovals, the accident (which hampered his ability to use the clutch pedal for several seasons) stopped Mears from being as competitive as he might have ultimately been. Rick Dole

Rick Mears, at his last celebration in victory lane at Indianapolis. This, his fourth win in 1991, tied Mears with A.J. Foyt, and Al Unser, Sr. Rick Dole

stood that. My brother and I had always raced together all of our lives and we had always worked together. At the end of the day we'd come home and pick each other's brains and say, "What are you doing here and what are you doing here." We'd both help each other because we thought if we could elevate ourselves to where all we had to do is race each other instead of everybody else on the track, then that would really be fun. I think I learned that team work at a very early age and when I came (to Indy Cars) where it really fit in. Because anything I ever did on a car the other drivers knew about it and I never held anything back. Then you get to race each other instead of the other guys out there"

So with that information and philosophy, Mears made his Indy Car debut in 1976 with an eighth place finish and took a pair of ninth place finishes later in the year, earning himself Rookie Of The Year honors. At the beginning of the next season, he finished four races in the top ten. Roger Penske offered him a part

time ride to fill in for Mario Andretti while Andretti was off in Europe with the F1 World Championship.

In 1978, Mears started his first Indy 500. He qualified on the front row at his first Indy 500, but was forced out with mechanical problems. He went on to win three races—Milwaukee, Atlanta and Brands Hatch. The following season, 1979, his skill level was such that he won the race at Indy from pole, then won two other events and finished in the top ten in each of the fourteen events, becoming the first CART Champion.

He won once and finished in the top five eight times in 1980 and then came back in 1981 to take six victories and the series title again. But in 1981, in a horrible fire in the pits at Indianapolis, Mears was burned about the face and neck. It would be the first of a series of accidents which would scar him and affect him for the rest of his life. In 1984, after repeating his title challenge yet again in 1982 and his Indy win in May of that season, he went to Sanair in Quebec and crashed hard, running his feet under the guardrail, nearly tearing them off as the car slid along. The accident took him out of operation until midway through the 1985 season.

By the time he called it quits in December of 1992, Mears had won 29 Indy car races from Mexico City to Brands Hatch, Great Britain. He had established forty pole positions, three championships and four Indy 500 wins (the latest being the 1991 win). He had remained not only loyal, but extremely profitable for Roger Penske, becoming one of the few drivers to remain with a singe team for sixteen seasons of racing.

But when the time had come for him to call it quits, he not only knew it, he knew why. Yet another crash at Indy in 1992 damaged Mears' wrist. It was yet another injury which would cause him to miss most of the season while the wrist was healing. Shortly afterward, he announced his retirement.

"When I was sliding upside down, the thought was going through my mind: "I don't need this." I had crashed before and the thought had never crossed my mind. So that was just another indicator. Weighing up things here and there it was just telling me it was time to go. You know when I missed the Nazareth race because of my wrist and I was sitting on top of the building watching the race. Eddie Cheever was standing up there talking to me and bouncing around—he didn't have a ride—and he said, "Doesn't this drive you nuts, watching it, not being able to be down there?" I got to thinking about it and said, 'No, it's not driving me nuts.'

"That was just another indicator that it was time to get out. It was just a lot of little things and it all pointed to desire. One of the key things was that I caught myself not taking it home with me. I always used to go back to the hotel at night and think a bit and come back the next day with two or three ideas about what we could do and try on the car. And it came to a point when I'd leave the track and I'd forget about it. I'd come back in the morning and say, "Okay, guys, where at are we at?' That wasn't the way it should have been done. When you start doing that you start making mistakes."

Mears in the pits. More often than not, Mears' advantage came from set-up strategies. Mears was a supreme tactician and a student of the competition. His cerebral approach was one of the reasons he and Penske got along so well. Rick Dole

Mears at the Meadowlands, 1990. Not one of the more satisfying seasons. He won only one race this season—at Phoenix—but still managed to finish third in the championship. Rick Dole

Smiling during Indy qualifying, 1990. Mears, even then, was a refreshingly approachable man who always had time for a fan, a crewman, or a question from the media. He was as respected and well-liked among the racing fraternity as he was with the general public. Rick Dole

"It was just a lot of different things adding up," Mears said. "And mainly the desire was going away. I just wasn't enjoying the driving as much. I mean I got into it as a hobby, not a business. I never dreamed of making a living at it, so it was enjoyment that drove me on, made me want to improve and go forward and generate the interest. And as the enjoyment of driving was going away then I just kept weighing all the facts.

"First of all, if your desire goes away you're not going to put your best foot forward. You always try a little harder with something you enjoy. I just thought that it wouldn't be fair for the teams or the sponsors if that started happening. So when that started going

away I just started weighing the facts. Everybody's talking about the crash at Indy and I had already pretty much made up my mind before that happened. That sped up the process a little bit. "

So Mears took a job in the Penske Team as an advisor. There's no title for his job at Penske, "I just kind of do whatever, wherever, whenever," he said. Of course, he still knows how to set up a car, and he still was able to help Roger Penske with feedback as to how to handle the strategy. So the decision was a natural. And in 1993, Mears did what he had always done in the past, except that he no longer got into the race car to do it.

"It's going very well," he said in 1995. "It was definitely the right decision. I haven't regretted it. You never know how things were going to go, but I've never regretted not being in the car because I feel involved. I could never have just walked away from the whole thing. That would have been impossible because I enjoyed the sport and the enjoyed the team I'm working with—I've been with them seventeen years now—so staying involved was critical. If I had walked away from everything, I would have missed it."

Mears admits he does still miss the driving from time to time. He missed the aggression part of it and the part about beating the pants off anybody who he raced against. There are few places he can still do that. And he misses doing it the way he did it; so perfect it was the best it could have ever been done.

"It was getting through the corner at its limit," he said. "That thrill of trying to get a corner as perfect as you can get it. Quicker than everyone else. It doesn't matter the speed of the corner or the speed of the track. It's all relative. If the average is eighty miles an hour and you can run eighty one and everybody else is eighty and below, that's exciting. And the competition was the main thing."

Mears still has a trace of the limp he received in Sanair in 1984, and a little scar tissue around the nose from the pit fire in 1981, but he has a lot of life left in him. As of this writing in 1995, Mears is happy being with Penske, still. But perhaps it will be time to eventually move on—to other challenges and other stages.

"I doubt very seriously about owning my own team," he said quietly. "You never say never, but right now I'm enjoying what I'm doing, so I haven't thought about anything else. And Roger has left the door open to let me do whatever I want, to let me be involved."

The final act is playing out on the stage of Rick Mears life. If he plays it anything like he played his seventeen years as a driver, it may be a long and similarly successful production. Stay seated.

Chapter 20

Harry Miller

Harry Miller, designer, builder, and supplier of some of the greatest race cars to ever run on the boards and bricks of America's speedways, had contributed to racing not simply technologically, but rather institutionally. Miller motivated a change in the fundamental structure of racing.

Although the name Miller appears on entry sheets at the Indianapolis Motor Speedway as early as 1913, it was in 1919 when Miller made his mark not just on American racing, but racing worldwide.

Blessed with a technical background and totally familiar with automotive design, his theories and his innovations came from firsthand knowledge of racing engines and racing cars. Originally a carburetor manufacturer and supplier, he first entered racing as carburetor supplier, then a fabricator of pistons and valves, and eventually came to create complete engines, then entire cars.

Adept in his own right, his ideas would be transformed onto paper by a team of master draftsmen—led by none other than Leo Goossen and Fred Offenhauser, creator of the famous "Offy" engine that would later dominate Indy. The two were fantastic technicians and designers. Miller imagined his creations, then explained them to Offenhauser and Goossen, who put them into production.

Where Miller's main competition, Fred Duesen-

Through his extensive, technical background in automotive design, Miller made his mark not just on American racing, but on racing worldwide. He started out producing carburetors, but he will best be known for his expertise in designing complete cars. Courtesy Bruce Craig

berg, relied on an abstract vision of what the perfect race vehicle should be, he was not blessed with the manpower, facilities or attention to order that Miller had. A look at the Miller shop in 1920 was like looking at a cafeteria, its benches spotless and its tooling in military style orderliness. Duesenberg made racing more a philosophy than a process. Led by his brother, August, Fred Duesenberg led a challenge to reduce the weight of the race car, and became obsessed with lightening the car from engine to chassis. To that end, Duesenberg used aluminum chassis frames with hardwood inserts to save weight. This design was far too crude for Miller, who used all steel for his frames.

Deusenberg was frugal and built race cars for a purpose other than for winning races—for the publicity gained and capitalized on the success with road car sales. Miller, on the other hand, produced the best race cars money could buy, eventually even using Duesenberg chassis to win the Indy 500 with a Miller engine.

The differences in philosophy between Duesenberg and Miller produced differences in the final product. Miller's cars were always more sophisticated, with more "moving parts." His components were always made of the finest alloys available, with each piece machined to very precise tolerances (Miller was one of the first men to use chrome-moly for fabrication of race cars). He would form simple pieces—such as con rods, wrist pins, etc.—from solid billets and machine them down to the right thickness, or cast seemingly insignificant parts to the exact shape he wanted. The cars were painstakingly assembled and created with as much attention as sculpture. But often his ideas were short of the genius that Duesenberg showed.

It was the Duesenberg straight eight, by the way, that Miller copied and eventually perfected to beat Duesenberg. Developed for their passenger touring cars, the Duesenberg engine debuted in 1919 and was a throwback to more reliable and simplistic engines of years earlier. Forsaking the dual overhead designs of the 1910s to a SOHC design racing engine (although originally a pushrod engine), the engine was cast as a single unit, incorporating crankcase, cylinders and combustion chambers. The Duesen-

berg's guts were easily accessible and the compression low, thereby keeping gasket failure to a minimum. The engine was successful—at the hands of Harry Miller.

Miller, who had experimented with four and sixteen cylinder engines, took the Duesenberg engine design—a 182 ci, SOHC cam eight, with battery ignition—and modified the bore/stroke relationship, shortening the stroke and increasing bore. The engine won in a Duesenberg chassis at the hands of Jimmy Murphy in 1922. It took Duesenberg until 1924 before he finally captured the Indy 500 after some ten attempts. The Duesenberg would win the Indy 500 twice more before racing's Golden Age would slide into oblivion at the end of 1929, with Miller taking the other three 500s. But that was not the end of the story.

From the beginning, Harry Armenius Miller was born in Wisconsin in 1875 of German and Canadian

Rare photo of (from left) Louis Chevrolet, Harry Miller, and Fred and Augie Duesenberg. Miller may not have been the most inventive of the four, but he was certainly the most savvy. He took ideas of the others and produced some of the most sophisticated and beautiful race cars the world had ever seen, thus inspiring the term "The Golden Age of Racing." Courtesy Auburn-Cord Duesenberg Museum

parents. By the time he was thirteen he had dropped out of school to work in a machine shop. His father, a minister and school teacher, was furious with Harry. He wanted his children to be educated, and Harry was clearly disinterested in academia. They fought often and the feud eventually forced Miller to leave Wisconsin for the west coast, where he ultimately settled permanently.

Working for a bicycle factory—as did Fred Duesenberg and Louis Chevrolet—Miller learned to machine parts for racing bikes. Also like Duesenberg, Miller mounted a small motor on a bicycle. Miller, too, was also involved in marine engines. He created a small engine that could be clamped to the back of a boat—an outboard—but failed to patent it. The outboard was very similar to what Oliver Evinrude began selling sometime later. Nevertheless, marine engines would be at least as important to Miller's name as automobiles.

In 1905, Miller created his first automobile. It was a crude thing that was mostly completed for personal use and not for sale. But he found he was very good at making that particular car run and as it evolved, he realized he had a flair for making slow cars fast and fast cars faster. By 1909, he had opened up his carburetor business in Los Angeles, and by the end of the decade, Miller's carburetors had become the most prolific at Indy. They had the reputation for being the best racing carburetors anywhere.

While he was moving toward making pistons, Miller met and hired Fred Offenhauser. Offenhauser quickly became a key in the Miller racing combination. With Offenhauser, Miller quickly embarked upon a career as an racing car engine manufacturer.

In 1919, Miller built his first four cylinder, the 183—which was a disaster. Cliff Durant, of Durant Motor Company, invested in the car and was so disgusted in its final performance, that he actually gave it away to Duesenberg driver Tommy Milton.

Milton tried to get the thing to work, but was unable to. He went to Miller and asked that a straight eight be installed. Miller had no such engine. Milton, who was becoming disenchanted with Fred Deusenberg's lack of financial acumen—meaning he was rarely paid for his driving—decided he had had enough of Duesenberg. He essentially stole the designs from the Deusenberg shop and took them to Miller, who reproduced them for Tommy Milton. In a convoluted story, the car had been disqualified because it was not, as it was touted, a Durant. Jimmy Murphy quickly jumped from the Duesenberg ship as well and fitted a Duesenberg with a Miller eight—and went on to win the 1922 Indy 500.

By the 1923 season the Miller 122 was available as an off-the-shelf model. The straight eight was quick and reliable, and in that season Jimmy Murphy, Tommy Milton, Eddie Hartz, Harlan Fengler and Bennett Hill won at least one of the eight races of the season, with Milton driving home to victory in the 500.

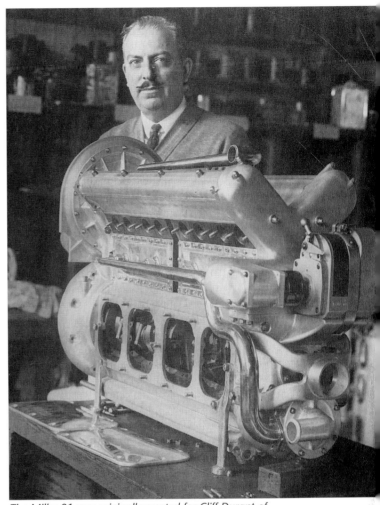

The Miller 91 was originally created for Cliff Durant of Durant Motor Company. The 91 reardrive had its first win at the hands of racer Frank Lockhart. Miller and his staff built about thirty-five 91 engines. Courtesy Bruce Craig

Eleven cars were entered in the May extravaganza. And so dominant were the Millers, that after the 1924 even Europeans virtually quit racing seriously at the Speedway until nearly thirty years later.

The engine evolved with superchargers and, along with its counterpart at Duesenberg, the eights won all of the 20 races entered in 1924 and 1925, with eight going to Duesenberg and twelve going to Miller (both 500s were won by the Duesenbergs).

To this day, the 122 is still a marvelous piece of racing machinery. In contrast to what it was competing against, the 122 looked as the Lotus 25 appeared almost forty years later, an unencumbered streamlined and lightweight little race car with more power.

In 1925, however, the 122ci displacement formula took its last breath. The engine which had been so dominant in the Miller was now obsolete under the new rules. That left a new era of expan-

Miller created his first automobile in 1905. It was a crude thing that was mostly completed for personal use and not for sale. Through his tinkering, Miller realized he had a flair for making slow cars fast and fast cars faster. He would go on to become a world-renown car builder. Courtesy Bruce Craig

sion and innovation. Miller was to lead this one hands-down.

The innovation this time was not just under the hood, but in the overall design of the car. Race cars had always been front engine rear drive. As far as the engine placement, Miller didn't see the wisdom in changing that, but as far as the rear wheels being driven, Miller saw an opportunity for change.

The first Miller 91, was actually created again for Durant, who raced the car with a driver named Dave Lewis. The following season Miller created and sold the 91s for the series. They were still hardly as powerful as the Duesenbergs. But luck handed the 91 rear-drive its first win at the hands of Frank Lockhart, who inherited the lead and won it in a rain-shortened event.

The 1927 race, however, was not won on luck but on technical superiority. The 91 front-driver was now the car to have. The small supercharged 91ci engines were much faster than anything else available. In retrospect, the car was so good that it actually put an end to what is now called the 'Golden Age of Racing.' The engines, with their small cylinders, were watch-like in their precision, and were putting out something near 250 horsepower, about 20-40 more than the best Duesenbergs.

Would-be racers were frustrated at the domination by Miller's cars and road car manufacturers were irritated at Miller because he had shut them out of a race that was supposed to be a showcase for them. From 1927 to 1929—20 races in three seasons—a Miller won all but one race, the 1927 Indy 500. In 1928, with a car that was rumored to have been running pure methyl alcohol, Leon Duray put his front drive Miller 91 on the pole of the Indy 500 with a 124mph average lap that stood until 1937—longer than any qualifying run since.

The Model 91 eight-cylinder engines were fetching $5,000 or more back in the twenties. His cars were going for fifteen-thousand or more and at his peak, he was selling more than he could make. Unfortunately for Miller, the next season ended all of that. In 1930, the beautiful workmanship of the 91s was obsolete again. The United States was in a depression, and racing was far too expensive. The rules were changed to appeal to the masses, and they did. The 1930s and the era of frugality at Indy changed the emphasis from a high-tech spectacle to a run-what-you-brung show. The new formula nearly bankrupted Miller.

He turned to his marine engines to survive the lean years, ultimately creating the Offenhauser, the world's most hardy little engine in the process. But that story is to be told in the chapter on Offenhauser and Goossen.

In 1935, Ford Motors recruited Harry Miller to build ten roadsters for use at Indy. The cars were based on the Ford Flathead engine and were built, in actuality, by Ford people. Miller was the head of the team. Miller, rejuvenated by the call, built masterpieces. The Miller-Fords all had front drive similar to the 91s, all independently suspended, and streamlined to the hilt. The cars, painted a beautiful black-and-white, were the best of the field.

The project was doomed from the start, however, since the steering knuckles were located too close to the engine. They overheated so badly, that they just seared together and made it impossible for the drivers to continue. Ford disbanded the operation after the race and sold the cars—which later showed up with various modifications at The Speedway.

Harry Miller died alone on May 3, 1943. His wife, who loved him dearly, had been kept at arm's length for several years as a cancerous growth had developed on Miller's face, inevitably taking his life. He refused to let her see him. In the end, his only friends were his animals—monkeys, parrots and dogs. So embarrassed of his disfigurement, he headed east, where he found no welcome. Miller had been insulting American manufacturers for years with his triumphs and, lately with his failure at Ford, the manufacturers were finally to pay him back. He could find no employment. He died nearly bankrupt and friendless.

Chapter 21

Pat Patrick

Pat Patrick sat at the Firestone press conference looking like a wise owl, big eyeglasses reflecting light in different directions as he moved his head slowly, taking it all in, processing the information, reserving judgment.

Firestone's PR man introduced Patrick as if he were a famous statesman or revered showman. The crowd deferred to Patrick and you could feel a sort of pregnant hush. A question was asked about how he felt the team would do in the coming season, what with all the intense competition in Indy cars.

He started slowly and quietly, but the words had a palpable weight. "Well," he said in that lispy southern twang, "If I could get a set of decent tires and my driver would try a bit harder we might be able to do something here." Then he smiled. "No," he said, "I'm thrilled with what's happening. I couldn't ask my guys for better."

And really, except for the small joke, you would expect no other answer from Patrick.

To look at Patrick, to hear the small voice come out of mouth of the man who looks like your favorite uncle, or the kind old gentleman who owns the deli down the street, your insurance man, your everyman, is to immediately understand Pat Patrick.

He is what he claims to be—the voice of reason, ready for a chat, an opinion and a reasonable word.

Businessman Pat Patrick in 1995. Patrick long ago shed his image of a millionaire oilman and adopted one of a team owner. On race weekends he can be seen in faded jeans or khaki pants and billed caps. Courtesy Patrick Racing

U.E. "Pat" Patrick doesn't need to do this racing thing. He's got enough money. In the early days in fact, they didn't just call him Patrick, but "Millionaire Oilman" car owner, the owner of Patrick Petroleum. In fact, if you realize that the car that took Gordon Johncock to his victory in 1982 was called an Indy Wildcat, you may just get the picture of who Pat Patrick really is: an oil wildcatter with the nose for success.

And like the mystical, larger-than-life men who stalked the plains of Texas, they made their fortunes not so much on science and technology as on feel. They could look at a piece of land and tell you if there was oil there. And it was the outguessing of nature that appealed to him.

Patrick's beginnings were as humble as any millionaire oilman's could be. He began racing as a major sponsor of an Indy car team through his oil company. He decided, what the hell, it might be nice to build a team. So he did. But unlike many monied folks who decide they like the hobby of auto racing, Patrick not only knew a great deal about it, he also had some loyalties at a very early stage in his career in racing. And as he had done as a wildcatter, he could look at a man and see the worth beneath the surface.

"I started in 1967 as a sponsor on the car," he said. "I was in that position for about two years. I became a

Pat Patrick with his driver Emerson Fittipaldi after the win at Indianapolis in 1989. It was the first win for Fittipaldi and the last for Patrick. As always, Patrick defers to his drivers and crew during the successes. Courtesy Patrick Racing

partner of the team in 1970, and then I bought the whole team in 1973. I took control of it. I won Indianapolis in 1974, and again in 1982 and again in 1989. And we finished second numerous times."

His first year was 1970, and he had hired Johnny Rutherford and bought an Eagle from Dan Gurney, whose products he remained loyal to for four seasons. The first season the team won no races, scored no poles and finished twelfth in the championship. The second season he ran Rutherford and Jim McElreath. Neither driver won a race. In 1972, he quit sponsoring the car via Patrick Petroleum and began making a business of it, finding other sponsorship. He hired Swede Savage and still was unable to win a race.

In 1973, finally, with a three-car team of Savage, Gordon Johncock and Wally Dallenbach, the team won six events including a fairy tale victory at the Indianapolis Motor Speedway. Patrick had struck black gold in only his third attempt. Dallenbach finished second in the championship.

In 1974, the team won twice and finished third in the standings. In 1975, Patrick created his first evolution toward the Wildcat with a DGS-Eagle Offy Wildcat. The team started out in some ways as a proxy for the Offenhauser engine. Patrick was extremely smitten with the little Offy as the Indy Car fraternity was moving toward the Ford powerplants. He refused to let the Offy die and sent his crew chief, George Bignotti, to update the engine to best the Fords.

The 1975 engines were created by Dale Drake's design people and delivered to Patrick prior to the Indy 500 for that year. Bignotti and Patrick had seen some flaws in the Goossen design. The slight changes they dictated to Drake had gained the engine another 50hp, and had increased fuel economy.

With Johncock and Dallenbach at their respective wheels, the new Offy was able to run up front for a good part of the race as Dallenbach led until he hit some debris from a crash and damaged the suspension. The life that had been breathed into the Offy immediately impressed the field and Drake was called upon to create some thirty engines for the next season. To make a long story short, under stress the engine couldn't take the punishment and was finally, mercifully, put out to pasture. But if it had breathed longer than it should have, it was Pat Patrick's doing.

The engine wouldn't work, but perhaps the car would. In 1976, the Eagle was dropped completely and the car was called simply "Bignotti-Wildcat." In it, Johncock won two races along with the USAC Championship. In 1977, the car was called the Wildcat/DGS-Offy. The DGS stood for Drake/Goossen/Sparks, or Dale Drake, Leo Goossen and Art Sparks, the creators of the final version of the Offy.

In 1978, costs were escalating; speedway purses were not. Talent was fleeing American racing, and most blamed USAC for the state of discontent. The USAC committee had a twenty-one member board, and team owners held only one spot on that board. They lobbied for changes and more input into the decision making process, but were flatly denied.

In November of 1978, a group of dissidents broke away from the USAC establishment and formed Championship Auto Racing Teams (CART). The board of directors, which was comprised of A.J. Foyt, Jim Hall, Tyler Alexander, Roger Penske and Bob Fletcher, elected Pat Patrick as the president.

The goals of CART were to market the series to the fans. Where USAC had operated in a sort of closed-door arrogance, CART would promote the series with the media and with the fan base. It would keep cumbersome administration down by making rules via the board and awarding a larger share of the purses to the participants. On March 11, 1979, CART staged its first event at Phoenix International Raceway.

Said long-time friend and crew chief Jim McGee, "Pat's done a great deal for Indy Car racing. Without Pat or Roger, it wouldn't be where it is today. Those two guys took it when it was absolutely on the skids. We were all ready to get out of racing then. I was getting ready to get out of Indy Car racing and go to work in another business because I could see that there was no way that it was going to be a successful way to make a living. He and Roger got a hold of it and formed CART and they turned this Indy Car racing into a business that is now a very good way to make a living. I think we owe both of those guys a debt of gratitude."

"What I'd like to be remembered for," Patrick agreed, "is founding IndyCar. The second most important thing was founding Indy Lights, which is a feeder series for the main event. A lot of good drivers like Paul Tracy and Bryan Herta came from Indy Lights—a lot of great drivers came from the series."

Patrick's founding of Indy lights has in fact helped the Indy Car series a great deal. He conceived of the series in 1986 as a feeder series for Indy Cars. The series has grown in popularity, with both fans and competitors turning attention to the series as a forum for future Indy stars. But his main achievement was CART and Indy Cars.

"In my opinion, it is the greatest racing in the world. I think that IndyCars put on the best open-wheeled racing anyplace, better than Formula One and Indy Lights and any open wheels there are. As far as racing in general, I think that NASCAR does a tremendous job of promoting their series, of marketing their series. Maybe not in Europe where the Europeans don't cater to the NASCAR folks, but I would think that our races, which are shown in 144 countries, are the most popular in the world.

"There's no question that if you take a product like this and manage it properly, it could be enormously successful. When we started it was obvious that oval racing wouldn't work. And that's all USAC was. So Roger and I took control of it and started racing wherever we could really, because at that time USAC controlled all of the tracks. We would do street

courses road courses or whatever and since then of course, the series has grown tremendously."

Although for the first three seasons there were only two wins for Patrick's team, those following years really were mostly dominated by two teams: Patrick and Penske. Patrick driver Gordon Johncock took the team to victory a few times in the 1982/1983 seasons.

Said Patrick: "Roger and I were friends and business partners prior to that time. Not close friends at the time, but we became close friends during that time, because it took a great deal of our time to make it work. We've been friends ever since. Used to be Patrick and Penske, those were the two teams to beat. Since I came back in, hell everybody can beat you now. There's a lot of competition."

In the next several seasons his driver line-up read like a who's-who of race car drivers: in 1982 he hired Mario Andretti; in 1983 Chip Ganassi; then Danny Ongias; Emerson Fittipaldi, Bruno Giacomelli, Bill Whittington, Kevin Cogan, Roberto Guerrero and Danny Sullivan. Most recently he hired Scott Pruett, who as this book was being penned won his first race in an Indy Car.

Patrick's favorite? "Scott is probably the best over-

Patrick and his favorite driver, Mario Andretti. "He would always go help get a sponsor and do personal appearances, sign autographs," Patrick said. "I liked Mario a lot." John Mahoney

Patrick at Indy in 1980, looking irritated. When Patrick and Roger Penske organized the fledgling Championship Auto Racing Teams series in 1978, Patrick was one of the most competitive teams on paper. Unfortunately, the team did not always convert good machinery and grid positions into wins. John Mahoney

advice, which he gave in his typical slow and thoughtful manner.

"I think some people look to me as maybe an elder statesman if that's a good way to look at it. I don't know about pearls of wisdom. We've got an awful lot of smart guys in this series. I've been around a lot and seen a lot of things happen and you get a feel for how to react sometimes when things around you aren't going the way you think they should."

Patrick is the kind of guy you inherently trust. You look at him and you see wisdom and intelligence, but more than that you see yourself. You see your own insight and understanding reflected in him. More accurately, he is not a mirror, but a catalyst. He makes you understand with his demeanor. And although he has his detractors as anyone else does, most people around him have a great deal of respect for Patrick.

"He's been a great guy to work for. He's been very gracious to me and my family," Jim McGee said. "Pat's got a lot of empathy for people as far as other things besides racing. He's the first guy to come to you when you have a problem, whether it's a death in the family or an illness or something like that. And very family-oriented. But he's still a hard businessman. He wants to win worse than anybody. He's got a way with people where people just flock around him. He's just a fun person to be with. But by the same token, he's very focused and very determined to win."

For now, Patrick is the paternal member of CART's racing family. He is no longer discussed as millionaire oilman Patrick, but just Pat Patrick. He is humble and humbling all at once. Gregarious and shy. But, like any good oilman should be, larger than life.

But Patrick's days may be numbered. Even as his new Firestone project seems to be gaining momentum, one gets the feeling that the well of youth is running dry and he will cap off his career some time soon. He's quit once already while dogged by poor performance from the Alfa-Romeo engine. And the following season he had trouble securing an engine deal for 1992, as well as difficulty finding sponsorship. So he dropped out for three years. Now, the competition is tougher than ever.

"I'd like to stay. I have a contract with Firestone through 1998 and I'd like to fulfill that, but at least through 1998. Depending on how things go, I'll stay around a little longer." Then he smiles with that all-knowing look and gives you a wink, telling you not to worry, that everything will be all right whether he's there or not. "I'm enjoying this now," he says.

And you just have to believe him.

all supportive and cooperative driver. As far as working with sponsors, personal appearances and so forth he's very good. In my opinion, Scott is a force to be reckoned with somewhere down the road. The next guy is Mario Andretti when he drove for me. He would always go help get a sponsor and personal appearances, sign autographs. Mario was a very, very professional driver. I liked Mario a lot."

The founding of CART aside, Patrick is still known as the voice of reason. During the CART/IRL feud that had erupted in 1995, Pat Patrick was asked by many in both media and administrative circles for his

Chapter 22

Roger Penske

On October third, 1993, Roger Penske had a lot on his mind. His drivers, Emerson Fittipaldi and Paul Tracy, were gridded one-two for the start of the Makita 100 at Laguna Seca. Although they had just missed winning the championship, the team was determined to finish the season off with a bang in front of a healthy contingent of Philip Morris corporate types where Penske sits on the board. On October 4, the following day, Detroit Diesel, which Penske had purchased as a small unprofitable off-shoot of GM, was scheduled for an IPO.

An initial public offering is hard enough to manage on its own, let alone the biggest and most successful Indy Car team in the history of the sport. But for Roger Penske, no challenge is great enough.

The team ended up finishing in first and second place in Monterey, with Paul Track leading flag to flag. Although they had lost the championship to Nigel Mansell and his unsinkable English fortitude, Fittipaldi and Tracy would finish second and third in the championship standings, with Tracy winning as many races as Mansell, five, and Fittipaldi winning another three. By the way, the IPO came off without a hitch, opening on the New York Stock Exchange and moving almost 20 percent in just the first day.

Roger Penske: the winningest car owner in the history of the Indianapolis track. Courtesy Marlboro Racing

Roger Penske was rich. Again.

Contrary to popular belief, Roger Penske *does* sleep. And he *does* fail. But certainly both are a rarity. Much about what you hear about Roger Penske is of his domination in whatever he does. And from that editorials abound. As anyone in his position often is, Roger Penske is blindly criticized for his unbelievable success, his almost uncanny knack for doing precisely the right thing in a vortex of confusion. *Nobody* can do what Roger Penske does without cheating, the thinking goes. *He must be authoritarian; unethical; a man so obsessed with getting his way he would commit murder; wound so tightly he squeaks.* Et cetera.

But it is in his failures—which albeit are rare—where one can see the true Penske personality. And for sure Roger Penske's biggest failure came in 1995, two years after that IPO, at the Indy 500.

To set the stage for the disastrous month of May, the previous season had seen a three-car Penske team steamroll the competition. The year following the IPO, Al Unser Jr. led the team to victory in twelve of sixteen races and finished second in three of the remaining four races of the championship. They had finished the season 1-2-3.

But then came May of the following season. Although the team wasn't quite on its game prior to

A youthful Roger Penske, captured around 1970. As always, Penske is focused and pre-occupied on whatever project he is working. Courtesy Judy Stropus

Indy, they had had success with Al Jr. winning at Long Beach. The Mercedes pushrod engine, which had swept pole the previous season was no longer being used. USAC had legislated against the engine by reducing the manifold presssure from 55 to 50. The team decided the engine wouldn't be competitive, so they didn't run it. The Penske chassis held running a standard Mercedes-Ilmor engine. And it was well off the pace.

Early in the month, the team had found they were lacking the downforce they desperately needed. If they increased the swept wing area, they lost top speed; but if they took out wing, the car left tire marks down the main straight off turn four at nearly 230mph. Pole day left both Penskes off the front row. At the end of the first weekend, the Penskes had still not qualified. Come the second weekend, and Team Penske was clearly struggling. Not only were they not quicker than they had been last weekend, but the competition had gone faster and they hadn't seemed capable of staying with any of them. The team pulled an older Penske chassis off the shelf and Al Jr. gave it a try. It was slower still. Emerson Fittipaldi used a spare Rahal Lola and was unable to find the sweet spot, settling for a poor place at the back of the grid. It was almost certain the qualifying speed wouldn't hold.

Stephan Johansson, in Tony Bettenhausen's *year-old* Penske got the car up to speed and just nipped Fittipaldi. Penske now had no cars in the field and with time running out, it was clear that he would only have one shot at it. Fittipaldi walked back to the garage

horribly dejected. Unser got back in the PC24 and sped around the track as the gun sounded. He was unable to find anything more and failed to get into the field.

In Penske's terms, it was a monumental defeat. The most successful owner in the history of Indianapolis would not be at the 1995 Indianapolis 500. It was a failure as great or greater than any Penske had ever had. But behind the story was the real Penske.

There were fundamental failures, but what they did to try to get the cars qualified was nothing short of heroic. "I'll tell you what," veteran Penske member Rick Mears said with pride, "there wasn't another team there that would have turned over as many stones as Penske did. I guarantee that. Indy was a combination of a lot of things. Hindsight is great. You can look back and see the mistakes. But for us, at the time, they weren't mistakes. You've got to figure in, that the year before we were having similar problems with the car, but we attributed it to the engine—the Mercedes pushrod motor.

"So we probably didn't work on getting that sorted out because we had enough horsepower to overcome it. We won the race. So when we came back with the regular motor, all of the sudden we had the same problems, but we didn't have the same horsepower to make up for it. That was a mistake. But we didn't know it. We figured it out a little too late. These cars are built in big pieces now and all work is done in such small defined areas. Not like the old days where you could just tear the tunnel out of it and get a piece of aluminum and shape a new one and try it overnight. Now you've got to spend hours and hours in a wind tunnel and make very small minute changes to accomplish gains now. So it was something that we couldn't respond to in time."

But Mears, who in 1995 acted as a consultant to Penske, watched the team try everything they could. Selfless acts that some would say were uncharacteristic of Penske. Mears says not so; he says that those days typified Penske's selflessness.

"One of Roger's strong traits is that he doesn't care if it's his name on the car or not. A lot of guys would say, 'This is my car, we're going to run it.' And it wasn't the first time. One of the years I won, the Penske wasn't working and so the last day before qualifying, we took a March out—one of the show cars; a year-old show car—and put it on the track and ended up qualifying on the front row. He's there to win races, just like we are.

"So you look back there were mistakes and we didn't know it. It was a crush to everybody, but you got to stand back and say, 'Hey, we aren't the first people not to make the show.' You know you can't cry about it. Roger said, 'Let's look at Milwaukee.'

"That's when he really gets going is in a situation like that. The organizing skills; getting two cars, transferring pieces, getting new people, keeping the people motivated. Then once the car was there he didn't

The 1971 American Motors Trans Am Javelin. Here Penske, at his own peril, stands in front of Mark Donohue and keeps him from moving off until the crew finishes. Donohue captured the Trans-Am Championship for AMC, the first for the manufacturer, winning seven of ten races that season. Courtesy Judy Stropus

want to put the drivers in cars that they didn't know how they went together, so he rebuilt every car that we got. And then went to put it on the track, and it rains for two days."

Roger Penske was raised in Shaker Heights, Ohio. He began his career as a sports car racer in Pennsylvania, where he met a young Mark Donohue. A national caliber road racer and champion in his own right, Penske saw the wisdom in letting someone else drive the cars while he prepared them, so he retired in 1964.

They formed a loose association which would eventually become one of the strongest partnerships in American racing history. In 1966, Penske hired Donohue to drive in a handful of Can-Am races, where he began winning and finished second in the championship behind John Surtees.

For the next few seasons, Penske had Donohue in

Roger Penske at the Indianapolis Motor Speedway in 1972. He would win the race for the first time this season.
Courtesy Judy Stropus

an SCCA Trans Am as well as in a Can-Am car. The SCCA had been Penske's major stomping grounds and he wanted to do as well or better than he had as a driver. Donohue and the Chevrolet-Penske would finish third in Can-Am behind Denis Hulme and Bruce McLaren. But by the following season they would utterly dominate the Trans-Am series, winning ten of thirteen races, finishing third and fourth in two of the other three. The eight straight wins and ten in the season would be a record that would stand unbroken through 1995.

In 1970, Penske moved to Indy, where Donohue would finish second in an impressive showing. Donohue won his first race in 1971 at Pocono, then following up two weeks later with a victory at Michigan. By 1972, Penske would win his first of ten races at The Brickyard. Donohue sat on the front row, took the lead in the late stages and won by a full lap over Al Unser. Right afterward it was back to road racing. Although Penske kept a team fielded for the Indy 500, Indy Car racing was not where Penske's heart was; it was in road racing. In F1. But after the young American was killed in practice for the Austrian Grand Prix, Penske lost interest in F1. Although he competed one more season without Donohue, it was as if his interest died as suddenly as his driver had. He moved back to the United States and began to solidify his hold on the Indianapolis.

He hired Jim McGee to run his team in 1975, but began a full-time effort for a full season in Indy Cars. He began an assault on American open-wheeled racing that would include taking the series away from USAC and making it an independent series based on both ovals and road circuits. Championship Auto Racing Series—CART—eventually to be known as Indy-Cars, was born, and Penske had fathered it.

Over the previous six seasons, his cars had only won six events in all races run. And three of those were at the hands of Donohue. In just four seasons he would win more than twenty races and have in his employ some of the most famous names in motor racing: Bobby Unser, Mario Andretti, Tom Sneva and Rick Mears.

Fifteen seasons later he would have 95 wins, ten Indy 500 victories and nine championships. His teams would be the best prepared, best funded and most strongly manned in the business. He would also form a NASCAR team, headed by Rusty Wallace, and would continue growing his auto dealerships and truck rental fleets, not to mention Detroit Diesel. At this writing, Penske was employing more than 13,000 people and generating $3 billion a year in sales.

With the exception of Mark Donohue, the person who shared the longest and most successful relationship with Penske was Rick Mears. Mears was hired by Penske at the end of 1977, mostly to fill in for Mario Andretti, who was racing in F1 at the time. Tom Sneva, who had been with the team for four seasons, had won a total of three races by the end of 1978.

Mears in eleven starts of the eighteen in the 1978 championship equalled Sneva's record. By next season, Sneva was out and Mears became Penske's fair haired boy, emerging as the winningest driver in Indy Car racing while he drove for Penske, winning Indy four times, capturing pole at Indianapolis six times, winning 29 races in his career and three championships.

Penske has his fans. And most of them are around him, working for him, remaining loyal in the day-to-day business of the team. Rick Mears, for one. Mears has been with Penske from almost the beginning of his career, a very unique situation in racing. And Mears appreciates his drive and commitment. Also his sensitivity and understanding.

"I think a lot of people really don't know him. It has really pissed me off over the years. He had a bad reputation, in terms of people saying, 'If I had that much money I could buy that too', or I had people come up to me and say, 'Boy, isn't he tough to work for?' I kept wondering why I was hearing this for all these years. Then it dawned on me one day: he *can* be tough to work for if you don't want to work. That's all that he asks is that you put your best foot forward. If you don't want to do that, then he can be a little tough to work for. So it is akin to a sour grapes thing. He's always treated his people very well. People don't

Penske and his driver in 1968. Penske hired Mark Donohue for the 1967 season to drive an SCCA Trans Am Camaro. Donohue would utterly dominate the 1968 Trans-Am series, winning ten of thirteen races, finishing third and fourth in two of the other three. The eight straight wins and ten in the season would be a record that would stand through this writing. Courtesy Judy Stropus

Mark Donohue slides into the Sunoco Ferrari 512M as Roger Penske moves around keeping an eye on things. The team would finish third, that year, 1971, with Donohue co-driving with David Hobbes. Courtesy Judy Stropus

Roger Penske outside one of his many auto dealerships. Penske's auto racing is only one aspect of his tremendous empire, which includes car and truck rentals, dealerships and ownership of Detroit Diesel engine manufacturing. Courtesy Judy Stropus

see that side of him sometimes. They just see him as a hard-nosed businessman. But he's got a big heart.

"He's a perfectionist. He has an attention to detail in everything no matter what it is. When he gets involved in something he just doesn't get into it to be a part of it, he understands it. Right from the word go. Detroit Diesel. I remember talking about it with him and he was like a kid with a new toy. He could tell you what they were doing to the engine, how they were modifying the injectors, the nozzles, the sizes. He explained the machines and what they were doing and how they were modifying the rods and everything else. He understands it inside out. The business aspects of it are the same way. And he knows how to motivate people. His natural self will motivate people. Whatever he does, he does his best.

"He's there to win, but if we've done everything we can do, 'That's fine,' he says, 'I don't mind getting beat. But I hate making mistakes.' It just drives him up the wall. But if we didn't make any mistakes and we did our best and we got beat, then that's fine. Now we just put our noses to the grindstone and improve for next time."

As this book is begin penned, Penske is hard at work for the 1996 Indy 500. You can be sure of one thing: Roger Penske may make mistakes, and he may find himself out of the Indy 500 again some day. But they will not be the same mistakes and it will never, ever be for lack of trying.

Chapter 23

Bobby Rahal

Modern race car drivers don't change a great deal. At least that's the way it seems from the outside. Stands to reason. How stylish can you make a Nomex suit?

But Bobby Rahal's outward appearance, more than most, has remained the same since he began Indy Car racing back in 1983. The mustache is still in the same shape, the hair—what is left of it—is the same color and has the same trim, and his body is still fit as ever. But Rahal has changed and grown as much or more than any man in the series.

Rahal's career in racing can be broken into three parts: a formative period, when he began racing, tried to break into European racing and then settled here with Jim Trueman; a period as a true hired gun, where he left Truesports and signed with Galles, just an employee for the first time in his career; and finally, his period of true independence, as ower of his own team. All three stages of Rahal's career are distinct.

Bobby Rahal was born January 10, 1953, in Medina, Ohio. He began racing as a teenager in his father's amateur status SCCA Lotus, and in 1970 his father convinced Canadian officials that Bobby was eighteen and entered him in his first novice event. By 1974, he had captured the B Sports national title and then moved to the amateur Atlantic class, which he neatly won, capturing the President's Cup as top amateur driver. In 1976 he teamed up with Jim Trueman and moved into pro Atlantic racing.

In 1976, 1977, and 1978, Formula Atlantic was the place for up and coming drivers. In the ranks of

In 1982 Rahal entered his first Indy Car event at Phoenix, where he started fifteenth and finished eighteenth. Four races later, in Cleveland, Rahal won. Courtesy IndyCar

the series were some of the greats like future World Champions Keke Rosberg, Gilles Villeneuve, and Price Cobb, among others. In that atmosphere, Rahal managed to finish second in the championship to Villeneuve, who went off to F1 the following season to drive for Ferrari.

Rahal would follow Villeneuve to Europe as well; not in F1 but in F3, then in F2 with Walter Wolf's F2 team—a nice step in the right direction. In 1979, Rahal won in F2 and also back home in the U.S., in Can-Am for Jim Trueman. Rahal finished fifth in the Can-Am standings. But for one reason or another, the rides in F1 didn't pan out for Rahal.

In 1980, he concentrated mostly on Can-Am, finishing fifth, then drove an IMSA sports car race in 1981, winning the Daytona 24 Hours in a Porsche 935 Turbo with co-drivers Brian Redman and Bob Garretson. In 1982, he entered his first Indy Car event at the opener at Phoenix where he started fifteenth and finished eighteenth. Four races later, in Cleveland, Rahal won. He then took another victory at Michigan and won the Rookie of The Year honors. He took second in points and was well on his way to becoming one of America's hot drivers.

Although he fared poorly in 1983, winning only once at Riverside and finishing in fifth in the championship, he had picked up some valuable relationships and some important experience. He had driven at Le Mans and had formed a relationship with the Wood Brothers, which would result in a ride for him in a stock car the next season. In 1984, he won back-to-back at Phoenix and Laguna Seca. He began a tradition at the California track which would be hard to break, winning four in a row at the Monterey track from 1984 to 1987. In 1985, he won three Indy Car races, an IMSA race, an IROC race, and finished third in the PPG championship.

By 1986, two things were clear: Bobby Rahal was destined to win the championship as well as the Indy 500; and Jim Trueman was going to die.

Trueman, who had seen Rahal through the thick and thin of his career, who had managed his career, provided him with great cars to drive and the means necessary—both physically and emotionally—was riddled with cancer. He had gone from a robust larger-than-life man who was prone to shouting and tempers to a frail fraction of a man.

The month of May saw Trueman at the track occasionally, and when he did show up, he looked so fragile that a gust of wind might finish him off. Under intense emotional pressure, Rahal qualified his Truesports March-Cosworth in fourth spot. Jim Trueman was literally on his deathbed when the race was cancelled due to rain. Several thought Trueman might not even see race day. But the following day the race was run and after twenty leader changes among

seven different drivers, Rahal emerged as the winner, at a record breaking 170.722mph, becoming the first driver ever to complete the race in less than three hours. On live TV, the first time ever, Rahal drank his milk and shared it with a tearful Jim Trueman, who found the strength in this, his ultimate achievement, the winning of the Indy 500.

Rahal, who trailed in the points with his classic early season failures, was in fourth place in points after three races. At Milwaukee, he started seventh and finished sixth. By the following weekend at Portland, Jim Trueman was dead.

Rahal dedicated the season to Trueman and went on to win five more races in a highly emotional season. He charged through a determined field which included the energized Michael Andretti and captured his first PPG Indy Car championship.

Still pumped with the success, Rahal and Steve Horne followed up and won their second championship in a row while winning three races and twelve top five finishes. Again, he nipped Andretti at the final race to win the championship. He also co-drove with German Jochen Mass to victory in a pair of IMSA GT victories in a Porsche 962. Rahal was driving a March

With the number-one plate in 1993, having won the PPG Cup in 1992. It was his first season as team owner in Rahal Hogan. With trucking magnate Carl Hogan, Rahal purchased all of Pat Patrick's equipment. With the Chevy engine contract, he became the first driver in PPG Indy Car history to win on a team of his own. Courtesy Miller Brewing

chassis in 1986 and a Lola chassis in 1987. But it was clear that that part of Rahal's life was over. There was no mentor in Jim Trueman anymore. He was on his own. By the same token, the successes were his too.

"Remember, he passed away in May and most the series was after May," Rahal recalled in 1995. "It was Steve Horne, myself—Mrs. Trueman was still obviously in a state of mourning. Maybe we all were to some degree or another. But there were a lot of changes that year where we all felt that our future was in our hands. In 1984 and 1985, we had Adrian Newey as our engineer. Of course Adrian is now with Williams as a designer. In 1985, I think we had seven pole positions and came within one race in 1985 of winning the championship and if Jacques Villeneuve hadn't hit me at Sanair, we would have won in 1985.

"Adrian, because of personality conflicts at Truesports, he didn't want to stay. So we started 1986 with our assistant engineer Grant Newberry, who's now with Penske, and Grant and Steve and myself basically had to make it on our own. It took us a while to get there, but once we got rolling it definitely built the confidence that we could win. We won six races from Indy onward. Since the fall, we won four of the last five races. We won Mid-Ohio, Michigan, Laguna Seca, Sanair and we were third at Elkhart Lake—we were on the pole at Elkhart. Yeah, there was a lot of confidence as the year rolled on."

In 1988, it was clear that Rahal's disposition had changed. He had failed to set any fast qualifying laps (something he had done every season since he began) and only won one race, the Pocono 500. The Judd engine was not to be as competitive as he had hoped and the Truesports team, now run by Trueman's wife Barbara, had lost the direction it had had under the Trueman. Rahal announced his decision to leave Truesports at the end of the season, calling it "The hardest decision I've ever had to make in my racing career." To most, however, it was not a surprise.

In 1989, Rahal drove for the Kraco team as Michael Andretti moved on to drive on the Newman-Haas team with his father. Rahal only won once and finished ninth in points. In 1990, the team merged with Galles Racing and with Al Unser Jr. Results were even worse than in he previous season as he failed to win any races. This was the first time in his career that had happened. In 1991, he won a lone race, but had a huge abundance of second spot finishes and ran with Michael Andretti down to Laguna Seca. Andretti, finally, took his first championship. Rahal was runner up. And was feeling second best.

In 1992, seeming preoccupied, Rahal announced his decision to drive for Patrick racing. It seemed as if he were seeking something. But nobody, perhaps not even he, was quite sure what it was. The partnerships of the past several seasons had simply not provided what Rahal needed for success. He was not unsuccessful, but seemed just off-base. After the announcement of his departure to Patrick, which looked like a

Another trophy. The 1995 season was not Rahal's best—but neither was it as bad as the two previous seasons. Dismal was 1994, the first season with Honda power. The team struggled all through 1994 with the engine, then abandoned it at the end of the season. That decision proved to be a bad one, since the following season, 1995, Honda had proven to become one of the best powerplants in the series.
Courtesy IndyCar

quick-fix for something deeper, Rahal finally solved the problem. He bought the Patrick team.

"I had actually signed with Patrick," Rahal said. "Pat was unable to put together an engine deal with Ilmor, and Miller Brewing had been burned by the whole Alfa-Romeo episode, so they weren't in any frame of mind to roll the dice on an unknown engine like the Cosworth XB. The previous DFS hadn't been a very good engine and it had sort of lived beyond its normal life, so to speak. It became very clear to me that I had to take control because if I didn't, God knows what would have happened to me. I certainly wasn't ready to retire.

"It's very clear in my mind that the driver most often represents the team. The sponsors create their value with their association with the driver and trying

Playing the crowd. Rahal walks back to the pits after having a problem on the course, but takes the opportunity to visit. Rahal knows the importance of pleasing sponsors as well as fans. As a racer he may have a hard time finding time to do things like this, but as an owner he knows it is essential to funding. Besides, it's nice to be noticed. Courtesy IndyCar

to draw any parallels, or use the driver as an example of that company's capabilities. I thought that, hell, taking it that next step, putting the sponsorship together to go out and do your own team was a log-

ical step really, compared to where I had been. Yeah, there was an obligation to that, but I guess I wasn't afraid to accept that obligation, and I think that a lot of drivers have always felt you can't do both. I think in 1992 we showed that you can.

"But it does take work. It isn't one of those things that you can go off and lay on the beach for two weeks. I'm in the office every day and you're intimately involved in the decision that goes forward with the team. But for me I've always felt that I'd much rather have control. The more control you have and the more influence you have, the safer your position. And I did not want my career to be ended because of decisions being made by somebody else."

With trucking magnate Carl Hogan, Rahal purchased all of Patrick's equipment at the end of 1991 and the Chevy engine contact. He went out the following season and whipped the competition's butt, becoming the first driver in PPG Indy Car history to win on a team of his own. He won four times and nipped Andretti for the fifth time at Laguna Seca (as well as Al Unser Jr.) for his third title.

The following two seasons were hardly repeats. In 1993, full of the initial success, Rahal bought out Truesports, which was trying to develop its own chassis. The chassis development stuttered and stammered until, at Indy, Rahal failed even to make the field. He

Rahal, head cocked over for the corner, takes the 1995 Lola-Mercedes. Notice the "Hogan" on the nose. Following this season, Rahal would strike out on his own. Looking back, it is clear that Rahal does his best on his own, when he is completely responsible for his team's results. Courtesy IndyCar

scrapped the car and campaigned a Lola the rest of the season, but by then, it was too late. Development time had been lost already. He won no races, but still finished fourth in the championship.

In 1994, running a Lola, he decided to try a new engine and tested and raced the Honda engine, which was at a very developmental stage. His best finish was a second. At the end of the season, he dropped the Honda, which turned out to be a bad choice, since Honda engines proved to be the pace of the field in 1995, winning their first event and leading several times.

The deciding moment of this third generation Rahal had to be the 1995 announcement that Rahal would now go it alone. Carl Hogan announced he would be leaving the partnership. Rahal was on his own. As this book went to press, Rahal's future was uncertain. Pundits are wondering, will he win again?

"I think I'm more excited than I have been in years. I felt this the other day, and people confirmed it within the team: there's a real enthusiasm and there just seems to be a different atmosphere. Somewhat lighter. I don't want to make it sound as though it's less serious. It's as serious and dedicated, but there's a kind of lightness. The politics within the team are going to be—well there won't be any frankly—or very nominal. In any partnership, there will be certain alliances. Everybody's got an idea about how things should be done. That can have a negative effect. But my sense is that work will be great and I have a lot of faith in people to do what they know how to do."

If one looks back at the three men Rahal has become in the past, it is clear that he does his best on his own. In Jim Trueman, Rahal was his own person. Encouragement by Trueman gave Rahal the tools he himself already possessed. He converted them into wins. He used the momentum to win two titles. In 1993, when he took control of the team, he did the same. But when it was clear that there was one too many cooks in the kitchen, Rahal struck out on his own.

First race of 1995, Rahal circles the temporary road course by himself. Rahal is usually a crowd favorite—although you'd never know it here as only a couple of people keep track of his progress. Rahal is known as a thinking man's driver. Courtesy IndyCar

Rahal will be up in the top, no matter what. But comforted by his own confidence, he just might stay there this time. Only time will tell.

Chapter 24

Eddie Rickenbacker

Eddie Rickenbacker never won a national championship, and he never won the Indianapolis 500. In terms of his driving ability, he was just average. His best run in any championship was third, and his total wins in championship races only numbered seven. Yet Rickenbacker was one of the most charismatic and important people in American racing. What he did for the prestige of open wheel racing in the United States can not be underestimated.

Rickenbacker was the Norman Schwartzkopff of the 1920s and the Ross Perot of World War Two. He was charming, talented and larger-than-life. He captured the imagination of the America public and cast a light on the Indianapolis Motor Speedway. Rickenbacker's story was less about cars than it was about Americana.

Born in 1890 of Swiss immigrants, Rickenbacker was one of seven children on a rural Ohio farm. His father, a paving contractor, was struck and killed by a piledriver wedge when Rickenbacker was twelve. He was forced to find a job in a glass factory, making about $3 a week, which was far more than what anyone else in the family was making. He never finished the seventh grade.

From glass he went to iron and from iron to being a machinist. And along the way, he discovered both the automobile and the inherent beauty in machining, writing, "I have always accepted without question the affinity between art and mechanics. People who are not exposed to both do not see the similarity. To take a piece of rough steel and transform it on a lathe into something that is not only shining and beautiful but also a part of an apparatus serving a useful purpose became, in my mind, even more fulfilling than a painting or sculpture." It was an aspect of his personality that would help him through life.

Following an industrial accident which kept him bedridden for almost a month, Rickenbacker was forced to ponder his existence, so to speak. What he realized was that more than anything else, he wished to become involved in auto manufacturing. A neighborhood shop saw the young man's potential and hired him to fix cars and occasionally machine new pieces.

Although the pay was decent, Rickenbacker decided that he wasn't going the right direction—or at least not quickly enough. He wanted to build new cars, not fix old ones. He enrolled in a correspondence course in mechanical engineering and went looking for work at the Frayer-Miller manufacturing plant in Columbus.

The plant was a small one which only produced a single car per day. And try as he did, he had a difficult time trying to convince them to hire him. So he quit his job and simply began working at the plant—for free. Leo Frayer was so impressed by the young man's

Eddie Rickenbacker was one of the most charismatic of race car drivers. He was charming, talented, and larger-than-life. The last race Rickenbacker drove was at Ascot, which he won. He never regretted moving out of racing, but he always regretted not having won the Indy 500. Courtesy Bruce Craig

Eddie Rickenbacker at the wheel of Duesenberg racer in 1914. The photo was taken outside the Santa Monica board track. Rickenbacker had always wanted to drive for Dueseberg, and did only up through this season. Note Augie Duesenberg standing to the mechanic's right elbow (in checked cap). Courtesy Auburn-Cord Duesenberg Museum

enthusiasm that he hired him. In a professional relationship that would last almost a dozen years, Rickenbacker eventually became Frayer's right hand man.

His first exposure to racing was during the Vanderbuilt Cup races at the turn of the century. Frayer had built four cars to compete in the 1906 Vanderbuilt Cup, which was a sort of American wake-up call that paid $10,000 to win. Frayer picked Rickenbacker to be his riding mechanic. That first experience was not as successful as it might have been, as the car's engine seized.

Frayer sold the company some years later and took Rickenbacker with him to the Columbus Buggie Company, which was owned by Clinton Firestone. Rickenbacker was put in charge of design of a touring car, then in charge of sales.

By 1910, at the ripe age of nineteen, Rickenbacker was making $150 a month and driving a car of his own. He had married that summer and had

enough disposable income to do as he pleased. And he pleased to go racing.

Dirt track racing had been proliferating around the countrysides. Drivers competed in mostly stock cars on small dirt rings. For Rickenbacker, the racing was justified by the potential in sales.

Rickenbacker built his race car by stripping his own street car down and began racing it. The first race he entered was a twenty-five miler in Red Oak, Iowa—where he promptly drove the car off the track and into a ditch. By the following week, he had repaired the Firestone-Columbus and won the next five of five races. A driver was born.

Rickenbacker raced all over Iowa and Nebraska and was selling cars at every stop. Leo Frayer had been following his success through the company and offered to pay him to drive against barstorming Barney Oldfield. He jumped at the chance and returned to Columbus. The race to enter, Frayer wrote Rickenbacker, was this new 500 miler that the Indianapolis Speedway was going to hold. The track had opened in 1909 and had held a three-day event of 43 different speed contests. Now it was keen on running a longer contest which could be viewed by spectators the entire time.

With Frayer at the wheel of the 1911 contest and Rickenbacker as co-driver and riding mechanic, Rickenbacker made his first appearance at the Brickyard. The duo finished eleventh. In 1912, Rickenbacker drove most of the way with his own riding mechanic, falling out with mechanical problems.

By 1913, Rickenbacker had moved to Duesenberg and was racing for the brothers. He began to bankroll some of the racing for the Duesenberg brothers, who were absolutely horrible about finances and organization. He won his first championship race and won enough local races to keep the team afloat, adding to his reputation as a good driver and a great mechanic.

Two years later he was in the position to buy out the Maxwell team. Short of cash, he approached The Speedway and Carl Fisher and James Allison, men who had helped bankroll the construction of the Speedway. He convinced them to put up the money and share in the prize money. They agreed, and with four cars, he raced the championship trail. He won five races in the Maxwells and won a very special race at Indianapolis

on labor day—a 100 mile event. The last race he ever drove was at Ascot Park—which he won. He never regretted moving out of racing, but he always regretted not having won the Indy 500.

When the war came he was 27 years old. As he had first lied about his age, adding years to get jobs, he now had to subtract years. A doctor friend wrote on the physical sheet that he was twenty five—and Rickenbacker was off to pilots school. His prowess in the sky was legendary and well beyond the scope of this book. When he had been given the title "Ace of Aces" by the American government, he only had seven confirmed kills to his credit. There was nobody who had downed eight enemy planes. In fact the record of seven was shared with three other men—all of whom had been killed after achieving seven. Rickenbacker finished up the war with 26 victories and 134 air battles, an incredible number of confrontations.

When he returned home he was a national hero. He could virtually write his own ticket. True to that goal he had set for himself in the hospital, what he wanted to do still, he decided again, was to build cars. Rickenbacker cars, with the Rickenbacker name on it.

The road to manufacturing success was somewhat more rocky than he thought. He had staked his reputation on four-wheel brakes which were not used by any manufacturer at that point. The brakes, however were not reliable and they failed miserably,

Rickenbacker with riding mechanic E.O. Donell. The Mason was unable to provide Rickenbacker with a win in 1913, the year this photo was taken. Courtesy Auburn-Cord Duesenberg Museum

dooming the company before it ever got going.

While trying to determine how to get out of debt and create a job for himself at the same time, he hit upon an idea: rejuvenate the Indianapolis 500. In debt and unemployed, he returned to Allison and Fisher, this time appealing to them to sell him The Speedway, which they did. Due to his notoriety he was given an odd loan.

"My option ran out, and Allison gave me a thirty day extension . . . " Rickenbacker wrote in his autobiography. "I hurried back to Detroit and put the package before (Frank Blair) at the Union Guardian Trust Company. He arranged to float a bond issue in the state of Michigan. We raised $700,000 in 6 1/2 percent bonds with only an hour to go before the options ran out. I kept 51 percent of the common stock—a bonus—and the bank took 49 percent for its effort in marketing the bond issue. On November 1, 1927, I assumed control of the Indianapolis Speedway and immediately went to work improving it."

The improvements he enacted were a repaving and a reconstruction of the walls around the track. He created an 18-hole golf course and improved the angles of the guardrails. The Speedway flourished under Rickenbacker's control and even managed to turn profits during the depression. But as the interwar period stoked the fires of The Speedway, the war that would follow would extinguish all flames. Rickenbacker had no interest in anything but the war effort.

"Important as the Speedway was, it became obvious as World War II got underway that all the fuel, oil, rubber materials and countless hours of time that would be consumed in the race and preparing for it would serve a more vital purpose in national defense. Following the 1941 race, I closed down The Speedway."

Under the direction of Wilbur Shaw, The Speedway was sold to Tony Hulman, and Eddie Rickenbacker moved on.

Eddie Rickenbacker didn't change much at Indy. He turned an old speedway in Indianapolis into a slightly more impressive facility, but with his name, he changed the sport and the event—the Indy 500—into a wholly American tradition. It was fitting that from the 1930s and 1940s when he owned the Speedway until the the early 1960s, the Indy 500 was almost exclusively American property, with few foreign winners. Rickenbacker died in 1973 at the age of 83. He was given a hero's burial.

Rickenbacker drove for the Duesenberg's starting in 1913. Two years later, with the help of sponsors, he bought out the Maxwell team. Courtesy Bruce Craig

At right
Eddie Rickenbacker will be remembered most for his contribution to the sport of open wheel racing. He purchased The Speedway in 1927 and immediately started making improvements. The Speedway flourished under Rickenbacker's control. Courtesy Bruce Craig

Chapter 25

Johnny Rutherford

Johnny Rutherford, "Lone Star JR," has always done things his way. The soft-spoken Texan is one of those insidious folks who, like a bad cough, will never go away. He just stays around and reminds his ex-competitors how committed to racing he was, and tutors his predecessors on secrets of longevity and survival.

Rutherford, who drove race cars almost as long as A.J. Foyt, who won twenty-seven races in 315 starts, with three Indy 500 wins and three Indy 500 poles, and who, at the age of 52, was the oldest driver to win a 500-mile race (Michigan, 1986), is still out there. Not competing now, but still driving, still keeping the IndyCar fields in line, driving series pace cars.

Like any youngster, Rutherford got interested in cars and racing through an experience with a relative in the formative years. "I first became interested in racing as a youngster nine years old. My dad took me to see a midget race and I really just sat up and took notice and said someday I really want to drive race cars."

But oval racing was not exactly what he had in mind at first. Like any kid, speed was only part of the equation. But, as fate is wont to do from time to time, circumstances conspired to put Rutherford on a different track—both literally and figuratively.

The social aspect of racing, what with the cars and the danger, brought him to drag racing initially.

Johnny Rutherford at the Indianapolis 500 in 1967. Rutherford was a popular and successful racer, winning the Indianapolis 500 three times in his racing career.
Bob Tronolone

"I kind of grew up with (drag racing). Reading *Speed Age* magazine and going to the races when it was available and then it got away form me. When I was older I did have cars and I did participate in early drag racing, because organized drag racing was just getting started in Texas.

"There was a hot rod club and I was there one night, and one of the guys said, 'I've got to leave early and go help my brother put an engine in his dirt track car'. I said, 'What's a dirt track car?' and he said, 'Yeah, they race every Friday night in Dallas.' And I immediately launched my first race car to race on dirt tracks and started racing in the spring of 1959. I've been hammering away at it ever since."

Rutherford began racing on the bullrings of central Texas shortly afterward, in the spring of 1959. At Devil's Bowl Speedway in Dallas, he made a name for himself in modifieds. By 1961, he had switched to Sprint cars, and by the following season, he had driven his first USAC race and his first Stock Car race.

"There was Lloyd Ruby and A.J. Foyt and Jim Mackelry and Eddie Hill and myself. We were the major racers to come out of Texas to gain any notoriety in big time auto racing as it were. There were a lot of good race car drivers in Texas that never did pursue going to the big time like we did, but it was kind of good. We had our Texas group, Foyt and Ruby,

Rutherford in the pits during the 1974 Indianapolis 500. This was Rutherford's first win at Indianapolis and perhaps his most memorable, starting in the twenty-fifth spot and making his way to the front and on to victory.
Bob Tronolone

Mackelry and myself running Indy Cars. I raced Mackelry and Foyt in sprint cars pretty regularly, and in midgets and stock cars on occasions. It was pretty diversified in what we were racing."

He made his first start in IndyCar in 1962 in the Hoosier Hundred in September. The following season, he started the Daytona 500 in 1963 in pole position, and ran the entire USAC championship season, finishing a respectable tenth in points. He was still driving his sprint car when time allowed, and was building a following.

In 1964, he crashed in an incident that would scar both the speedway as well as Rutherford. Running well back, Rutherford tailed the field as it tried in vain to catch Jimmy Clark's Lotus, as Clark drove away with ease. By the end of the first lap, Clark was nearly a hundred yards ahead of the pack. Dave MacDonald, running behind the main pack, attempted to get caught up and powered through the fourth turn. The back end slid, the car spun inside and smacked the wall. His car exploded into flames and then ricochetted back across the track. Eddie Sachs, with nowhere to go, plowed straight into MacDonald. He was killed instantly. With huge flames and giant clouds billowing off the asphalt, Johnny Rutherford—as well as Bobby Unser and Troy Ruttman—drove right through the accident as it was happening, actually hitting Sach's car. His hands were burned and his car was too damaged to continue. The injuries would be a recurring theme in Rutherford's career.

In 1966, he took the wall at Ohio's Eldora Speedway like a hurdler, vaulting over it and breaking both

Rutherford in the Chaparral 2K at the Indianapolis 500 in 1980. Rutherford would go on to win the event, his third and final Indianapolis victory. Bob Tronolone

Johnny Rutherford with the Borg-Warner Trophy, a wreath, and milk—or its suitable substitute, at any rate. Courtesy Goodyear Tire

arms as he landed. He remained out of racing until 1967, then the next year he crashed in Phoenix and badly burned his hands once again.

In 1969, he ran fourteen races, winning no events, and finished eleventh in the standings, then came back in 1970 to finish out of the top ten. In 1971, he finished his first Indy 500 after having crashed or breaking down in every other event. He was still unable to get close to winning it, and in 1972, he finished seventh in points and 27th at Indy due to a broken connecting rod.

His luck changed in 1973 with his teaming with McLaren. For the first time in his career, he started the 500 on the pole, setting a new track record in the dynamic new car in the process. Although he didn't win the 500, he did win a race that season—his first since 1965. The following season however, he finally won *the* race, the Indianapolis 500.

"Of the three wins, I think the first one would have been the most satisfying because we had the energy crunch and a new chief stewart in Tom Binford at The Speedway. That year was the energy crunch in 1974, and we had bought an engine early on qualifying morning, in practice, and went to the garage to change it and Binford said we had to be in line by eleven o'clock in our position, which we weren't. We were changing the engine. So he put us back at the end of the line, which relegated us to the third day of qualifying. Because of the energy crunch, they compressed the four days of qualifying into two because we were trying to save fuel and thinking about the people who had to drive to the track, and they didn't want them to have to drive

Bearing the number one in 1981 after capturing the 1980 Championship. Driving Hall's Chaparral-Cosworth, Johnny Rutherford would capture only one race this season, the first event here at Phoenix, and finish fifth in points. Courtesy Pennzoil Racing, Deke Houlgate

for two more days of it. They made it easier on the fans.

"Anyway, we qualified second fastest in the field, but it was the third day so I was in the twenty-fifth starting spot. Pole was in the ninth row. The car was so magnificent that day, the McLaren M16. And it was just *perfect*. They dropped the green flag, and in twelve laps I was running third from twenty-fifth. I moved to the lead. Foyt and I had a tremendous battle in the middle stages of the race. His engine let go, and he developed an oil leak and I went on to win the race. My first one."

He went from there to win again in 1976 with McLaren. His third and final 500 victory was in 1980, the season of his first and only championship. He became both the only two-series champ in history as well as the only multi-time Indy winner to win only a single championship in either series—CART or USAC. The Hall Pennzoil Chaparral was one of the best cars he had ever driven and he made the most of it.

"The third win in the Chaparral was dominating. I was quickest every day and sat on the pole. I led most of the laps and won the race. It was a different kind of a feeling. The middle one, the 1976 victory, was the rain-shortened one. The shortest race in history of The Speedway. I walked into victory lane in the rain. They all had something about them, but I would say that in 1974 was the most gratifying."

Like his peers, Rutherford made the transition from dirt to pavement successfully.

"That's a whole new program when you go to pavement. Everything you've learned on the dirt you've got to forget. You have a tendency to drive into the corners too hard, and you get sideways, and you have to stay straight and smooth on the pavement. Some guys make the transition and some guys don't. I seem to have made it. The first time I drove on a proper paved track I sat on the pole and won the race. I figured out pavement and the feeling that you had to have on the pavement as opposed to the dirt fairly quickly."

He was not able to do as well between ovals and road courses as the Unsers, Andretti, and Foyt had done, and it ultimately did him in.

Rutherford is a humble man who seemed to be as relaxed and confident when he was in the cockpit as he is, now, out of the cockpit. In the mid-nineties and in semi-retirement, Rutherford was driving the pace cars for the Indy Car series and enjoying the racing scene as he always had. And he knows how he wants to be remembered: "I think being a strong competitor. Always being one that pleased the fans. That they always enjoyed watching me race because of my style or whatever. I've enjoyed racing very hard. I'm just a guy who liked to go racing and liked to drive hard, and hopefully the fans enjoyed what I did."

They always did.

Rutherford, who grew up on the dirt tracks of Texas and Oklahoma, was one of the few drivers who proved successful in pavement racing. Courtesy Pennzoil Racing, Deke Houlgate

Chapter 26

Wilbur Shaw

Wilbur Shaw, winner of three Indianapolis 500s, three AAA Indy Car championships and eventual general manager of The Speedway was one of America's last great barnstormers. But with inherent recklessness also came a great sense of responsibility, one which ultimately perpetuated and forged a tradition in American racing which would live to become a legacy for sportspersons and sports fans in the United States.

Born on October 31, Halloween Day, 1902, Shaw was raised by a father who, himself, was a sort of reckless man inspiring a sense of adventure in his son.

His father, who eventually divorced his mother while Shaw was quite young, taught him to use his hands. His mother taught him religion and discipline. With those tools, Shaw was ready to take on the world.

Growing up in Indianapolis, he fell in love with automobiles in 1916 while he had a part-time job fitting batteries in Stutzs. He eventually landed a job with Bill Hunt, a race car builder with a shop close to The Speedway, and realized that batteries were nothing compared to race cars. With Hunt, Shaw attended his first race. Several hours later, Shaw was was left stranded and dazed; Hunt, who was racing that day,

A classic shot of Wilbur Shaw at rest. Shaw was one of the few racers to make a successful transition from pre-war racing to post war racing. Shaw poses here in the first crash helmet. Courtesy Bruce Craig

crashed and was taken to the hospital.

Nevertheless, he was determined, after that day, to become a race car driver. For another season, until he was eighteen, he toiled with Hunt until he decided to build his own car, a jalopy with which he felt he would earn his reputation and eventual fortune. In his spare time, he built the car on the second floor of Hunt's building in Indianapolis. If the assembly of the car was a difficult and arduous task, removing the damned thing from the second floor turned out to be nearly impossible.

Shaw removed a second story window, loosened and removed bricks around the casement and rolled the car down a makeshift ramp of 2x12' planks—which broke just as he was a couple feet from the ground. The car survived, and he took it to the Hoosier Motor Speedway outside Indianapolis, where he was promptly booted out for entering such a bucket of bolts at such a young age.

Determined to show the owner of Hoosier Speedway how capable and talented he in fact was, he took the car to Lafayette, Indiana's fairgrounds Speedway. Bill Hunt qualified the car for him, realizing the kid was going to kill himself in traffic. It would be better, Hunt was certain, for this stubborn youngster if at least he start-

Perhaps Shaw's greatest success was assisting in the sale of The Speedway to the Hulman family, thus preserving it so it could still be enjoyed for generations to come.
Jack Mackenzie

ed up front. So Hunt qualified the car second, and Shaw started the dirt track race on the front row.

The race started, and the car gained speed quickly, but by the second corner, he was history.

"The car started skipping sideways," Shaw said in his autobiography, *"Gentlemen, Start Your Engines."* "Then it slid into a rut, and I was riding on my two right wheels with no knowledge of what to do under such conditions. After about fifty feet of this involuntary stunt driving, the car leveled off again and the wheels hit the ground with a jolt. It seemed as if the whole frame was being twisted out of shape as another rut grabbed at the right wheels and this time the car did a complete roll, taking a big section of the fence with it."

Shaw went back to the owner of the Hoosier Motor Speedway and apologized, asking for advice. So taken with the humility of young Shaw, Mr. Dunning, the owner of Hoosier, hired him to drive a Frontenc-Ford. After several sessions of tutoring, Shaw was to race back at Lafayette where, to everyone's surprise, he began winning. A few months later he was winning most of his races and was being paid appearance money at different tracks. By 1924 he had won the National Light Car championship.

By 1926, Shaw had the opportunity to drive for several prominent car owners, but not on AAA sanctioned tracks or events—of which the Indianapolis 500 was a part. In those days, drivers had alliances, something similar to CFL and NFL football players of today. If you raced in one series, you didn't race in the other.

But the bigger purses were in the AAA championship, and Shaw finally talked organizers into allowing him to do both. By 1928, he was to start the first Indianapolis 500 of his career. He raced an old Miller 91, which had been re-stroked from a 122, and he qualified in the seventh row, finishing fourth.

Married at the beginning of the previous season, his 1927 season was to be horribly interrupted by the premature birth of his daughter and the subsequent tragic death of his wife. The motivation to race was to leave him until he accompanied Frank Lockhart to Daytona Beach for a speed record attempt where Lockhart was killed.

Shaw failed to finish his second Indy 500 race, as his machine, a car lent to him, broke down. He did, however, manage to win his first AAA sanctioned race, but by the following season he was having trouble paying bills. The local tracks needed Shaw to boost revenues, and he needed them to make a living, but the AAA was now determined to make an issue of drivers who contended both series, banning drivers who did not contend all AAA races exclusively.

By the following season, Shaw had mended the schism between himself and the AAA, but was not allowed to return to the Speedway until June 1, which of course meant missing the race. Married again by 1930, Shaw was to begin racing boats by coincidence as the prospect of seeing a Miller marine engine had initially lured him to a local dock. The regulations at The Speedway had changed completely by 1930, and the standard cars were now useless. The new cars had to be big enough to accommodate a riding mechanic—even if there was no riding mechanic. He won two races that season in a Smith-Miller, a 183ci car.

In 1931 Shaw went to drive for Duesenberg. Although Duesenberg had long since departed from the glory days of the twenties, Shaw was smitten with the idea of driving for the legendary company—as perhaps a driver of this epoch would like to drive for Ferrari. Shaw was to win no championship races in either 1931 or 1932. His only performance of notoriety was when he sailed over the wall at Indianapolis.

By 1934—after having raced at Monza in 1933 and wrecking his car—Shaw decided he needed to build his own car. In 1935, he contested his own car and by 1937, Shaw would win his first Indianapolis 500 and go on to win the three-race AAA Championship. In 1939 and 1940, Shaw would win the Indy 500 twice more and win the championship in 1939, finishing twice in second spot overall in 1938 and 1940.

The World went to war once more and Eddie Rickenbacker, the owner of The Speedway, became president of Eastern Airlines and had become increasingly involved in politics and the defense movement. As auto racing took a backseat to his patriotism, the Speedway floundered. When it reopened, it was under the command of three-time Indy winner, Wilbur Shaw.

During the war, Shaw was testing tires for Firestone at The Speedway and was apalled at how the track had deteriorated.

He worried that the symbol of American racing was withering into nothing, and he approached Rickenbacker about a sale. Rickenbacker, who had little time for The Speedway at that juncture, agreed. Shaw went about finding a suitable syndicate of buyers, avoiding the offers of most of the corporations due to what he felt was their insistence on making The Speedway a huge billboard for their products. Then he found Anton Hulman, a manufacturer of non-automotive products. Hulman, Shaw felt, would not whore out The Speedway.

Hulman purchased it from Rickenbacker on November 14, 1945, for something rumored to be about $700,000, and appointed Shaw as general manager. He retired as driver and oversaw the renovation of the track, the guardrails and the grandstand area, which was finished literally as the gates were being opened to the first race in 1945.

Although worried about the turnout for the first race under new management—the first race in five seasons—the race was a huge success.

Wrote Shaw: "It's difficult to describe the mingled emotions I experienced at that instant. I had a tremendous feeling of satisfaction for my part in making the big show possible again. The record-breaking turnout was particularly gratifying. . . . Almost overshadowing these thoughts was a feeling of envy as I looked over the starting field. I could see every driver in the cockpit of his car, tense and impatient to get under way. Many were old rivals of mine . . . I felt like

Wilbur Shaw in his 1937 Indianapolis 500 winning Gilmore Special. This victory was the only one in a three race season. Shaw poses with mechanic Jigger Johnson. He won the championship over Ted Horn and Bernd Rosemeyer. Courtesy Auburn-Cord Duesenberg Museum

a helpless little boy about to burst into tears, because his playmates had grabbed all of his toys and were running away with them. Then I glanced at the pace car and realized, for one lap at least, I'd be out in front of the pack. Turning back to the mike, and taking a deep breath, I gave the traditional command: 'Gentlemen, start your engines.'"

The race was a success. The Speedway, under Shaw, survived and evolved into what it is today, largely because of Hulman's purchase of it in 1945—largely from the impetus of Shaw.

On October 30, 1954, while flying out of the Chrysler Corporation's private proving ground outside Chelesea, Michigan, where he had done a special testing of a pair of road cars, his plane's wings iced over. At 4:19, it crashed to earth in a corn field outside Decatur, Indiana. Shaw, his pilot, and a friend were killed instantly.

At left
Shaw being congratulated by fans after his 1939 Indy 500 victory. Shaw was a long-time Indianapolis resident, and was always smitten with the race and its traditions. Courtesy Bruce Craig

Wilbur Shaw in 1940 in the Maserati. He won his third Indy 500 in this car, which was his last. He won the race three times and the AAA championship three times as well. Courtesy Firestone

130

Chapter 27

Tom Sneva

In racing, a profession where confidence is paramount, Tom Sneva is flush with the stuff. Sneva had confidence in his abilities as a driver, faith in his abilities as a mechanic and an engineer, and self-assurance as a spokesperson. Two of the three helped him. One trait may have actually shortened his career.

"(Tom) and I are very much alike in some respects," Bobby Rahal said. "I'm not afraid to say what's on my mind . . . and unfortunately for Tom, he was even less afraid," Rahal laughed.

A few years later and Sneva might have been a voice of wisdom. After all, most of what he complained about and campaigned against was eventually changed, but he had a way about him that was not altogether diplomatic. Frankly, he rubbed people the wrong way—especially his employers.

"A lot of people felt that way," Sneva said while relaxing at his golf club in Phoenix, Arizona. "Like Gordon Johncock once said, 'If there were ten guys in the elevator and nine of them pushed the up button, I'd push the down button. And it sort of looked like that at times, but I was always really trying to look after the drivers . . . And if (my opinions) didn't fit with the car owners then they would get upset, and if it didn't fit

Sneva's 1980 season. He finished second in the championship and won one race—in Phoenix, near his current home. He finished 19th at Indy and led for several laps early on in the event. John Mahoney

with USAC (then they were upset)."

"I was the first guy to go 200 miles an hour, and at the press conference I'd tell them, 'Hey, we're going too fast, we don't need to be doing this.'" he said. "It got pretty frustrating after a while. When you were trying to help the drivers as a group and you couldn't even get the support of the drivers because they weren't smart enough to figure out that might be good for them.

"The problem is that the guys who are the most powerful are the guys who are doing the winning. The guys who are doing the winning are on top of the world and are getting the most money and they don't think they need much change, but it's only because they don't have enough foresight to look down the road a few years and say, 'Hey, maybe in a couple of years I won't be on top and maybe if I make these changes it will help me prolong my situation or help the drivers as a whole.'

"It was always safety. But it was always either safety or competition related. That's what put me sideways with Penske. Roger always wanted to win—so did I. But I thought it would be better that we win by a car length not a lap. So I was always advocating ways to make the

Tom Sneva in the cockpit of his 1983 Texaco Star, a Patrick entry. He would win at the Indianapolis Motor Speedway as well as the Milwaukee Mile. After being released by Penske, Sneva's career actually accelerated. He finished fourth this season. Courtesy Texaco Racing, Hank Ives

The ex-school teacher with the win he sought for so long. Sneva had to be the sentimental favorite in 1983, when he won the Indy 500. He started on the second row and passed Al Unser, Sr. on the 191st lap for the lead and the win. Courtesy Texaco Racing, Hank Ives

competition closer and working on safety and Roger was always looking for a bigger advantage, which you can't blame him for that.

"In the mid-eighties we were tearing up guys' legs left and right. I wasn't any rocket scientist, but I'd say things like, 'Hey, we need to move the driver back in the car,' or 'We need to add to the front of the car.' They did all these things about two years later. But at the time we had all these engineers and experts had all their own ideas on how to make it safer for the drivers. Two or three or four years later they ended up doing what I brought up before that. I wasn't a good enough salesman to convince them that was needed. In the meantime how many drivers legs did we chew up? Now obviously we've got it all better. But I was that guy"

Understand now?

His comments had the effect of shortening his time spent at Penske, and he frequently turned up new people who wished he would just shut up. But whatever he said—in fact maybe because of what he said—Tom Sneva was still a crowd pleaser. After coming up short so many times, when he fianally won the

Indianapolis 500 in 1983, Sneva was for sure the sentimental favorite.

"I would like to think so. We did get along good with all the fans. I think it was a good day at Indianapolis. It was a big race with the Unsers. There was a little bit of controversy with Al Jr. blocking for his dad late in the race. But it was a fun day."

Sneva began racing in 1969, driving stock cars in a local track in Spokane, Washington. In 1970, he moved to modifieds and was the Canadian American Modified Racing Champion in his first season. He also became the Greater Inland Empire Racing Champion in both 1970 and 1971. In 1971, he drove his first USAC Championship race, the Trenton 300, and finished 21. But it was two years later before he raced again, starting his second race in 1973 in Texas, dropping out with mechanical problems early in the race. Although he passed his rookie test in 1973, he made no attempt to qualify for the Indianapolis 500. He raced at seven Championship races that season, finishing only as high as tenth. He drove a sprint car that year also and won six mains.

1983 Indianapolis 500. Sneva passes Rick Mears, his ex-teammate and goes on to win the event. Mears finished third that year in the Patrick/Bignotti car. John Mahoney

Although he was a driver, and a damned good one, Sneva was also a father and a husband. Driving as fun as it was, was not paying the bills. In real life Tom Sneva was a schoolteacher.

"I taught for three years. I was a like a principal teacher in Jr. High and then one year I taught high school level. I was sort of like the head of the math department, but that was only because I was the only math teacher at high school. I was a rookie in 1974. The district gave me the month of May off in 1973 to go back and take the rookie test. That was pretty nice of them. We went back and didn't have any money, but passed the test but then never got a chance to qualify because we broke all of our parts. We only had one motor. It was a pretty low budget deal.

"When I got back the (education department) said, hey you got to make this decision whether or not you're going to stay in education or go race. I had two small kids and a wife and no future in racing—so I gave up school teaching to see if I couldn't make it in racing," Sneva said tongue-in-cheek.

And he did make it in racing. In 1974, Sneva was the fastest rookie at the Indy 500, but was forced to

drop out again with mechanical problems after 94 laps. He contested the entire championship and finished seventeenth in the championship.

In 1975, Sneva signed on with Penske Racing. He qualified in fourth spot and clipped a competitor's tire, launching himself into the guardrail. The car caught fire and was destroyed in one of the most spectacular incidents at Indy. He missed the Milwaukee race the following weekend, but was back at the next race at Pocono, and right after that won his first Indy Car event at Michigan. He finished sixth in the standings that season.

In 1976, Sneva won no races and finished eighth in the championship. At Indy he qualified on the front row but finished only sixth. In 1977, he posted the first 200mph lap in Speedway history with a 200.535mph run.

It happened as a big surprise. Penske had just hired Mario Andretti, who was really the number-one driver for Penske Racing. Sneva was, as he says, "sort of B guy." Andretti and a few other drivers had been running speeds up to the 199s in "Happy Hour" as the track was cooler and quicker than during the mid-

Sneva and his boss at the time, Roger Penske. Although Sneva's results were exemplary, he was never able to win the Indy 500 with Penske. And Sneva admittedly had a tendency to create problems for himself within his teams. Penske let him go soon after this season. John Mahoney

day, but nobody had cracked the barrier. Sneva was back at about 197 or so. Penske wanted him to run Andretti's set up so they switched the car to what Andretti was running. Sneva actually did quite well with the set up, but spun coming off turn four. He hit the wall and smacked the right side of the car. And the crew had to rebuild the car overnight. In the meantime, Sneva, Andretti and Penske were having a powow.

"We had a big meeting that night, and Mario announced that nobody was going to run 200mphr the next day; it was going to be too hot, and they wouldn't get in during happy hour and all this other stuff. Anyway, my guys worked all night and put the right side back on our car and I told them, 'Let's put *my* set up back on it instead of Mario's,' because I liked it. And we go out the next day and there was only one guy who ran 200mph and that was the B driver on the Penske team." Sneva finished second that year.

He did, however, manage to win two races on the championship trail that season, ultimately capturing the championship title. In 1978, Sneva repeated the championship winning season, but oddly, didn't win a single race that year—becoming the first and only driver since to do so. He finished second six times and third four times to finish ahead of Al Unser. He was also quickest in qualifying six times, including at the Indy 500, where he posted the Speedway's first 200mph lap.

In 1979, he won no races again in either CART or USAC championships and finished second in USAC and seventh in CART standings. In 1980, he finished second again in USAC and third in CART. In 1981, he won twice in CART, but only managed an eighth

place in the year-end standings. In 1982, he won two races again and finished fourth in points.

But at the Indy 500, he had luck worse than Andretti. He had been successful. He had won two championships and had qualified on pole twice. "We finished second three times," he said "Twice was with Penske and backing up a spot and the third time was starting with a small independent team and going all the way through the field and finishing second to Rutherford in 1980, which I think is my best effort ever at Indy."

But nobody paid any attention to that race. It was just another runner-up finish for Sneva, who, many thought, would never win the Indy 500. But in 1983 things changed. In 1983, driving the Texaco Star owned by Pat Patrick, Sneva was clearly the class of the field. By the end of the race, he was catching Al Unser who was trailed by his son Al Jr. Although Al Jr. was not in contention for the win, he was clearly interested in keeping his father out front. Lap after lap, Sneva, who was absolutely the sentimental favorite on that day, was kept at bay behind the younger Unser. Al Unser was getting away. Finally, on the 191st lap, Sneva pulled out and around both Unsers and inherited the lead, which he never relinquished. Sneva had won his first Indy 500.

Although he won a career high four races in the 1984 championship and finished runner-up in the standings to Mario Andretti, Sneva's career would begin to wind down sometime after that Indy 500 win. In 1985, he finished tenth in points with no wins, driving for Dan Gurney. In 1986, he won no races again and finished tenth. In 1987, he lost his ride mid-way through the season. In 1988, he started only two races, the Indy 500 and Michigan, failing for the first time in sixteen seasons to post a top-five finish. In 1989, he ran a half-dozen races for the Granatelli team, but posted poor results and left the team mid-season. That was the last season in racing for Sneva, who returned to Arizona to manage his family's golf course interests.

Sneva still talks as he did when he was ranting and raving back in the early 1980s. He still has a fire and enthusiasm which will make you love him or hate him. And ultimately, it is that which tended to do him in with the people who held an opinion of the latter.

Said Jim McGee, Sneva's chief mechanic during his time at Penske: "Tom was a very, very good race car driver, but he was much in tune with wanting to set the car up himself. He always had trouble with either the mechanics or the engineers because he knew what he thought he wanted and he would have a tendency to steer them that way and he could be difficult. But he was a fun guy. We always had a good time together."

Rahal said, "On an oval Tom Sneva was as good as anyone and better than most. I don't know personally if he was a good engineer type or if he could sort out a car, but let's face it, the guy was quite good on the mile ovals and he was gutsy and a great driver."

But contrary nature aside, Johncock said, "I can tell you one thing: Tom always stood on the gas. He knew one way to go, and he was fast. I liked Tom, and he was obviously a very quick driver."

Sneva is now happily retired from driving and making his living as a golf course owner. He just opened a new place in Phoenix called Victory Lane, to go with the golf course called The 500 Club. The new facility is a six-diamond soft ball field, with sand volleyball courts and batting cages, with a sports bar in the middle of the entire thing. Sneva is there quite often—probably telling anyone who will listen about the dangers of the fast pitch.

Sneva (left), Tom Bigelow (center) and Gary Bettenhausen were honored at the Annual "Last Row Party" at the Indianapolis Press Club. Even in the bad times, Sneva was a good sport. The three poorest qualifiers still managed to finish 2nd, 8th, and 3rd respectively. John Mahoney

Chapter 28

Danny Sullivan

Y ou can call Danny Sullivan "Hollywood" if you want. He doesn't care. Because this Indy Car champion and Indianapolis 500 winner knows that he's not just for show.

Danny Sullivan, for a time, became Indy Car's poster-boy, the Burt Reynolds of motor Sport. He was a model, an actor and a spokesperson for the sport of racing. He was, the publicists said, the prototype race car driver. He had the classic good looks of a Cary Grant, the schoolboy image of a Robert Redford, the oratory skills of David Frost and the nerve of Chuck Yeager. He just looked like he belonged in his role as a superstar race car driver and playboy. But Sullivan had a hard road to get where he did.

"Danny is a classic case of somebody who made their way with talent," ESPN commentator Derek Daly said. "When he was in a good situation, he was able to rise to the occasion. Danny is a start name in racing. He has won very, very big races by being mentally strong and being able to rise to the occasion—like the Indy 500."

"Hollywood" Danny Sullivan in 1993. The title was a burden to the man who had persevered through many years of odd jobs so that he could pursue his dream. Courtesy Galles

When you see Sullivan, when you hear about him and all that he is supposed to be, you are often overwhelmed by the steamroller of an image. But Sullivan's image is not very close to Sullivan's true persona.

Sullivan was born in Louisville, Kentucky, on March 5, 1950. He attended Kentucky Military Institute, and played sports, lettering in swimming, track, football and soccer. Once he graduated, he went to the University of Kentucky for two semesters in business before dropping out. He went to New York where he worked a variety of odd jobs, including cab driver and a waiter at Maxwell Plum's. (He also worked as a lumberjack in the Adironondacks as well as a chicken ranch hand). On his twenty-first birthday a family friend and mentor gave Sullivan a scholarship to Jim Russell Driving School in Great Britain. Directionless, Sullivan had once said that he wanted to be a race car driver. The doctor decided to force the issue.

"If I have to look back at the end of my career and say there was one person who made it all happen, it was Frank Faulkner." Sullivan said. "He was the one who got me to go to the driving school and helped me get going. It started as a whim. Literally. I was bumming around in New York. But the minute I sat down in that car for the first time, I knew it was everything I ever wanted to do in my life. As a kid I didn't follow cars. I didn't follow racing. I didn't go to races. I didn't know anything about racing. I just said, 'Man, that looks like fun, I'd like to try that.'"

The following season, bankrolled partly by Faulkner, Sullivan was racing. His first racing was in a

In 1986, the year after his now-famous spin-and-win Indy 500 victory. The car is different, but the livery is the same. Of that incident Sullivan shrugged and said, "It wasn't so much that I was forced to come in (at Indy); I could have kept going. I slightly flat spotted the tires and that brought out a yellow flag because of the spin so it was as good a time as any to come in and make sure nothing was broken and put new tires on." Courtesy Miller Brewing

British Formula Ford outing in 1972. In 1974, he finished second in British Formula 2 and the following season finished fourth in the prestigious European F3 championship, scoring four wins and four poles.

In 1976, he raced in F2, then moved to sports car endurance racing in 1977. In 1978, he raced in Formula Atlantics in New Zealand and in 1980 and 1981 he raced in the Can-Am series, finishing no worse than sixth in points for three consecutive seasons. In 1982, he debuted in Indy Cars with a impressive third place at Atlanta.

In 1983, after almost ten years of toiling, Sullivan got his chance to drive at the pinnacle, in F1. He drove the entire season for Ken Tyrrell, having never before been behind the wheel of a Grand Prix car. His best finish was a fifth at Monaco, not bad considering his inexperience. At the end of the season, he left to go back to the United States—to Indy Car racing.

"My background was I started in Europe and I really wanted to be successful in F1," Sullivan said. "The problem is that nothing is ever black and white. What happened was I had a good year and Tyrrell wanted me to stay there, but they were losing Benetton as their sponsor because (Tyrrell) didn't and wouldn't get a turbocharged engine. What happened was that Ken (Tyrrell) told me, 'If I don't have a sponsor, I might have to take a paid driver for the second seat, so I can't even guarantee that you're going to be there.' So Doug Shierson comes into the picture and offers me a ride and offers me a lot of money, and I

got to tell you I went up to Frank Faulkner's house in Berkeley, California, and sat up there for three days and made the toughest decision in my life. When I look back on it, would I have liked to have stayed in Formula One? Sure. But do I regret the decision? Absolutely not.

"It would be very hard for me to say that I was disappointed in what I did the first year I didn't drive in F1. I drove for Tyrell in 1983. In 1984 I won three races. I signed for Penske in 1985, and the second race I did I won the Indianapolis 500."

In 1992, he moved to Galles alongside Al Unser Jr. Here he poses with team owners Rick Galles and Maurie Kraines at winter testing in California. He finished seventh in the series in 1992. Courtesy Galles

On his twenty first birthday, a family friend and mentor gave Sullivan a scholarship to Jim Russell Driving School in Great Britain. From there a career was born. Courtesy Galles

narrowly missing Mario Andretti, whom he had just passed for the lead, Sullivan pitted, changed tires and raced back to the checkered flag.

Much to the chagrin of Mario Andretti, Sullivan went back out after the yellow, caught Andretti, passed him, and went on to win the race.

Andretti credited the win to dumb luck. So did Sullivan, who claimed afterward that he was just holding on for dear life. When he found that he had failed to hit anything, he just did what was natural: he pointed the Penske the right direction and planted his foot on the throttle.

That win, that incident, secured Sullivan's immortality and began the legend. It was a thrilling moment, watching the man wrestle with the car and bring it home for the victory. It was also the biggest race of the year and, gee whiz, this guy is pretty damned photogenic. It was the beginning of "Hollywood" Danny Sullivan.

"I've always felt that the thing both hurt and helped me. I lived in LA in an area—actually on Rockingham Drive down the street from OJ (Simpson)—but I lived in an area where it was more common to see a famous person than if I had lived in Indianapolis. The reason I lived there was because the guy I originally drove for out in California was a guy named Garvin Brown—the heir to Brown-Forman distilleries, Jack Daniel, Early Times and so forth. Garvin had an apartment out here, and he said, 'Just stay with me.'

"Well he knew a lot of the people because he'd been there for ten years. Garvin got around and knew a lot of people. Consequently when I started doing well and had some success I invited people to Long Beach, whether it was Kurt Russell or Don Johnson or people like that. Then I met Michael Mann who pro-

That win, the Indy 500, was probably the most dramatic 500 in modern history, accomplished after a spectacular spin at full speed on the 120th lap. After

Sullivan has the respect of most of the Indy Car regulars because of his commitment to racing. Sometimes he is not brilliant behind the wheel, but usually he keeps the pressure on. Either way, he was never given a break he didn't deserve. Courtesy Galles

As most American road racing drivers did in the seventies, Sullivan wished to go racing in Europe. His first racing was in British Formula Ford in 1972. In 1974 he finished second in British Formula 2 and the following season finished fourth in the prestigious European F3 championship. In 1983, after almost ten years of toiling, Sullivan got his chance to drive at the pinnacle, in F1. At the end of the season he left to go back to the United States—to Indy Car racing. Courtesy Galles

duced *Miami Vice,* and he invited me to be on the show and who's going to turn down being on a hit show?"

In 1986, Sullivan began his ill-fated career in acting, appearing in the then hot *Miami Vice* series as, surprise, a race car driver. He also appeared on "All My Children." Anybody who saw the shows—including Sullivan—realized that as good looking as the man was, there was no way he was going to make it as an actor. He gave it up and went back to racing full-time.

In 1986, he won two races and finished fourth in the series points. In 1987 he finished ninth. In 1988 he won his first championship, taking four events and scoring in the top ten in eleven of fourteen races. In 1989, he broke his arm at Indy, but still drove the car on Memorial Day to the 28th spot. He won two races that season and finished seventh in points.

In 1990, his career began to wane slightly at the end of the season, in which he won twice. He was released from Penske. In 1991, he joined Pat Patrick and Alfa Romeo, which was an ill-fated effort from the start as the Alfas were always down on power. In 1992, he moved to Galles alongside Al Unser Jr and

won only once, at Long Beach, in a controversial move that put his teammate out of the race. He finished seventh in the series.

In 1993, he won once again and finished twelfth. In 1994, he left Indy Car racing altogether when Galles decided to focus on Adrian Fernandez. He went looking for a ride in NASCAR and found it, but also found limited success. He drove in a few select races, but had no noteworthy finishes. In 1995, he was back in the seat with a ride at Pac West alongside Mauricio Guglemin. He did well but won no races with the new team.

And although he continues to do modeling for sunglass companies and other products, Sullivan has really been relegated to a driver first and foremost, which is what he wants to be now anyway.

"I've raced him for years," Bobby Rahal said in the mid-nineties, well after Sullivan's major success with Penske. "I think he can be very quick on a given day. A guy you could race pretty close with and never worry about him doing something foolish. With all the appearances and side showed to death had a negative affect, but I think Danny on any given day was

In 1986 Sullivan began his ill-fated acting career, appearing in the then hot "Miami Vice" series as a race car driver. Realizing that he wasn't going to make it as an actor, he gave it up and concentrated on driving—and won the Indy Car title two years later in 1988. Courtesy Galles

right there with the best of them. I think Danny did a lot for racing. He sort of took racing out of the pits and made it mainstream entertainment.

"I get along with Danny very well," Rahal continued thoughtfully. "Racing is what he loved doing. Forget all the Hollywood stuff and what have you; certainly that was all there, but when you would have a

Sullivan in his Tyrrell in Holland, 1983. This was Sullivan's only season in F1. He had been competitive for Tyrrell, but had failed to convert any drives into wins. His best finish was a fifth at Monaco. He contested all fifteen races of the 1983 season. Tony Sakkis

glass of wine with him . . . maybe it was two glasses of wine . . . but it was always racing. Yeah, Danny was always interested in the personalities of the people involved, but Danny was interested in racing and I think that's something that a lot of people think of when they think of him."

The Hollywood nickname is around less now than it used to be, but it is still around. And he still looks like the poster boy—or man, now in his late forties—for auto racing.

But in all, Sullivan has remained actually a relatively humble man. He is always ready for an interview and signs autographs as if he is paid to do so—which he is not. With the fame and success has come, finally, wealth. Sullivan now lives in Aspen, Colorado, and hardly thinks about the days as a taxi driver—unless, of course, he is reminded about them by journalists.

Racing for its own sake is still what motivates him, and he will always be thankful for the opportunity to have driven—and won—in some of the great races and great cars of the sport. But through all the hype and glitz, there is no doubt that he earned the seats with nothing more dramatic than his driving ability.

"You're wearing a couple of hats there," Sullivan said of his role as a spokesperson for his sponsors, "but ultimately, I'm a race car driver and what I like to do is go fast."

Chapter 29

Al Unser, Jr.

Journalists, like lawyers, tend to ask leading questions. Long-time writers, especially for afternoon newspapers, don't look at the hows of an event as much as the whys. They care not that the race was run in one hour and fifty minutes and the margin of victory was nine seconds and that the prize money was worth so much. What they care about is the human emotion behind the event. What part of the human spirit was evoked to defeat the challengers?

Drivers, like any other sportspersons, are deluged after an event by the media, asking about the hows and the wheres and the whys. But the news reporter's profession, with its eternal deadlines and space considerations, is such that creativity is distilled into a science. Passion is a formula that must be elicited and regurgitated before 8 P.M. for the early edition. Sometimes the angle is a stretch; occasionally reporters ask questions expecting certain answers.

Then comes Al Unser Jr.

"Al," a journalist asked Al Jr. after he won the Marlboro Challenge in 1989, "when you're out of the championship fight, do you tend to maybe relax a bit, think of the race as opposed to the championship, go for the glory for once?"

Unser looked up, sort of confused, a blank look on his face. "No," he said, simply.

Unser in Marlboro-Penske colors. Said Penske teammate Emerson Fittipaldi, "I'm learning from him all the time. I watch him all the time, learning where he is quick and where I can improve. There are many things he does better than me. He will be as famous as his father. No doubt about it."
Courtesy Marlboro Racing

Next question.

Alright, maybe phrase it differently.

"Do you perhaps put more on the line now that there's less to lose? Let's face it Al, you've never done this well at this racetrack."

"No," he said plainly. "I race every race the same. I try to win every race, every week."

Vintage Al Jr.: no nonsense. No pandering, no favorites, and no apologies.

If you want candor, ask Al Unser Jr. a question. He's as diplomatic as the next guy, but he doesn't give anything away for free. And probably because of it—some say despite it—Al Unser Jr. is one of the most respected men in Indy Car racing. He is smart, he is experienced, and he is honest. Most of all, however, he is fast.

"I'm learning from him all the time," Penske's teammate and two-time World Champion Emerson Fittipaldi said. "I watch him all the time, learning where he is quick and where I can improve. You never can convince yourself that you are the best and the quickest otherwise you are not going to be. There are many things he does better than me.

"I give you an example; when we come back from the track we have lap charts of a lap around the track—where you can compare driving styles where I'm gaining on him, where he's gaining on me—I'm

Rick Galles saw the potential in the young Unser after he had won two championships—in Super Vee and in Can-Am—and began assembling a single car team. Al Jr. finished seventh in points in his first season as his father won the championship, then became the youngest driver at the speedway to have gone over 200mph. Here he drives the 1983 Galles Eagle Cosworth. Courtesy Galles

always learning something from those." Fittipaldi stopped and pondered a second. "He will be as famous as his father. No doubt about it."

Perhaps to say that about Al Unser Jr. is to give him the credit he has sought from the beginning. Blessed or blighted by the name Unser, Al Jr. admitted to only racing to get the attention of his father and uncle. He had snowmobiles and go karts as a kid and was proficient in both even before he was a teenager. Although fascinated with speed, it was not an all-encompassing desire to become a race car driver.

Unser's cousin Bobby Jr. instilled in him a competitiveness that he had never had. Al Jr. had no brothers and it was his cousin Bobby who was so enthusiastic about racing. Al Jr. was somehow caught up in the emotion. The karts had proven to be great experience for Unser, and so he decided to race sprint cars. The racing was just part of the competitiveness. It could have just as easily been baseball.

But his father was a race car driver, and he wanted to be good in what his father did. So for the first few seasons—when he was about fifteen years old—

he raced with his father's blessing and backing. More importantly, he raced for his father's attention and respect.

In sprint cars he proved successful, and from there went to the World of Outlaws and did well. But he was soon trying to get out and into pavement racing. He now says he wishes he had stayed longer, but like everything Al Unser says, he has already dealt with it and there are few emotions lingering from the topic.

In 1980, Al Jr. began racing SCCA Super Vees. By the next season he had signed with Rick Galles and was campaigning a full season. He won four of nine events and won the championship. Galles moved him into a Can-Am car. Again, he won four of nine and won the championship. In August of 1982, Al Jr. started his first Indy Car race at Riverside driving for Jerry Forsythe. At twenty years old, one of the youngest to ever climb into a championship car, he finished fifth.

Galles, a long time Albuquerque native, saw what he had with the young Unser and began assembling a single car Indy Car team. That first season, Al Jr. finished seventh in points, watching as his father won the championship.

After becoming the youngest driver at the speedway to have gone over 200mph, Al Jr. found himself in the late stages of the 1983 Indy 500 with Al Sr. leading. With Tom Sneva the fastest car on the track, and Al Jr. in the position to block Sneva' advance, he did just that, making his car as wide as possible, holding up Sneva for several laps. And when the race was over Al Jr. admitted to "trying to help dad."

But if Al Unser Jr. began racing to satisfy his father he got serious about racing because of the Speedway, and the Indy 500. And still, today, the Indy 500 has a special place in his heart—an emotion that seems strangely unlike him.

"It's the oldest race in the world," he said at the end of his 1995 season where he was runner-up to Jacques Villeneuve. "It's the crown jewel of our sport. It's really the fastest racetrack. The challenges put in front of you at Indy during the month of May are incredible. And they come from all sides. Mario has a quote that he said some years ago that kind of sunk in: 'The god's eyes are upon you at Indy.' And they are. The Indy 500 can make you a great race car driver—which it has definitely done for me and my family. It can also break you from greatness or whatever. Its a very fickle place and the pressures are just incredible. They just never cease to happen. Everybody's always looking at you; the press, the fans, everything. You literally get pulled eight or nine different directions in the month of May. That's what makes it tough. It's just three weeks worth of racing, and it's just incredible."

The Speedway has in fact had a special meaning to the Unser family, and they have persevered better than any other family in the history of the place. As 1996 was starting, Al Jr. had won twice, Al Sr. had won four times, and uncle Bobby had won three times. On the tragic side, his uncle Jerry was killed there in 1959. Mostly, however, the track had been good to the family. "The experience Dad had at that place—and just with racing in general—has helped. He shared everything with me, and it definitely helped."

And what is it about the place? Why this profound respect for these particular two and a half miles of pavement?

It was the size and the magnitude of the event, he says. The sheer number of people. And there he was—there his father was—right in the middle of it all.

"His car was just so big and beautiful," Al said about his first experience at Indy. "It was awesome. As a nine year old boy it was really something. I went to the seventy-two 500 and the seventy-three 500 and then I did not go back again until 1982 because I was racing."

It would take him ten years before he, too, would win at The Speedway. Prior to that, there was winning elsewhere.

At Galles in 1993. Al Jr. moved back to Galles in 1988 and won four races and finished second in the championship that first season, then followed up in 1989 with the spectacular last lap Indy loss to Emerson Fittipaldi. Eva Vega

When Rick Galles talked of running two cars, Al Jr. felt the team was not in the position to win races with two cars. He left to drive for Lotus, a deal which fell apart just before the season began. He found himself without a ride. Ironically, a seat was left vacant at Shierson. Unser took the seat and took Shierson to the final race at Miami, losing the championship in the closest year-long battle ever, 151-150. The championship contender and ultimate winner was his own father. Courtesy Shierson

In 1984, Al Jr. won his first Indy Car race at Portland. Fittingly, it was on Father's Day. He finished sixth in the championship that year. At the end of the season, Rick Galles talked of running two cars, and Al Jr. realized the team was not in the position to win races with one car, let alone two. He left to drive for Lotus, which was going to bring a car to the U.S.

The deal fell apart, and he found himself without a ride. Ironically, a seat was left vacant at at Shierson by John Paul Jr., who was having legal problems. The deal, brokered by his father, put Al Jr. into a Shierson Lola-Cosworth and in a championship fight down to the final race at Miami. He lost the championship in the closest year-long battle ever, 151-150. The championship contender and ultimate winner was his own father.

In 1986, Al Jr. finished fourth in points in Indy Car but became IROC Champion—the youngest ever. He also co-drove a 962 Porsche to victory at the 24 hours of Daytona. In 1987 he won Daytona again, but failed to win a single Indy Car race.

In 1988, back with Galles, he won four races and finished second in the championship, then followed up in 1989 with the spectacular last lap Indy loss to Emerson Fittipaldi.

In 1990, he finally won the championship, which had seemed to unfairly elude him the previous seven seasons. In that year he won six times. Two years later he would win the most important race of his life, the Indy 500. For the first time in his life, the emotion was

Number One accepts his number one. A win at Mid-Ohio in 1995. Defending the championship he had clinched the previous season, Unser came up just short of winning back-to-back championships, losing in 1995 to Jacques Villeneuve. Courtesy IndyCar

Below
The Indianapolis Motor Speedway has had special meaning to the Unser Family. By 1995, Al Jr. had won twice, Al Sr. had won four times and uncle Bobby had won three times. Here, Al Jr. takes a pit stop. Courtesy IndyCar

too much. Nerves a wreck, Unser cried tears of joy. He had done it. He had won the Indianapolis 500. The third Unser do do so.

Unser would win the 500 again as well as the championship—both in the same season—in 1994. Ironically, he was driving for the team that had brought success to both his father and his uncle: Penske.

Now, on the eve of his fourteenth season in America's premier racing series, Unser looks as serious as he did when he started. He seems to be a perma-nent member of the Penske stable and is carrying on a tradition that he seemed destined for from the moment he was born.

"I didn't want to do anything else, "Al Jr. said at the last race of 1995. "I just wanted to race. My son on the other hand, I think he wants to do other things. Which is great; which I'm all for. Racing is a very tough business and you have to sacrifice a ton in order to go do it."

There is no doubt that he has done that. And he'll be the first to tell you.

Blessed or blighted by the name Unser, Al Jr. admitted to racing to satisfy his father initially. As he became successful, his desires changed and he began racing for himself. The result by 1995 was two championships and two Indianapolis 500 victories.
Courtesy IndyCar

Chapter 30

Al Unser, Sr.

Al Unser stood in pit lane at the Indianapolis Motor Speedway in 1987 with that look. The look that seems part scowl and part annoyance. The look that warns all but the right people away. Unsuited, he watched as drivers moved out onto the track for practice. He was not a part of the show.

Having signed a contract for three 500 mile races for Roger Penske for the 1985 season, the season in which he won the PPG Championship, and again in 1986 where he won none of the three races entered, Al Unser found himself in totally unfamiliar territory. Winner of three Indy 500s, three championships and numerous races, he had no ride for the 1987 Indianapolis 500.

Although offers had come in, none of them were acceptable to Unser, who had spent all or parts of the previous four seasons with the Penske team. Unser held out for something more like the Penske operation. By the middle of the month, he'd found something like Penske. In fact he found Penske.

Penske had announced over the winter that he would run Danny Ongias—not Unser—in the third car at Indy. Ongias, however, crashed hard in practice at the Speedway in the first week, and the medical staff at The Speedway sug-

Al Unser, Sr. is one of the most renowned Indy Car drivers in the history of the sport. But although he won four Indianapolis 500s and three championships, Unser was never given quite the recognition he deserved, due to his reserved style. Bob Tronolone

gested that Ongias stay out of the car for the rest of the month. Unser had a job.

The team had been running Penske chassied cars. The PC16, however, had shown little of the speed the Marches had shown, and Roger Penske pulled the PC16s and replaced them for the Indy with Chevy-Marches. All were replaced except for Unser's car, which had no time to be converted, so he qualified and ran a March-Cosworth. This car was a show car which had been taken out of competition after a year. It was shipped to Indianapolis and made race-ready for Unser Sr. Mears qualified on the front row the first weekend and Unser qualified on the second weekend well into the middle of the field.

The race started, and Unser barely managed to miss hitting a spinning car in the first corner of the first lap. Then on the restart he lost several more positions. By the end of 100 miles he was down a lap to leader Mario Andretti and running solidly mid-field, not looking much like a three-time winner, let alone a four-time winner.

But he began making progress. Although not as quick as Andretti or second place man Roberto Guerrero, he was proving to be the pace of the rest of the field. By half way, Unser had made it into the top five

Unser in the new Hall-Chaparral, shaking the car down at Phoenix. In 1979, Unser drove away from the field in the Chaparral 2K at the start, but dropped out due to mechanical difficulties. Courtesy Pennzoil Racing, Deke Houlgate

and with three-quarters of the race run, he found himself third behind Andretti and Guerrero.

Twenty laps from the end, Andretti succumbed to some of his traditional Andretti luck and Guerrero, who pitted, was blighted with an overheated clutch and no power. Unser inherited the lead and a few minutes later, the win. His fourth win at Indy. And although the accolades would come, the jobs would not.

Al Unser was a lot of things, but what he wasn't was a publicity hound. He was a confident man who liked to show his skill on the race track rather than at press conferences. To some, he looked aloof, even angry. But to pigeonhole Al Unser is to say you know the man by the way he looks, which you just can't.

"I think he's a very private person," Bobby Rahal said of Unser. "He's not Mr. Personality with everyone. He's all business. There's only one thing and one thing only that's really motivated him that I can see and that's racing cars. I look at Al Jr., and I see them as very similar types of people: both conservative people on and off the race track. Junior's a very conservative driver, I think. But Jr.'s a better racer than a qualifier. And I think Al's like that too. He's not a one-lap-wonder

who can sort of hold his breath for one lap and that would be it. He was a good racer."

"But Al's an awfully private guy," Rahal said. "I can say that Al Unser is probably one of the most underrated drivers. He's won Indy four times, but the only guy you ever really hear about is A.J. Foyt. Or Mario Andretti gets more coverage, and he's only won it once. I think Al is so quiet that maybe he never got the credit he deserved. Speaking from a popular standpoint, I think he was a better road racer than he ever got credit for. He led at Elkhart Lake in seventy-four or five, whenever they had the Formula five-thousand race. He was beating Mario. But I think Al's demeanor probably caused people not to give him the credit he should have gotten. But there was no doubt that he was one of the best. When I look at a number of the best people I've raced against he'd be in that handful. Tough but fair, extremely talented in every thing he tried."

Parnelli Jones, who hired Unser in 1969, said virtually the same thing; that the man was very quick and almost snuck up on his competition.

"Al Unser Senior was the best Indy driver I ever

had," Jones said. "A car owner couldn't have a better driver than Al. He wasn't as flashy as Bobby, but he was always there, and he would beat you on quickness. He's a lot quieter, for one thing. He doesn't like to do public speaking and things. Not outward all the time. Bobby is a lot different. Al's just quick. He's not somebody you notice like Bobby. He's not sliding the car around all the time. He's not flashy or anything; he just keeps putting it down the road. We won a lot of races. We won Indy twice."

To go over Unser's achievements is to see at once fantastic fortune. At the same time it was a series of situations that had him coming up just short, having to use all his facilities to get to where he wanted to be.

Son of racer Jerry Unser, nephew of Louis, brother to Bobby, Louis and Jerry Unser, and father of Al Unser Jr., Unser was born into a racing family. But he was so much younger than his older brothers that he was almost on his own. His brothers did their thing and he did his. Although he was a part of the family, his racing was far more elementary than theirs, and they paid little attention to him.

His first race at the Speedway was fraught with disappointment, first because the Speedway told him he didn't have enough experience, and that he couldn't take his test; then, after he had passed his rookie test with Frank Arciero in a car that didn't want to make the field, he was unable to qualify.

Forget winning the race. When the Maserati engine destroyed itself while Unser attempted to qualify, Unser was finished. Until A.J. Foyt, who was a rival of Unser's, offered him his backup car.

There was no reason for it. There were veteran drivers to whom Foyt could have offered the car to, but he chose this kid from Albuquerque. Unser qualified the car on the last row and raced Foyt's car to finish ninth, four laps down to winner Jimmy Clark.

Pennzoil's anatomy of a pit stop, with Al Unser Sr. on lap forty-four of the 1979 Indianapolis 500. Unser stops the car on the mark. Tire changers and refuelers are ready. In less than five seconds the refueling hose is attached and the right side wheel men start to work. Both front and rear right side tires are changed, the car is topped off. And Unser screeches out of the pits thirteen seconds later. Courtesy Pennzoil Racing, Deke Houlgate

Al Unser's main theme was that he did things himself. He had some fortuitous breaks, but as any executive will tell you, opportunity is nothing without preparation. And Unser was always prepared.

From the start of his career, he was always involved in the cars, always curious as to how they ran. He'd been operating his own shop when he was not racing. It was a street car repair shop like his father's, which he'd bought and built on his own in Albuquerque. From an early age Unser knew what went on beneath the hood of a street car, and eventually what was going on in any of his race cars.

By the end of his career, he was one of the very best drivers in the series for giving feedback on the cars. Porsche hired him for just that purpose late in his career—although the relationship was doomed since Porsche listened to him, but failed to make any of the changes he suggested. (When the car debuted, Al Unser was all but publicly vocal about the arrogance of Porsche's crewmen; the chassis of the Porsche was scrapped a few months after Unser left Porsche, and the engine was withdrawn a few years later with only minimal success).

After driving for Foyt in 1965, Unser drove for Andy Granatelli in 1966 with Lotus and Jimmy Clark. After being engaged in a dual with Gordon Johncock

Unser Sr. in Victory Lane at the 1970 Indianapolis 500. This was his first Indianapolis victory. Unser Sr. would go on to win three more 500s, making him only one of three drivers to have won the Indianapolis 500 four times, the other two being A.J. Foyt and Rick Mears. Bob Tronolone

for a good portion of the race he spun out and ended his day. He finished second three times that season and was fifth in points. In 1967 he finished second

Driving the Chaparral racing Lola in 1978, Unser speeds to his third 500 win. Unser rarely won in the car, in fact he only won two other races in the car that season. Astonishingly, the races he won were all five hundred milers. Courtesy Ford Racing

Al Unser's first win for Penske, and his last win at the Indianapolis 500. The March Cosworth was provided to him at the last minute by Roger Penske and he made the most of it, starting mid-pack and driving to the front. The win was surprising, since Unser was not even qualified until late in the month. Courtesy Ford Racing

again in five races including the Indy 500, with no wins, and finished fifth again in the standings. He also raced USAC stock cars a dozen times and won once, with a final points tally which put him fourth.

In 1968, Unser drove the Daytona 500 and finished fourth, earning Rookie Of The Year honors. He then went back to Indy Cars and with Parnelli Jones and George Bignotti and won an astounding five races in a row, finishing third in points. In 1969, in the infield during practice for the Indianapolis 500, Al Unser fell and fractured his leg. In all the racing he had done, a fall on a motorcycle finally sidelined him from the Indy 500.

But by mid-season he was back and winning races, finishing runner up to Mario Andretti that season. In 1970 he made up for the mistake and captured both the pole for the Indy 500 as well as the race itself. Then he capped that off by winning ten races, tying A.J. Foyt for most races won in a season, and winning the championship. His Brother Bobby was runner up. Al Unser repeated as winner of the 500 in 1971, and looked as if he would repeat the championship, as he won five of the first six races. But he failed to score a single point in the last half of the season and finished fourth. He also contended six stock car races that season and won once.

In 1972, he finished fourth in points and won in stock cars. In 1973, he won once in the Indy Car and finished first in the Championship Dirt Title series, which had become a separate series in 1970. He was fourth in 1974. Unser won in Formula 5000 in 1975, as his team, VPJ, concentrated on F5000 more than Indy Cars, finishing third in points. He also won in the Championship Dirt Series, finishing ninth. In 1976, he finished fourth in Indy Car with two wins, finished second in Formula 5000 with one win, and in 1977, he won once and finished fourth in the standings. He also won in IROC. And in 1978, he won the Indy 500, the Pocono 500 and the Ontario 500, the Triple Crown of Championship racing.

In 1979, he was fifth with one win in Indy Cars. In 1980, he won no races in Indy Car, but won once in Can-Am. In 1981 and 1982, he won no championship races, but came back in 1983 with Penske and finished second at the 500, with some help from his son, and he won at Cleveland. In 1984, he won no races. Then he won the championship in 1985. Unser won his fourth and final Indianapolis 500 in 1987.

Through it all, Al Unser, Sr. has become a legend of American racing. He has, along with his brother Bobby, A.J. Foyt and Mario Andretti, proven that the best drivers in the world are adaptable. That they can win on dirt ovals, gravel road, paved ovals, and a paved road course and in cars ranging from heads-up sprint cars to Can-Am cars, and everything in between.

Unser was born with talent and drive, no doubt about it. But he made the most of it. A few lucky breaks and he became one of only three four-time winners of the Indianapolis 500. Ironically, with one or two more he might have gone down in history as the all time best. With a bit more horn-blowing, he might have been the most memorable of them all.

Author's note: While doing an advance for the local paper, I spoke with Unser's son, Al Unser Jr., in September of 1995 prior to the Laguna Seca Grand Prix. In passing, I asked the most expedient way for me to get a hold of his father. Al Jr. gave me a phone number. After trying for some time to get a hold of his father, leaving messages and such, someone finally answered the phone. It was Al Unser, Sr.

"Hello," the voice said.

I knew it was Al. His de-nasal voice and sort of run-on of words is unmistakeable.

"I'm looking for Al Unser," I said.

"Uuhh," the voice said, "He's not here right now."

"Is there a good time to call back?"

"Well . . . what did you need?"

I identified myself as the person who had called earlier, the writer for the San Francisco Chronicle *and one-time writer for the* San Francisco Examiner, *where, I hoped, he might remember talking with me previously. I explained I was trying to do a project on Indy car drivers and wanted a word with him.*

"Give him a call tomorrow. He should be here then." He said. "He should be here around noon."

As I hung up, I realized there would be no interview. I also realized he knew that I knew who'd answered the phone. It was a polite way of him telling me to leave him alone.

But just for the hell of it, I called the next day at noon.

There was no answer.

Al Unser Sr. in the pits at Indy in 1992. Unser, then and now as a retired driver, is a private man who was more at home in a cockpit of a race car than just about anywhere else on earth. Rick Dole

Chapter 31

Bobby Unser

If Al Unser began racing as a result of his older brothers' interest in racing, and winning because of an hereditary strain of racing gene, then Bobby Unser had the gene in spades. But where Al had an unbounded natural talent, Bobby's success came more from his determination. Bobby Unser was always a fierce competitor, not just in Indy Cars, but in *anything*.

Parnelli Jones remembers once when they were running a dirt track car and . . . "One time we were at a midget race at Colorado. It was quarter-mile track and we asked, 'What's the track record.' They told us something like sixteen-thirty-four, or something. So we got out there and were running, and Bobby's driving the car, and I'm driving the car, and we get down to about sixteen-eight or sixteen-seventy or something. But we can't get it down to close to the track record. So we tore the car all apart and put it back together. He was *so* mad. Come to find the next night that the track record was *seventeen*-thirty-four. We were way under the track record."

Said Gordon Johncock: "He was a hell of a competitor. We had one altercation at Milwaukee. If that's all the trouble we had in all those years of racing, I'd say that's pretty good. But we tangled wheels in turn three at Milwaukee. Just a racing incident. It's a possibility I was leading and he tried to come under me and

Bobby Unser was perhaps the most colorful of the Unser clan. He was outgoing and flashy, unlike his brother, Al. Bobby was always fast and he was always intense. When he wasn't the best, he gave it all he had, and paid the penalty many times. Bob Tronolone

I just didn't know he was there. I don't really remember. But I do remember he was really upset. He kind of blamed me at the time."

Bobby Unser, the third of four boys, was as interested in racing as any Unser ever was. He watched his uncle demolish the competition at Pike's Peak and helped his brother Jerry prepare his cars in the early fifties. His father had helped tune cars, and Bobby, with his father, drove the 1952 Carrera Panamericana when Unser was only fifteen years old.

His uncles had not just won at Pike's Peak, but dominated there. At an early age, Bobby, too, learned to fix different cars and he and his brothers began fiddling with motorized gadgetry. Bobby's father traded some mules for a Ford and the brothers had their own car—which they could drive only out in the desert.

By the early fifties the Unser boys had established themselves as the local talent at the short tracks across New Mexico and Colorado. They rarely saw their Uncle Louis, but in 1955 their father had taken all three boys (with Al in tow) to Pike's Peak. The boys all brought their own cars and raced in the event for the first time, finishing third, fourth, and fifth. The beginning of a new generation was at hand.

Pike's Peak eventually became one of Bobby Unser's properties. Not literally, of course, but he had

Bobby Unser in his Eagle-Drake-Offenhauser. Unser's determination was famous, and he was chronically intense. Here, at Milwaukee, he sat on pole but failed to win the race. Russ Lake, Milwaukee Mile

won there in so many different classes and so many different forms that Unser really can be considered king of the hill.

If Al began racing to follow in his brothers' footsteps, Bobby did it more as a challenge. Racing was a way of life, certainly, but winning was a challenge Bobby Unser took almost personally. The challenge really began at the hill, at Pike's Peak. And it was one of the main reservoirs of confidence which propelled Bobby Unser to the top of the pinnacle of the sport of auto racing.

In 1915, the three brothers, Bobby's uncles and father, bolted a sidecar on a motorcycle and drove to the top of Pike's Peak, the first time it had been done. The following year a wealthy Coloradan paid to have a road built to the top of the mountain. The first "Race To The Clouds" was held, and the Unsers became fascinated with the race. By the end of the decade, they were regulars at the Pike's Peak Hillclimbs. Bobby's uncle Jerry finished second from 1926 through 1929; Louis finished second in 1930; Jerry finished third in 1931, but in 1934 Louis finally won the event. It was

the first of many for the Unser family.

In 1936 (the race wasn't run in 1935), Louis won, then won again in 1937, 1938, 1939, and 1941. The war stopped racing for the next four years, but when it resumed in 1946, there was Louis, winning in 1946 and 1947. He won one last one in 1957.

Bobby Unser had been watching—or hearing about the Hill—since he was younger. He had won a pair of modified stock car championships in the early fifties and by 1955 was ready to take on the Unser tradition, to take on Pike's Peak. His father took all four of the boys (Al was unable to race) to Pike's Peak to race.

Louis—through either genuine concern for his nephews or from fear of being beaten by them—insisted that their cars be slowed down. Their father agreed.

From that moment on, Bobby Unser would make sure that he beat his uncle.

And eventually he did. He won thirteen Pike's Peak hillclimbs in everything from a four-wheel drive Audi to an Eagle-Offy, with an overall Pike's Peak record in 1986. And if his commitment to besting his uncle at Pike's Peak is any indication, his commitment

Bobby Unser prior to the 1975 Indy 500. He would win the race that year. The relationship between Gurney and Unser deteriorated by the end of the year, but twenty years later, Gurney still calls him one of the best drivers he ever worked with. Courtesy Dan Gurney's All American Eagles

to be the best driver in *any* car was just as intense. Where Al is smooth and almost invisible, Bobby was always obvious. He conceded readily that he wasn't as good a driver as his younger brother, but that he was far more determined.

Bobby Unser's career in Indy Car competition began in 1963 at the Indianapolis Motor Speedway in a car that was too old, too slow and too heavy to make the race. It afforded Unser his rookie test, which he passed easily. That ride—the one which got him into the race—was actually suggested by none other than Parnelli Jones.

"I got Bobby his first ride at Indianapolis," Jones said. "In 1963, his first year, I fixed him up for a ride in the Novi and fixed him up for a ride in the Vita-Fresh Orange Juice car. I took that Vita Fresh Orange Juice car and I was the fastest in 1963 all during practice. I took that car and had it second quick. I wanted him to drive *that* car. But I had already fixed him up with Andy (Granatelli) and he had driven both cars, and Bobby's dad wanted him to drive the Novi, so he made the decision to drive the Novi, and of course he crashed it in the first turn."

Actually it was the first turn of the third lap. Regardless, Unser would stay on with Granatelli for three years in a futile attempt to win something—any-

thing with the Novis. In 1966, he went to Bob Wilke's team and, ironically, won his first win in USAC Championship cars at none other than Pike's Peak, which was part of the USAC championship. He then won his first speedway race at Mosport in 1967, pulling together a string of top ten finishes that put him into third place for the year end championship tally. By the following season he was comfortable with winning and he had won four of the first five—including the Indy 500—and would win the championship over Mario Andretti by a mere 11 points, 4,330 to 4,319. In 1969, he drove an Eagle Offy to a single win and another third in the standings. In 1970, he won once again and finished second in the championship to his brother Al.

Bobby Unser joined forces with Dan Gurney and the All American Eagle team in 1971. And in 1971 and 1972, Unser led quite often and won six of twenty two races of the two seasons, but more often than not the car would break down. But rarely was anybody quicker than Bobby Unser on a flying lap in those two stellar seasons. In fact, Unser was on pole fifteen of those twenty-two occasions.

By 1975, Unser would win only three other races in forty-three tries. Unlike his 1971-1972 seasons, for the next three he would post pole positions far less frequently. He did, however, manage to win his second Indy 500 with Gurney along with the 1974 championship.

"Our lifestyles never quite jived," Gurney said, downplaying the acrimony that was evident in the team even to outsiders. "I enjoyed him and he was a brave and capable driver. He was sharp and we learned a lot together and went through a lot.

"When he left he tried to leave us prostrating. He has a vindictive side to him. But he was a genuine leader. He would go beyond honorable in business. But still, I paint him a ten."

In 1976, Unser left Gurney and ran for two seasons with the Fletcher Cobre Tire team. He used an Eagle chassis and won only one race. The following season he won no races and departed for Penske, where his drive and competitiveness were to serve him well alongside Roger Penske.

Unser said that he enjoyed his time with Roger Penske more than at any other time in his career. Penske was a man who had as much drive and was as motivated as Unser. When Unser asked for changes Penske made them immediately. And of course, he had the funds to spend. The team flourished while Unser drove, winning yet another Indy 500—the third for Unser as well as for Penske at the time. He also managed to finish runner up twice and win eleven races in thirty-seven starts.

Bobby Unser's final win, somewhat fittingly, was the Indianapolis 500 in 1981. It was, sadly, not decided until October of 1981. Although Unser had led for most of the race and had sat on the pole for the start, he had been disqualified after the race for an alleged infraction mid-race that could have and should have been handled by a stop-and-go penalty. With about forty laps left in the event, Unser pitted under yellow. Second place man Mario Andretti also pitted. When they took on fuel and tires and headed back out to the track, Unser led Andretti. The pace car had collected the leader and bunched the pack. As Unser tried to keep Andretti at bay the two sped out onto the track and passed several cars which were grouped behind the pace car. They pulled into the line, but had in fact passed cars—an illegal move.

The Penske team had never been informed of the error and Unser went on to win the race, hands-down. But afterward, Speedway officials penalized

Unser a full lap for passing under yellow, handing the win to Andretti, who had also passed under yellow.

The decision was challenged by Penske and almost five months later the ruling was overturned and Unser was finally given his due. He had won the May extravaganza in Autumn.

He retired at the end of the season and ran his own team for a single season, realizing he hated it, and signed for one season with Pat Patrick. But as he practiced the car prior to the season-opener, it was clear that his motivation was not as strong as it once was. He resigned before it ever got going and has been retired ever since.

Bobby Unser will always be remembered as one of

1979, with Penske at the Speedway. Bobby Unser said he enjoyed his time with Roger Penske more than at any other time in his career. Penske was a man who was motivated as much as Unser was. When Unser asked for changes, Penske made them immediately. And of course, he had the funds to do so. Russ Lake

the best in American motor sports. He was always fast and he was always intense. When he wasn't the best, he gave it all he had and paid the penalty many times.

"I've had great times with Bobby," Parnelli Jones said. "He's a great driver and he's had nine lives. He's wrecked a lot of cars, I'm telling you. But when he really got it together, he was unbelievable."

You can still watch Bobby Unser compete. He does it each Sunday of any network broadcast Indy Car event. His insight is refreshing and his candor unique. But most of all, his jabs at Sam Posey make it worth watching. Even in broadcasting, Bobby Unser has given up none of the competitiveness.

At left
In the Penske in 1981. This was Unser's final season. It was also his final win at Indy. It was, sadly, not decided until October of 1981. Although Unser had led for most of the race and had sat on the pole for the start, he had been disqualified after the race for an alleged infraction. The decision was challenged by the Penske team and almost five months later the ruling was overturned and Unser was finally given his due. He had won the May extravaganza in Autumn. He retired at the end of the season. Russ Lake

Unser in 1972 in the Olsonite Eagle. The car gave Unser the pole fifteen of twenty-two occasions over the course of two seasons and gave him a victory six times. But more often than not, the car broke down. Rarely was anybody quicker than Bobby Unser on a flying lap in those two stellar seasons. Bob Tronolone

THE RECORDS
AAA CHAMPIONSHIPS: 1909-1955

1909
1. George Robinson
2. Louis Chevrolet
3. Joe Nikrent
4. Bob Burman
5. Bert Dingley
6. Harris Hanahue
7. Ralph DePalma
8. Eaton McMillan
9. Harry Grant
10. Jack Fleming

1910
1. Ray Harroun
2. Joe Dawson
3. Al Livingston
4. John Aitken
5. Harry Grant
6. Tom Kincaid
7. Ralph Mulford
8. Billy Pearce
9. Bob Bruman
10. Franklin Gelnaw

1911
1. Ralph Mulford
2. Charles Merz
3. David Bruce-Brown
4. Ray Harroun
5. Hughie Hughes
6. Eddie Hearne
7. Len Zengle
8. Bert Dingley
9. Harvey Herrick
10. Louis Disbrow

1912
1. Ralph DePalma
2. Teddy Tezlaff
3. Joe Dawson
4. Hughie Hughes
5. Ralph Mulford
6. Charles Merz
7. Spencer Wishart
8. Erwin Bergdoll
9. Eddie Pullen
10. Mortimer Roberts

1913
1. Earl Cooper
2. Jules Goux
3. Ralph Mulford
4. Ralph DePalma
5. Spencer Wishart

6. Gil Anderson
7. Louis Disbrow
8. George Hill
9. Barney Oldfield
10. Billy Carson

1914
1. Ralph DePalma
2. Eddie Pullen
3. Barney Oldfield
4. Rene Thomas
5. Eddie Rickenbacker
6. Earl Cooper
7. Ralph Mulford
8. Arthur Duray
9. Gil Anderson
10. Tom Alley

1915
1. Earl Cooper
2. Dario Resta
3. Gil Anderson
4. Eddie O'Donnell
5. Eddie Rickenbacker
6. Ralph DePalma
7. Barney Oldfield
8. Bob Burman
9. Tom Alley
10. Billy Carson

1916
1. Dario Resta
2. John Aitken
3. Eddie Rickenbacker
4. Ralph DePalma
5. Earl Cooper
6. Wilbur D'Alene
7. Tommy Milton
8. Pete Henderson
9. Frank Galvin
10. Ralph Mulford

1917
1. Earl Cooper
2. Louis Chevrolet
3. Ralph Mulford
4. Eddie Hearne
5. Tommy Milton
6. Ira Vail
7. Dave Lewis
8. William Taylor
9. Cliff Durant
10. Ralph DePalma

1918
1. Ralph Mulford
2. Louis Chevrolet
3. Eddie Hearne
4. Ralph DePalma
5. Cliff Durant
6. Omar Toft
7. Dario Resta
8. Tommy Milton
9. Dave Lewis
10. Earl Cooper

1919
1. Howard Wilcox
2. Eddie Hearne
3. Gaston Chevrolet
4. Roscoe Sarles
5. Tommy Milton
6. Cliff Durant
7. Joe Boyer
8. Arthur Klein
9. Ralph Mulford
10. Louis Chevrolet

1920
1. Tommy Milton
2. Jimmy Murphy
3. Gaston Chevrolet
4. Ralph DePalma
5. Roscoe Sarles
6. Eddie O'Donnell
7. Rene Thomas
8. Eddie Hearne
9. Joe Thomas
10. Ralph Mulford

1921
1. Tommy Milton
2. Roscoe Sarles
3. Eddie Hearne
4. Jimmy Murphy
5. Joe Thomas
6. I.P. Fetterman
7. Eddie Miller
8. Ralph DePalma
9. Earl Cooper
10. Frank Elliott

1922
1. Jimmy Murphy
2. Tommy Milton
3. Harry Hartz
4. Frank Elliott
5. Bennett Hill

6. Eddie Hearne
7. Jerry Wonderlich
8. Roscoe Searles
9. Earl Cooper
10. Ralph Mulford

1923
1. Eddie Hearne
2. Jimmy Murphy
3. Bennett Hill
4. Harry Hartz
5. Tommy Milton
6. Harlan Fengler
7. Jerry Wonderlich
8. Earl Cooper
9. Frank Elliott
10. Dave Lewis

1924
1. Jimmy Murphy
2. Earl Cooper
3. Bennett Hill
4. Tommy Milton
5. Fred Comer
6. Harry Hartz
7. L.L. Corum
8. Harlan Fengler
9. Phil Shafer
10. Jerry Wonderlich

1925
1. Peter DePaolo
2. Tommy Milton
3. Harry Hartz
4. Bob McDonogh
5. Earl Cooper
6. Frank Elliott
7. Dave Lewis
8. Fred Comer
9. Ralph Hepburn
10. Phil Shafer

1926
1. Harry Hartz
2. Frank Lockhart
3. Peter DePaolo
4. Bennett Hill
5. Frank Elliott
6. Fred Comer
7. Dave Lewis
8. Norman Batten
9. Peter Kreis
10. Earl DeVore

1927
1. Peter DePaolo
2. Frank Lockhart
3. George Souders
4. Leon Duray
5. Harry Hartz
6. Earl DeVore
7. Babe Staff
8. Tony Gulotta
9. Dave Lewis
10. Cliff Woodbury

1928
1. Louis Meyer
2. Ray Keech
3. Lou Moore
4. George Souders
5. Bob McDonogh
6. Fred Frame
7. Norman Batten
8. Cliff Woodbury
9. Billy Arnold
10. Bill Spence

1929
1. Louis Meyer
2. Ray Keech
3. Wilbur Shaw
4. Fred Frame
5. Cliff Woodbury
6. Cliff Bergere
7. James Gleason
8. Fred Winnai
9. Frank Brisko
10. Myron Stevens

1930
1. Billy Arnold
2. Bill Cantlon
3. Bill Cummings
4. Russ Snowberger
5. Deacon Litz
6. Wilbur Shaw
7. Louis Meyer
8. Dave Evans
9. Frank Farmer
10. Herman Schurch

1931
1. Louis Schnieder
2. Fred Fame
3. Ralph Hepburn
4. Russ Snowberger
5. James Gleason

6. Bill Cantlon
7. Ernest Triplett
8. Lou Moore
9. Chester Miller
10. Bill Cummings

1932
1. Bob Carey
2. Fred Frame
3. Howard Wilcox
4. Russ Snowberger
5. Bill Cummings
6. Cliff Bergere
7. Mauri Rose
8. H.W. Stubblefield
9. Zeke Meyer
10. Ira Hall

1933
1. Louis Meyer
2. Lou Moore
3. Wilbur Shaw
4. Chet Gardner
5. H.W. Stubblefield
6. Dave Edwards
7. Bill Cummings
8. Tony Gulotta
9. Mauri Rose
10. Billy Winn

1934
1. Bill Cummings
2. Mauri Rose
3. Russ Snowberger
4. Al Miller
5. Kelly Petillo
6. Joe Russo
7. Lou Moore
8. Frank Brisko
9. Bill Canton
10. Billy Winn

1935
1. Kelly Petillo
2. Bill Cummings
3. Wilbur Shaw
4. Floyd Roberts
5. Billy Winn
6. Chet Gardner
7. Bill Canton
8. Louis Meyer
9. Ralph Hepburn
10. George MacKenzie

1936
1. Mauri Rose
2. Louis Meyer
3. Ted Horn
4. George MacKenzie
5. Tazio Nuvolari
6. Wilbur Shaw
7. Jean-Pierre Wimille
8. Chet Miller
9. Antonio Brivio
10. Ray Pixley

1937
1. Wilbur Shaw
2. Tek Horn
3. Bernd Rosemeyer
4. Ralph Hepburn
5. Louis Meyer
6. Richard Seaman

7. Bill Cummings
8. Rex Mays
9. Cliff Bergers
10. Ernst Von Selius

1938
1. Floyd Roberts
2. Wilbur Shaw
3. Chet Miller
4. Ted Horn
5. Chet Gardner
6. Bill DeVore
7. Duke Nalon
8. Joel Thorne
9. Hurb Ardinger
10. Jimmy Snyder

1939
1. Wilbur Shaw
2. Jimmy Snyder
3. Ted Horn
4. Babe Stapp
5. Cliff Bergere
6. George Barringer
7. Mauri Rose
8. Joel Thorne
9. Frank Wearne
10. George Connor

1940
1. Rex Mays
2. Wilbur Shaw
3. Mauri Rose
4. Ted Horn
5. Joel Thorne
6. Bob Swanson
7. Frank Wearne
8. Frank Brisko
9. Mil Hansen
10. George Robson

1941
1. Rex Mays
2. Ralph Hepburn
3. Cliff Bergere
4. Floyd Davis
5. Chet Miller
6. George Connor
7. Frank Wearne
8. Mauri Rose
9. Tony Bettenhausen
10. Paul Russo

1942—1945
NO RACING

1946
1. Ted Horn
2. Emil Andres
3. George Robson
4. Jimmy Jackson
5. Rex Mays
6. Louis Durant
7. George Connor
8. Tony Bettenhausen
9. Duke Dinsmore
10. Luigi Villoresi

1947
1. Ted Horn
2. Bill Holland
3. Mauri Rose
4. Charles VanAcker

5. Rex Mays
6. Tony Bettenhausen
7. Walt Brown
8. Emil Andres
9. George Connor
10. Paul Russo

1948
1. Ted Horn
2. Myron Fohr
3. Mauri Rose
4. Bill Sheffler
5. Duke Nalon
6. Lee Wallard
7. Bill Holland
8. Mack Hellings
9. Emil Andres
10. Charles VanAcker

1949
1. Johnnie Parsons
2. Myron Fohr
3. Bill Holland
4. Walt Brown
5. George Connor
6. Rex Mays
7. Paul Russo
8. Lee Wallard
9. Johnny Mantz
10. Emil Andres

1950
1. Henry Banks
2. Walt Faulkner
3. Johnnie Parsons
4. Cecil Green
5. Tony Bettenhausen
6. Duke Dinsmore
7. Paul Russo
8. Chuck Stevenson
9. Jack McGrath
10. Bill Schindler

1951
1. Tony Bettenhausen
2. Henry Banks
3. Walt Faulkner
4. Jack McGrath
5. Mike Nazaruk
6. Johnnie Parsons
7. Lee Wallard
8. Manuel Ayulo
9. Andy Linden
10. Paul Russo

1952
1. Chuck Stevenson
2. Troy Ruttman
3. Sam Hanks
4. Duane Carter
5. Jack McGrath
6. Jim Rathman
7. Paul Russo
8. Bobby Ball
9. Jimmy Reece
10. Henry Banks

1953
1. Sam Hanks
2. Jack McGrath
3. Bill Vukovich
4. Manuel Ayulo
5. Paul Russo

6. Art Cross
7. Don Freeland
8. Chuck Stevenson
9. Jimmy Bryan
10. Tony Bettenhausen

1954
1. Jimmy Bryan
2. Manuel Ayulo
3. Jack McGrath
4. Bill Vukovich
5. Jimmy Reece
6. Bob Sweikert
7. Chuck Stevenson
8. Sam Hanks
9. Mike Nazaruk
10. Don Freeland

1955
1. Bob Sweikert
2. Jimmy Bryan
3. Johnny Thomson
4. Tony Bettenhausen
5. Andy Linden
6. Jimmy Davies
7. Pat O'Connor
8. Pat Flaherty
9. George Amick
10. Walt Faulkner

1956
1. Jimmy Bryan
2. Pat Flaherty
3. Don Freeland
4. George Amick
5. Jimmy Reece
6. Johnny Boyd
7. Bob Veith
8. Rodger Ward
9. Sam Hanks
10. Johnny Thomson

1957
1. Jimmy Bryan
2. Jim Rathmann
3. George Amick
4. Pat O'Connor
5. Jud Larson
6. Andy Linden
7. Johnny Thomson
8. Johnny Boyd
9. Sam Hanks
10. Elmer George

1958
1. Tony Bettenhausen
2. George Amick
3. Johnny Thomson
4. Jud Larson
5. Rodger Ward
6. Jimmy Bryan
7. Eddie Sachs
8. Johnny Boyd
9. Don Branson
10. AJ Foyt

1959
1. Rodger Ward
2. Tony Bettenhausen
3. Johnny Thomson
4. Jim Rathmann
5. AJ Foyt

6. Eddie Sachs
7. Don Branson
8. Johnny Boyd
9. Len Sutton
10. Paul Goldsmith

1960
1. AJ Foyt
2. Rodger Ward
3. Don Branson
4. Jim Rathmann
5. Tony Bettenhausen
6. Gene Force
7. Johnny Thomson
8. Len Sutton
9. Lloyd Ruby
9. Bobby Marshman
10. Paul Goldsmith

1961
1. AJ Foyt
2. Eddie Sachs
3. Rodger Ward
4. Shorty Templeman
5. Al Keller
6. Jim Hurtubise
7. Len Sutton
8. Bobby Marshman
9. Dick Rathmann
10. Parnelli Jones

1962
1. Rodger Ward
2. AJ Foyt
3. Parnelli Jones
4. Don Branson
5. Bobby Marshman
6. Jim Hurtubise
7. Len Sutton
8. Jim McElreath
9. Eddie Sachs
10. Don Davis

1963
1. AJ Foyt
2. Rodger Ward
3. Jim McElreath
4. Parnelli Jones
5. Don Branson
6. Jim Clark
7. Chuck Hulse
8. Roger McCluskey
9. Jim Hurtubise
10. Johnny Rutherford

1964
1. AJ Foyt
2. Rodger Ward
3. Lloyd Ruby
4. Don Branson
5. Bud Tingelstad
6. Parnelli Jones
7. Bobby Marshman
8. Norm Hall
9. Johnny White
10. Bob Harkey

1965
1. Mario Andretti
2. AJ Foyt
3. Jim McElreath
4. Don Branson

158

5. Gordon Johncock
6. Joe Leonard
7. Bobby Unser
8. Roger McCluskey
9. Jud Larson
10. Jim Clark

1966
1. Mario Andretti
2. Jim McElreath
3. Gordon Johncock
4. Joe Leonard
5. Al Unser
6. Bobby Unser
7. Don Branson
8. Chuck Hulce
9. Billy Foster
10. Bud Tingelstad

1967
1. AJ Foyt
2. Mario Andretti
3. Bobby Unser
4. Gordon Johncock
5. Al Unser
6. Lloyd Ruby
7. Jim McElreath
8. Roger McCluskey
9. Joe Leonard
10. Bud Tingelstad

1968
1. Bobby Unser
2. Mario Andretti
3. Al Unser
4. Lloyd Ruby
5. Bill Vukovich
6. AJ Foyt
7. Dan Gurney
8. Gary Bettenhausen
9. Mel Kenyon
10. Jim Malloy

1969
1. Mario Andretti
2. Al Unser
3. Bobby Unser
4. Dan Gurney
5. Gordon Johncock
6. Wally Dallenbach
7. AJ Foyt
8. Bill Vukovich
9. Mike Mosely
10. Lloyd Ruby

1970
1. Al Unser
2. Bobby Unser
3. Jim McElreath
4. Mike Mosely
5. Mario Andretti
6. Roger McCluskey
7. Gordon Johncock
8. Art Pollard
9. AJ Foyt
10. Wally Dallenbach

1971
1. Joe Leonard
2. AJ Foyt
3. Bill Vukovich
4. Al Unser

1972
1. Joe Leonard
2. Bill Vukovich
3. Roger McCluskey
4. Al Unser
5. Mark Donohue
6. Mike Hiss
7. Johnny Rutherford
8. Bobby Unser
9. Sam Sessions
10. Mike Mosely

1973
1. Roger McCluskey
2. Wally Dallenbach
3. Johnny Rutherford
4. Bill Vukovich
5. Mario Andretti
6. Mike Mosley
7. Gordon Johncock
8. Gary Bettenhausen
9. Lloyd Ruby
10. AJ Foyt

1974
1. Bobby Unser
2. Johnny Rutherford
3. Gordon Johncock
4. Al Unser
5. Jimmy Caruthers
6. Bill Vukovich
7. Lloyd Ruby
8. AJ Foyt
9. Wally Dallenbach
10. Steve Krisloff

1975
1. AJ Foyt
2. Johnny Rutherford
3. Bobby Unser
4. Wally Dallenbach
5. Bill Vukovich
6. Tom Sneva
7. Roger McCluskey
8. Steve Krisloff
9. Pancho Carter
10. Gordon Johncock

1976
1. Gordon Johncock
2. Johnny Rutherford
3. Wally Dallenbach
4. Al Unser
5. Mike Mosley
6. Bobby Unser
7. AJ Foyt
8. Tom Sneva
9. Mario Andretti
10. Johnny Prsons Jr.

1977
1. Tom Sneva
2. Al Unser
3. AJ Foyt
4. Johnny Rutherford

5. Lloyd Ruby
6. Bobby Unser
7. Gary Bettenhausen
8. Mark Donohue
9. Mario Andretti
10. Wally Dallenbach

1978
1. AJ Foyt
2. Bill Vukovich Jr.
3. Tom Bigelow
4. Larry Dickson
5. Gary Bettenhausen
6. Jim McElreath
7. Jerry Sneva
8. Dick Simon
9. Roger McCluskey
10. Sheldon Kinser

1979
1. Rick Mears
2. Bobby Unser
3. Gordon Johncock
4. Johnny Rutherford
5. Al Unser
6. Danny Ongias
7. Tom Sneva
8. Tom Bagley
9. Wally Dallenbach
10. Mike Mosley

1980
1. Johnny Rutherford
2. Bobby Unser
3. Tom Sneva
4. Rick Mears
5. Pancho Carter
6. Gordon Johncock
7. Bill Alsup
8. Al Unser
9. Gary Bettenhausen
10. Vern Schuppan

1981
1. Rick Mears
2. Bill Alsup
3. Pancho Carter
4. Gordon Johncock
5. Johnny Rutherford
6. Tony Bettenhausen Jr.
7. Bobby Unser
8. Tom Sneva
9. Bob Lazier
10. Al Unser

1982
1. Rick Mears
2. Bobby Rahal
3. Mario Andretti
4. Gordon Johncock
5. Tom Sneva
6. Kevin Cogan
7. Al Unser
8. Geoff Brabham
9. Roger Mears
10. Tony Bettenhausen Jr.

1983
1. Al Unser
2. Teo Fabi
3. Mario Andretti
4. Tom Sneva

5. Gordon Johncock
6. Wally Dallenbach
7. Mario Andretti
8. Pancho Carter
9. Tom Bigelow
10. Mike Mosley

1984
1. Mario Andretti
2. Tom Sneva
3. Bobby Rahal
4. Danny Sullivan
5. Rick Mears
6. Al Unser Jr.
7. Michael Andretti
8. Geoff Brabham
9. Al Unser
10. Danny Ongias

1985
1. Al Unser
2. Al Unser Jr.
3. Bobby Rahal
4. Danny Sullivan
5. Mario Andretti
6. Emerson Fittipaldi
7. Tom Sneva
8. Jacques Villeneuve
9. Michael Andretti
10. Rick Mears

1986
1. Bobby Rahal
2. Michael Andretti
3. Danny Sullivan
4. Al Unser Jr.
5. Mario Andretti
6. Kevin Cogan
7. Emerson Fittipaldi
8. Rick Mears
9. Roberto Guerrero
10. Tom Sneva

1987
1. Bobby Rahal
2. Michael Andretti
3. Al Unser Jr.
4. Roberto Guerrero
5. Rick Mears
6. Mario Andretti
7. Arie Luyendyk
8. Geoff Brabham
9. Danny Sullivan
10. Emerson Fittipaldi

1988
1. Danny Sullivan
2. Al Unser Jr.
3. Bobby Rahal
4. Rick Mears
5. Mario Andretti
6. Michael Andretti
7. Emerson Fittipaldi
8. Raul Boesel
9. Derek Daly
10. Teo Fabi

1989
1. Emerson Fittipaldi
2. Rick Mears
3. Michael Andretti
4. Teo Fabi

5. Bobby Rahal
6. Rick Mears
7. Al Unser Jr.
8. John Paul Jr.
9. Chip Ganassi
10. Pancho Carter

1990
1. Al Unser Jr.
2. Michael Andretti
3. Rick Mears
4. Bobby Rahal
5. Emerson Fittipaldi
6. Danny Sullivan
7. Mario Andretti
8. Arie Luyendyk
9. Eddie Cheever
10. John Andretti

1991
1. Michael Andretti
2. Bobby Rahal
3. Al Unser Jr.
4. Rick Mears
5. Emerson Fittipaldi
6. Arie Luyendyk
7. Mario Andretti
8. John Andretti
9. Eddie Cheever
10. Scott Pruett

1992
1. Bobby Rahal
2. Michael Andretti
3. Al Unser Jr.
4. Emerson Fittipaldi
5. Scott Goodyear
6. Mario Andretti
7. Danny Sullivan
8. John Andretti
9. Raul Boesel
10. Eddie Cheever

1993
1. Nigel Mansell
2. Emerson Fittipaldi
3. Paul Tracy
4. Bobby Rahal
5. Raul Boesel
6. Mario Andretti
7. Al Unser Jr.
8. Arie Luyendyk
9. Scott Goodyear
10. Robby Gordon

1994
1. Al Unser Jr.
2. Emerson Fittipaldi
3. Paul Tracy
4. Michael Andretti
5. Robby Gordon
6. Jacques Villeneuve
7. Raul Boesel
8. Nigel Mansell
9. Teo Fabi
10. Bobby Rahal

Index